COLLEGE STUDY
STRATEGIES

COLLEGE STUDY STRATEGIES

Thinking and Learning

Marcia L. Laskey and Paula W. Gibson
Cardinal Stritch College

Allyn and Bacon
Boston • London • Toronto • Sydney • Tokyo • Singapore

*Thanks to our students, families, and staff
for all their contributions and support*

Vice President, Humanities: Joseph Opiela
Editorial Assistant: Kate Tolini
Marketing Manager: Lisa Kimball
Editorial Production Service: Chestnut Hill Enterprises, Inc.
Manufacturing Buyer: Suzanne Lareau
Cover Administrator: Suzanne Harbison

Copyright © 1997 by Allyn & Bacon
A Viacom Company
Needham Heights, MA 02194

Library of Congress Cataloging-in-Publication Data

Laskey, Marcia L.
    College study strategies : thinking and learning / Marcia L. Laskey and Paula W. Gibson.
        p.   cm.
    Includes bibliographical references and index.
    ISBN 0-205-19152-5 (alk. paper)
    1. Study skills.   2. Critical thinking—Study and teaching (Higher)   I. Gibson, Paula W.   II. Title.
LB2395.L38   1997
378.1'7'02812—dc20   96-34290
                                                         CIP

Printed in the United States of America

10   9   8   7   6   01   00

CONTENTS

PREFACE

We began to put material together for our study skills class because we could not find a book that fit our philosophy and met our objectives. We included all the information we believed our students needed to know and provided enough practice exercises for them to apply the strategies.

Slowly the information we collected began to evolve into a book. Our students' input helped us define the direction of the book that is a reflection of their needs.

We received enthusiastic responses from our students and colleagues. Many of our colleagues asked us when they would be able to purchase our book. This response prompted us to consider publication. *College Study Strategies: Thinking and Learning* is the result of a great deal of work and constant revision. We have learned much during this process and feel that we have written a text designed to help students find their way through academia. We believe that a solid foundation of strategies is basic to doing well in college. This text will assist students who enter college without this basic information, both recent high school graduates and returning adults who may be out of touch with learning and studying.

The content of this text includes study skills that address both visual and auditory modes. A Critical Thinking chapter has been included to help students learn how to process information and how to think logically, which is essential to college learning. The emphasis of the Critical Thinking chapter is integrated throughout the book. We also have included some diagnostic tests in the Learning Styles chapter so that students may develop their metacognitive skills. The chapter on Questioning Strategies That Lead to Critical Thinking is not found in most other textbooks, but it is an important strategy because learning to ask questions is vital to active participation and learning. We hope that these unique features and the basic study strategies will benefit students beginning their college careers.

ACKNOWLEDGMENTS

We want to thank Mary Pulvermacher for her secretarial support; Gene Laskey for his computer expertise and endurance; Ben Gibson for his artwork; Rachel Laskey, and Drew and Patrick Gibson for their supportive listening and encouragement; and Florence and Herbert Barland for their conviction that we have what it takes. We also want to thank all of the faculty, staff, and administration of Cardinal Stritch College for their faith and confidence in this project. We acknowledge the contributions of reviewers of this book: Jim Cebulski, University of South Florida; Helen Gilbart, St. Petersburg Junior College; and Kathryn E. Moore, St. Louis Community College at Meramec.

COLLEGE STUDY STRATEGIES

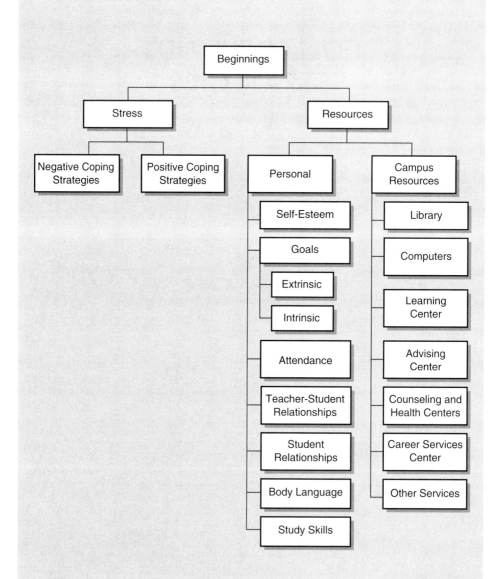

1

BEGINNINGS

Nothing great was ever achieved without enthusiasm.
—RALPH WALDO EMERSON

Key Concepts

Body language   Nonverbal communication.

Extrinsic motives   Reasons for a person's actions or beliefs that come from outside the person.

Intrinsic motives   Reasons for a person's actions or beliefs that come from a person's own values and goals.

Repercussions   Indirect results produced by an action or event.

Stress   Any physical, chemical, or emotional factor that causes bodily or mental tension.

Study skills   Strategies that are used to unlock the mysteries of learning. For example, highlighting is commonly used to delineate the main idea and key details.

Syllabus   A schedule of classes, tests, and assignments.

As you begin your college career, you will discover that learning certain strategies and understanding what college life is all about will ease your adjustment to higher education. It is to your advantage to assess your goals, attitudes, learning style, and academic strengths and weaknesses as you begin this new experience. In a sense, when you enter college you leave your old life behind. Even if you take only a few courses, the focus of your life changes as you encounter new ways of thinking and new experiences. You will probably view your old job, neighborhood, friends, and school in a new light as you become involved with college life, which has its own values, assumptions, customs, traditions, and activities.

Adapting to this new environment demands extra physical and mental energy as you learn new information and develop new skills. Adjusting to these changes can create stress. However, by using the academic and personal strategies presented in the following chapters, you can cope with this stress and ensure that college will be an enriching, productive experience.

STRESS

Stress is emotional and physical tension, which accompanies any positive or negative change. Learning to deal with stress is an important beginning in adjusting to your new environment. You can't avoid stress entirely, but you can change your response to it. The best place to start is to recognize what you can control and what you can't. You can't control other people, and you can't control every event that happens; however, you can control how you respond to people and events.

In today's rapidly changing world, almost everyone experiences stress. Some amount of stress is positive because it helps you achieve what you need to by increasing the adrenaline that gives you the energy to attain your goals. However, too much stress prevents you from being effective because it creates tension, which makes you less able to deal with the situation at hand. Entering college and adapting to a new lifestyle are stressful. Meeting new acquaintances, perhaps living away from home, and entering new social situations can all be difficult. Academic demands, deadlines, and exams add even more stress. In fact, the first year for all students is a venture into the unknown that can be quite terrifying. Too much stress may cause you to feel tense, anxious, uncomfortable, or even depressed. You might have the feeling that you will never be able to cope with this new situation.

Any physical, chemical, or emotional factor that causes bodily or mental tension results in stress. Stress can be manifested either physically or psychologically. Physically, the body responds as if there were a threat—the heart beats faster, breathing becomes rapid, muscles tense, and other changes occur. Stress can also result in symptoms of physical illness, such as stomach discomfort, nausea, headaches, and fatigue.

Psychological symptoms of stress can appear as depression or the inability to act. Other symptoms include rigid behavior and excessive worry. The way you react to stress is important. If you are able to deal with it in a positive way, you will feel you have some control over the stressful situation. If you are unable to do so, you will feel lost and out of control.

Determining the cause of your stress is the first step toward coping with it. Situations, such as lacking career goals or indecision about changing careers, can cause stress. Academic concerns about grades, exams, finishing papers on time, and being able to complete all the assigned reading also create stress for college students. Difficult relationships with roommates, friends and family can also create stressful situations. Finally, financial worries about whether there will be enough money for next semester's tuition can contribute to stress.

Negative Coping Strategies

There are both negative and positive ways to cope with stress. Although negative strategies may offer temporary relief, they do not help in the long run. Negative coping strategies include using alcohol and drugs, which ease the feeling of stress by dulling your feelings and lessening your self-awareness. However, they produce only a temporary release from the actual stress. Moreover, if alcohol and drugs become a way of life, you will no longer be able to function effectively in school and your focus will be on escape, not learning.

Becoming antagonistic, acting aggressively, and blaming others for your problems are other negative coping strategies that shift responsibility away from you, but these tactics are self-defeating because they alienate other people and don't solve the problem at hand. For example, you may blame a teacher for a poor grade, but, in reality, you are the one responsible. Stress can only temporarily be reduced by using negative coping strategies, so it is important to find positive alternatives.

Positive Coping Strategies

There are many positive strategies for dealing with stress. Once you identify the cause of your stress, whether it is an exam or a social relationship, then you can deal with it. If it is school related, perhaps prioritizing your time and organizing your tasks will help to alleviate some of the stress. Or you may need to seek extra academic support. If the stress is emotional, you may want to find someone to talk to, either a friend or a professional counselor.

Other strategies involve changing your response to the stress by setting realistic goals, reducing the number of your obligations, being more positive, and using positive self-reinforcement. For instance, tell yourself that you can handle the situation, and then develop a plan to deal with it. Good physical health, regular exercise, and healthful eating and sleeping routines also play a part in helping you cope with problems more effectively. Chapter 9, which deals with testing, presents more strategies for relieving anxiety. However, if you find that you are unable to develop a plan for dealing with the problems causing you stress, seek the advice of a counselor on campus for support.

In summary, positive coping strategies include:

- Prioritizing your time
- Organizing tasks
- Seeking academic support
- Finding someone to talk to
- Setting realistic goals
- Reducing obligations
- Using positive self-reinforcement
- Maintaining healthful habits

Complete the activities that follow to identify areas of stress in your life and to gain insights and strategies for dealing with some stressful situations.

◆ EXERCISE A: ASSESSING YOUR COPING RESOURCES

Complete the following self-evaluation to evaluate your personal resources for dealing with stress.

How Vulnerable Are You to STRESS?

Have you found yourself feeling "out of control"? Do you feel overwhelmed with too many tasks to do in a short amount of time? If this sounds familiar, you may be suffering from some form of *STRESS*. Take this test to determine what resources you use to cope with stress. Score each item from 1 (almost always) to 5 (never), according to how much of the time each statement applies to you.

_____ 1. I eat at least one hot, balanced meal a day.

_____ 2. I get seven to eight hours sleep at least four nights a week.

_____ 3. I give and receive affection regularly.

_____ 4. I have at least one relative within fifty miles on whom I can rely.

_____ 5. I exercise to the point of perspiration at least twice a week.

_____ 6. I smoke less than half a pack of cigarettes a day.

_____ 7. I take fewer than five alcoholic drinks a week.

_____ 8. I am the appropriate weight for my height.

_____ 9. I have an income adequate to meet basic expenses.

_____ 10. I get strength from my religious beliefs.

_____ 11. I regularly attend club or social activities.

_____ 12. I have a network of friends and acquaintances.

_____ 13. I have one or more friends to confide in about personal matters.

_____ 14. I am in good health (including eyesight, hearing, teeth).

_____ 15. I am able to speak openly about my feelings when angry or worried.

_____ 16. I have regular conversations with the people I live with about domestic issues, such as chores, money, and problems that stem from daily living.

_____ 17. I do something for fun at least once a week.

_____ 18. I am able to organize my time effectively.

_____ 19. I consume fewer than three cups of coffee, tea and/or cola drinks a day.

_____ 20. I take quiet time for myself during the day.

_____ **Total**

To obtain your score, add up the figures and subtract 20. Any number greater than 30 indicates that you have insufficient resources to deal with stress and are vulnerable to it. You are seriously vulnerable if your score is between 50 and 75, and extremely vulnerable if it is greater than 75.

◆ **EXERCISE B: IDENTIFYING STRESSFUL SITUATIONS**

Form a group, and develop a list of stressful situations that are common to college students.

_____

_____

_____

◆ **EXERCISE C: FINDING SOLUTIONS TO STRESSFUL SITUATIONS**

With your group, think up some solutions to three of the stressful situations you listed in Exercise B.

_____

_____

_____

◆ **EXERCISE D: COPING WITH YOUR OWN PERSONAL STRESSFUL SITUATIONS**

What areas in your life are causing you stress now? Fill in the following chart to discover the causes and possible solutions to feeling tense and anxious.

	Event or Problem	*Emotional or Physical Signal*	*Coping Strategies*
1.			
2.			
3.			

RESOURCES

Using your personal and campus resources won't make you totally immune to stress, but doing so will provide a foundation for you and give you a sense of control over your life. Your personal resources include your self-esteem, your goals, and your behavior.

Personal Resources

Self-Esteem
Your most important, enduring resource is you—your belief in yourself as a capable, unique, and worthwhile person. This basic belief, often referred to as self-esteem, is based on our judgment of ourselves, not on other people's assessment. Our self-esteem is partially determined by our past relationships with family, friends, and coworkers.

If your experiences in these areas are largely negative, then your self-esteem may be lower than it should be.

Complete the following checklist to determine your level of self-esteem and confidence.

◆ **SELF-ESTEEM CHECKLIST**

	Always	*Often*	*Rarely*
1. I have trouble making decisions.			
2. I find myself bragging or exaggerating the importance of my role.			
3. I feel shy when I meet people for the first time.			
4. I worry about what other people think about me.			
5. I feel possessive in my relationships with friends and/or family members.			
6. It is difficult for me to acknowledge my mistakes.			
7. I "put people down" so I can feel "one up."			
8. I feel self-conscious about my looks.			
9. I blame myself for things that go wrong, whether it's my fault or not.			
10. I am hesitant to express my opinions and feelings.			

"Almost always" or "often" answers to more than half of these questions may indicate that your level of self-esteem needs attention.

It's easy to get trapped in a cycle of low self-esteem. Figure 1-1 on page 8 illustrates how you can get caught in this cycle.

If you are caught in any of these negative messages, you need to make changes to reflect a belief in yourself. Here are some steps to take to raise your self-esteem:

- Speak up for yourself. Your ideas and opinions are worthwhile. No one can "put you down" unless you give them permission to do so.

FIGURE 1-1   Cycle of low self-esteem.

- Don't put yourself down. Nobody is perfect. Everyone has strengths and weaknesses, and everyone makes mistakes.
- Learn from your failures and mistakes. Try to see negative experiences as a chance to learn; then the negative becomes positive.
- Encourage and praise yourself and others. A positive attitude can change your perspective and give you energy and hope.
- Be good to yourself. Take care of yourself physically, and take time for yourself. Learn to enjoy yourself and your unique feelings.
- Respect yourself. You have unique abilities and talents. Make a list of the things you do well.

Goals

Your goals are an important expression of who you are, and setting clear goals can relieve stress by giving you a sense of control over your life. Before you can utilize the techniques offered in the following chapters and apply them to your course work, you need a focus: Why are you attending college? What do you want to gain from the experience? These questions can make students uneasy and uncomfortable because they are often difficult to answer. You may be in college because all of your friends are going to college, your family expects you to go to college, or maybe no other option, such as getting a job, seems as appealing as continuing your education. On the other hand, you might not have been in school for a long time and have decided to pursue an education to advance your career. Whatever the reason you have chosen to come to college, examining your motives can be a good point to begin learning more about yourself.

If your reasons came mostly from the outside pressure of family and friends, then your motives are largely extrinsic. For example, your family may continue to offer rewards, such as praise or money, for college success and punishment, such as disapproval or lack of funds, for poor performance. Friends and spouses may offer approval for your success in college or criticism for failures. **Extrinsic motives** can only be effective if the pressure from outside continues. They do not provide long-lasting or sustained support for your achievement. More important than extrinsic motives are your own values and the personal satisfaction you get from achieving your goals.

Your own goals and the sense of satisfaction you get from achieving them are **intrinsic motives.** Some intrinsic motives might include preparing for a satisfying career, gaining more information about the world, developing social skills and meeting new people, or living independently from your family. Of course, you may be one of the many college students who are unsure of their goals and whose motives are probably a mixture of extrinsic and intrinsic factors. In fact, few people rely totally on intrinsic motives and are absolutely positive of their exact long-range goals.

If you fall into this category of one who is somewhat unsure of his or her goals, remember that you have good company. In fact, one aim of an education is to provide an avenue for exploring different interests and goals. Even though you may be unsure of your long-term goals, you can set short-term goals that will be attainable during the first semester of college. Some of these short-term goals might be to miss no more than two classes in each course, to study for each test, to turn in papers on time, and to find a tutor for a difficult course.

The following exercises offer a chance to discover your own long-term goals and to set the short-term objectives necessary to achieve them.

◆ **EXERCISE E: DETERMINING YOUR MOTIVES FOR ATTENDING COLLEGE**

For the next fifteen minutes, free write, answering the question "Why Am I in College?" (To free write means to write as continuously as you can without regard to organization or punctuation.)

◆ **EXERCISE F: RANKING YOUR MOTIVES**

1. Reread your free writing. Underline four of your strongest reasons for attending college.

2. Share these goals in groups of four. Report to the class on any goals members of your group have in common.

◆ **EXERCISE G: CREATING A VISION FOR THE FUTURE**

Even if you do not know exactly what you would like to be doing in ten years, you can describe your ideal vision of the future.

1. Describe two or three possible scenarios of where and what you would like to be doing in ten years.

   _____

   _____

   _____

2. Choose one scenario, and list the steps you need to take to achieve this goal.

   _____   _____

   _____   _____

   _____   _____

3. List which steps you are willing to commit to.

   _____   _____

   _____   _____

   _____   _____

Attendance

Your behavior is another personal resource you control, and attending classes regularly and punctually is an important factor for success in college. As Woody Allen said, "Ninety percent of success is showing up!" Believing that you can skip class without any **repercussions,** or effects, is a common myth. If you do not attend class on a regular basis, you will miss some vital information needed to understand a new concept or to do well on an exam. Notes from a classmate are not as effective as your own because your knowledge base and learning styles are different. Therefore, what you need to know may not be in your friend's notes.

Lectures are most valuable when they reinforce a previously introduced idea. If you have read the related text or attended a prior lecture in which the idea was being introduced and discussed, then the lecture will enhance the concept you are already familiar with. If you do not regularly attend lectures, you will not benefit from the logical sequence of ideas, which will make learning new concepts more difficult. It is difficult to learn new information when you do not fully understand the prior concepts that are the building blocks to new knowledge.

Excessive absenteeism also leads to poor test scores. For example, you may not be aware that there is going to be a test or quiz and, therefore, will not be prepared properly. Excessive absenteeism may also have a negative effect on your teacher, which could also result in a lower grade in the course. Some professors lower your grade automatically after a specific number of absences. This information is usually stated in your **syllabus,** or your instructor will make this clear the first day of your class.

Teacher-Student Relationships
Another important resource is teacher-student relationships. Instructors, professors, and teaching assistants are all resources for students. If possible, try to develop a relationship with your instructor by seeking assistance with course work when needed. Always be polite and respectful toward faculty, but do not hesitate to ask questions or challenge ideas presented in class. All teachers are required to establish office hours when they are available to meet with students. Office hours and other important information can be found in your syllabus, so read it carefully. (See Treasure Hunt for Campus Resources, page 17.)

Keep in mind that teachers, as is true of everybody else, like to be treated with respect, courtesy, and consideration. Teacher-student relationships in college differ from those that exist at the high school level. Although your college teacher is an expert in a particular subject, there will be a greater flow of discussion and exchange of ideas in college. College teachers want students to think critically and to develop ideas of their own.

Another factor to be considered is that teachers ultimately are the people who evaluate and grade you; therefore, common sense demands that you show them respect. One way you can establish a relationship with your teacher is to make positive comments and ask questions either in class or during your professor's office hours about assignments, material covered, or related information. Be sure your questions are pertinent and timely. If you disagree with a teacher about a grade or feel your instructor has made a mistake in grading a paper or test, be sure to communicate this situation privately and in a positive manner. Keep open a line of communication with your instructor. Not only will this enhance your learning, but it will also enable you to achieve the best grade possible.

Student Relationships
Relationships with your fellow students are another important resource because they can provide general emotional support as well as support for individual classes. Study groups can be formed, or you can pair with another student so that you will be able to share ideas and information. Your friendships with other students can also make

classes more enjoyable and less stressful. Try to get to know at least one or two other students in each of your classes, and remember to provide support for them in return by listening and helping. Another way to meet people and develop friendships is to get involved with campus activities. By contributing to campus life, you will make it a more interesting place to be and you will develop a strong network of friends.

◆ **EXERCISE H: TEACHER-STUDENT SCENARIOS**

In groups, discuss the following scenarios. Write down your options or conclusions to the problems in the space provided.

Scenario 1
You are in class and have just finished a discussion on a poem that the class read for an assignment. You know this poem is going to be on your exam, but you disagree with your teacher's analysis. How would you handle this situation?

_____

_____

_____

Scenario 2
You consistently receive C– on papers returned. Your instructor seems to ignore your questions and to treat you with disdain. What could you do to improve this situation?

_____

_____

_____

◆ **EXERCISE I: STRATEGIES FOR GOOD RELATIONSHIPS**

In groups of three or four students, share your past problems and frustrations with teachers. Choose two experiences, and develop solutions to both that might have helped alleviate the problems.

◆ **EXERCISE J: MEETING CLASSMATES**

Choose a partner, and interview each other so you can get acquainted. You might ask the following questions:

1. Age
2. Background information
   a. Education
   b. Work experience
   c. Family status
3. Major
4. Reasons for coming to school
   a. Career goals
   b. Major area of study
5. Academic strengths and weaknesses

After gathering as much information as possible about the student interviewed, you will be asked to introduce your partner to the class and to share the information you have gathered.

Body Language

Another personal resource is **body language.** It transmits messages without words. Body language reflects your emotional state, that is, your attitudes and feelings toward others. The receiver of these non-verbal messages judges you by your body language. Facial expressions, stance, and movements—all enrich and elaborate the message you send. For example, if you sit erect and seem interested in the lecture, you will be sending a positive message to the teacher. So sit upright, and get interested in what is being said. It will help you have a more positive attitude, and you will probably do much better in the class than if you slump in your chair and act as if you have better things to do. If you slump in your seat, with eyes down, you will send a negative message. Fidgeting, clock watching, and nonpurposeful actions transmit disinterest and boredom and will be reflected in your grade.

Facial expressions also send nonverbal messages because they reflect your feelings. If you are bored or dislike an instructor or a course, your facial expressions will probably show what you are thinking. Your facial expression provides your instructor with cues for interpreting your interest or disinterest in the lecture or in the discussion that is taking place. Instructors react more positively if you appear to be participating in the lecture. Often just a nod of your head or smiling at the right time will show that you are actively participating in the class even if you haven't responded orally. Being alert in class definitely leaves your teacher with a positive impression, particularly in small classes and in classes where participation counts.

Study Skills

Study skills refer to those strategies that help you learn and get the most out of college. It is important for you to evaluate your study skills realistically. Doing so will help you perform better in classes, select your major, and know in what areas to seek help. Often students overestimate their skills and, as a result, do not make good decisions about studying and getting assistance from instructors, tutors, and learning centers. The following pretest will help you determine the strengths and weaknesses of your study skills.

◆ STUDY SKILLS PRETEST

Take this pretest to evaluate your study skills. Write *T* for "true" or *F* for "false" in the blank before each statement.

_____ 1. If you read slowly and carefully, you do not really need to take notes to remember the information presented.

_____ 2. Rereading a chapter before a test is usually better than reviewing your notes.

_____ 3. When highlighting or underlining in your textbook, you should mark almost every line so you can go back and review.

_____ 4. Writing notes on textbook material increases your understanding and memory of the material.

_____ 5. Reading college textbooks is easy and enjoyable.

_____ 6. Writing short summaries of textbook sections when studying a chapter assignment can help you understand and remember the material.

_____ 7. You always use the same study strategy when studying.

_____ 8. If you cannot write in a book, you should make outline notes in a notebook.

_____ 9. You use mapping as a note-taking device when you need to see the relationship of the parts of the ideas in the assignment.

_____ 10. You reread the chapters for every test.

If you marked *T* for 1, 2, 3, 5, 7, and 10, you need to work on building your study skills. Numbers 1, 2, 3, 5, 7, and 10 are false. If you marked between three and six of them *T*, you need to reevaluate your study skills. If you marked fewer than three *T*, review your study skills to become a more effectual student.

Campus Resources

Using campus resources can make the transition to college life easier for both recent high school graduates and adults returning to the academic environment. First, identify people, offices, and departments that offer support. Then, determine their various locations, hours, and services offered.

The Library and Computers

Two resources that you need to be aware of are the library and computer lab. Both have become so important in education that they are promoted as a selling feature at many institutes of higher education and are often the first stop for prospective students in a show-and-tell tour of a school. Some large schools have wired, or are considering wiring, laboratories, libraries, and dorms with a network that would permit students and faculty to communicate via the computer with each other, with the school, with other libraries, and with millions of other students, faculty, experts, and laypersons via the Internet and the World Wide Web at any time of the day or night. Check your school to see what is available so that you can utilize the computer for writing papers, practicing skills, and for general use. If you are not computer literate, consider taking a basic computer course to familiarize yourself with the computer. Computers are no longer an elective option but are a necessary tool in helping with your college career.

Library Electronic Card Catalogs.   The personal computer (PC) is as important to today's student as pencils, erasers, and books are. In addition to its obvious uses for writing papers and reports, the computer is an important research tool. School libraries have, or shortly will have, replaced card catalogs with electronic files. When you search the electronic card catalog, or on-line catalog, you often have access to two or three other cooperating libraries in the same community, far more information than was ever contained in the old oak card catalog.

If you find it difficult to use an on-line catalog, ask the librarian for assistance. However, in general, all you have to do is press a key or designated letters. You will then be able to locate needed information by entering either the author, title, or subject you wish to locate. If the resource you need is located in another library, a few additional key strokes can order the book to be transferred to your own library in a day or so.

The searching capabilities of electronic files are faster and better than any mechanical scheme you might otherwise use. In some electronic card files, you have the capability of browsing through the shelves. The file will give you information on the books that are physically on the shelf on either side of your target book. You can quickly consider these other books as additional sources for the information you are seeking, the same as you would if you were physically standing in front of the shelf.

The electronic card catalog also contains information on videos, government documents, sound recordings, and other audiovisual material.

Other Library Information Files.   In many schools you will find PCs, or similar terminals, connected to data banks that permit searching newspapers, magazines, and other periodicals for articles and items that you will need to research an assignment. The data banks are huge and up to date. The search is so fast you won't have time for a snack while it is going on, and an on-line printer will be available to provide you with a copy of the item or items you find for inclusion with your report.

Other Library Resources.   The library offers many other resources for students. The librarians are available to answer questions, to help you learn how to use the computer indexes, and to find books and articles you may need for assignments. Often, professors put books on reserve in the library. Students can then use these selected readings to supplement the textbook assignments and to broaden their understanding of a subject.

There may be study rooms available in the library, where you can work with other students. Study carrels offer a quiet, private place to work uninterrupted when the dorm room or your home becomes too distracting. The library may have information available on career options, available scholarships and grants, and graduate schools. All of these services make it well worth your time to visit and explore the library on campus.

Learning Centers

Another campus resource is a tutoring or learning center. Often learning centers offer academic support, peer tutoring, testing, and counseling. If you have any academic difficulties or disabilities, a learning center can offer the extra assistance you may need to be successful. Learning centers have become an important part of most colleges today and offer help to many students in many different ways. If you begin to feel overwhelmed or are dissatisfied with test scores, have difficulty writing papers, or need help with understanding math, using the services of a learning center can be very helpful.

Advising Center

Speaking to an advisor or seeking out a counselor at an advising center is important in choosing courses, planning your schedule, and choosing your major. Advisors are aware of the various options and opportunities that courses and majors offer. In many schools it is mandatory to meet with an advisor before scheduling classes, so be sure to use this service to your advantage.

Counseling and Health Centers

Two other important areas to be aware of are the counseling and health centers. The counseling office may be located in the health center or nursing office, depending on the size of the school. When stress becomes too much to handle or you are having personal difficulties, the counseling center can offer support by helping you to talk about and work out your problems. Health problems are often related to stress, so using the health facilities is also important. Another reason to use the health center is to discuss any physical disabilities. The health office or nurse should be notified of your disability so assistance can be provided when and if it is necessary.

Career Services Center

Another important area to seek out is the career services center. This office can often help you choose a major, find areas of interest, and discover where your aptitudes lie. Career service counselors can discuss the opportunities available in different fields, which may help you decide on a major. This office often helps students find internships and can assist with writing résumés and interviewing for jobs when that time arrives.

Other Services

Other areas of support may be the financial aid office, Registrar, dean of students, student government, and various clubs and activities. Finally, be sure to read the college catalog and student handbook for a full picture of the unique resources available on your campus.

◆ **TREASURE HUNT FOR CAMPUS RESOURCES**

With a partner, answer the following questions. Find the answers as quickly, quietly, and efficiently as possible.

1. What are the names of two people who work in the financial aid office?

   _____

   _____

2. Get signatures from one member of the advising center staff and one member of the learning center staff.

   _____

   _____

3. Go to the career services office, and ask for a pamphlet on careers.

4. Obtain a pamphlet describing a service of the library.

5. Find the computer lab, and write down the hours it is open.

_____

6. Go to the bookstore, and find out how many different types of sweatshirts your school has.

_____

_____

7. What is the name of the registrar?

_____

8. Bring back a signature from the office that handles students' special physical and learning needs.

_____

9. Get a nurse's signature from the health center.

_____

10. What is the name of the president of the college?

_____

11. Who is the dean of students? What service does his or her office offer?

_____

_____

12. List five organizations and activities on campus you might get involved in.

_____   _____

_____   _____

_____   _____

CRITICAL THINKING

You will learn more about critical thinking in the next chapter, but the first step to thinking critically involves honest self-assessment. Based on the exercises you did in Chapter 1, write a description of yourself at this point in your life. Include the categories shown here. Try to write at least three or four sentences describing yourself in each area.

1. Behavior: Academic, social, and interpersonal performance.

_____

_____

_____

2. Emotions: Feelings, both positive and negative.

_____

_____

_____

3. Physical fitness: Energy, wellness, habits.

_____

_____

_____

4. Beliefs: Values, convictions, expectations.

_____

_____

_____

5. Interpersonal skills: Relationships with family, friends, or instructors.

_____

_____

_____

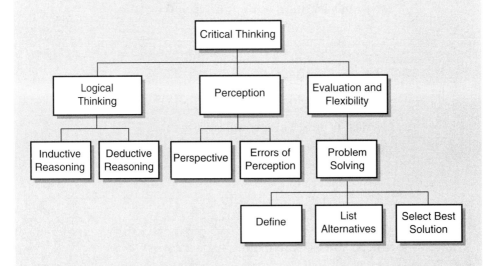

2

CRITICAL THINKING

There is nothing either good or bad but thinking makes it so.
—WILLIAM SHAKESPEARE,
Hamlet, *Act II, Scene 2*

Key Concepts

Ad hominem   Attacking a person rather than dealing with an issue.

Critical   Exercising or involving careful judgment.

Critical thinking   A complex concept that refers to a collection of cognitive activities that work together.

Deductive reasoning   Logical reasoning that moves from the general to the specific.

Generalization   A principle, statement, or idea having broad application.

Inductive reasoning   Logical reasoning that moves from specific facts to a general conclusion.

Perception   The way one views the world.

Stereotyping   A belief about a group without recognizing individual differences among members of the group.

Syllogism   A three-sentence chain of reasoning that includes a major premise, a minor premise, and a conclusion.

Thinking   A mental activity that involves forming concepts, solving problems, and engaging in reasoning.

When entering college, you will encounter many new challenges, ideas, and experiences. In order to respond productively to these new situations, you need to use effective thinking strategies. You already use many of these strategies, but becoming aware of a set of attitudes and strategies sometimes referred to as critical thinking can help make your college experience more profitable. The word *critical* means using careful judgment or evaluation. Accordingly, a critical thinker evaluates by asking questions, analyzing, or trying to make sense of a situation or problem. The word *thinking* involves the formulation of ideas, which includes forming concepts, solving problems, and reasoning. **Critical thinking** is a complex concept that refers to a collection of cognitive activities that often work together. In a sense, it involves thinking about thinking. Learning to think critically can involve the following cognitive abilities:

- Problem solving
- Logical thinking
- Perspective and perception
- Analysis
- Evaluation of ideas
- Decision making

You cannot succeed as a student by memorizing and spitting back information. You must apply what you have learned, and this involves critical thinking. For example, what good is it for a nursing student to memorize information about drugs but not be able to understand and apply the information when working in a hospital setting? Memorization might help you to make the right decision, but thinking critically is more likely to ensure a better outcome. Once you have grasped the theoretical elements of the information presented or read, you need to be able to apply the information. Tests, exams, and discussions require that you apply the information that you have learned, and this is where critical thinking becomes paramount to success in college.

Critical thinking is also important in college because you will be asked to absorb and integrate an extensive variety of information which will assist you in seeing the whole picture. Although you may feel that the many of the courses you taking are not related to each other, there are, in fact, processes that are common to them all. Critical thinking is one of these processes.

Critical thinking not only plays a role in your professional aspirations but also affects your entire life. You need to learn to think critically when making decisions in all areas of your life. Good decisions are generally based on sound, logical thinking. An example of acting illogically is choosing to major in science when this is the most difficult area for you to understand. In contrast, logical thinkers will ask themselves the following questions when choosing a major: What am I good at? What are my interests? What career will satisfy me the most? What are my strengths and weaknesses? Critical thinking can help you to make better decisions, to learn more effectively, and to apply and analyze what you know.

Not only do you as a critical thinker need to activate your cognitive skills, but you also need to be an active participant in the thinking process. Active participation means engaging in a dialog with yourself or others to decide what your basic thoughts are and to analyze how you came to these conclusions. Were your conclusions based on available facts and information, or were they based on what others told you? By thinking about and sorting out available information, you will be able to begin the process of problem solving, which is an important part of thinking critically.

Another area in which critical thinking is important is your social life. Critical thinkers think for themselves and are not easily swayed by peer pressure. You will be exposed to many different types of people with many different values. You will need to make decisions that may affect your whole life. Will you be pressured into drinking or taking drugs? Will you focus on your social life, or will you work on building your academic skills? Whether you are entering school as a returning adult or a traditional-age student coming from high school, the decisions you make are important ones and need to be thought out carefully. Critically thinking is vital to all parts of your life.

There are two kinds of thinkers: passive thinkers and active thinkers. Passive thinkers do not exercise their mental powers but rather follow others and often base their decisions on their first emotional response. An active thinker, such as Mr. Spock in *Star Trek*, thinks logically and only comes to a conclusion based on objective reasoning. Which type of thinker are you? Look at the characteristics of the active and passive thinkers listed below. Can you identify the characteristics that best fit your thinking? Can you add to this list?

Passive Thinkers	*Active Thinkers*
Not thinking for yourself	Engaging in the practice of solving problems, achieving goals, and analyzing issues
Allowing events to control you	
Allowing others to do your thinking	Getting involved
Not making decisions for yourself	Taking initiative
Believing everything you hear and read	Analyzing and evaluating what you hear and read
Avoiding decisions and goal setting	Realistically making decisions and setting goals

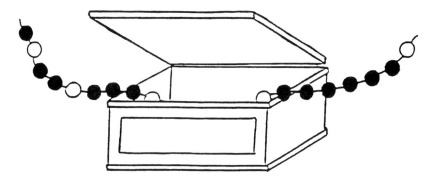

FIGURE 2-1   **How many pearls are hidden in the jewelry box? How many pearls are on the string?**

The information in this chapter will help you become a critical thinker. Begin with the following brain teasers, which require you to reason, problem solve, and analyze. (The answers to the brain teasers are on page 40.) Can you answer the questions posed in Figure 2-1?

Each of the items in Figure 2-2 illustrates a common phrase. For example, in the first item, the letters of the word *notebook* are placed in a spiral, so the configuration illustrates "spiral notebook." Can you figure out the phrases for all seventeen illustrations?

LOGICAL THINKING

The ability to think logically is one of the components essential to critical thinking. Logic is a form of reasoning that helps you find the connection between ideas and decide what the connection means. There are two kinds of logical reasoning: inductive and deductive. **Inductive reasoning** moves from the specific to the general; **deductive reasoning** moves from the general to the specific. As illustrated in Figure 2-3, words are general when they refer to groups or classes; words are specific when they refer to specific individuals, objects, or events.

In order to clarify these two types of reasoning, one needs to understand that a **generalization** is a principle, statement, or idea having broad application. There are two types of generalizations: faulty and valid. A faulty generalization is an erroneous or partly erroneous statement about a group or class of ideas or occurrences, things, and/or persons. Often, generalizations are faulty because they are based on insufficient evidence. For example, if a student takes one course from an ineffective teacher, the generalization "All the teachers are incompetent at this school" is faulty because it is based on only one experience, which may not be representative. Faulty generalizations can also arise when they are not based on

FIGURE 2-2   See how many other phrases you can decipher. The answers are on pages 40–41.

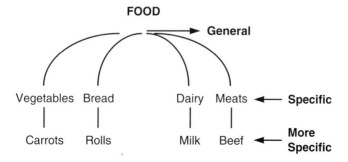

FIGURE 2-3   Moving from general to specific.

fact, have no person of authority backing up the information stated, and are not specific. In contrast, a valid generalization is based on integrated facts and sound evidence. When hearing or reading a generalization, consider the reasons for the statement and the examples used to support it. These reasons and examples are the evidence for a generalization or an assumption. The following list of questions can help you evaluate the evidence:

1. Is the evidence based on fact?
2. Is the evidence based on sufficient examples?
3. Are the reasons and/or examples logical and convincing?
4. Is the writer or speaker who presents the evidence reliable?

Examples of faulty and valid generalizations are illustrated in the following statements.

Example	*Type of generalization*
Old people never feel good.	Faulty
City children do not get enough sunshine.	Faulty
Some babies cry all the time.	Valid
Students who study generally get good grades.	Valid

The first two statements are faulty because they are absolute statements that are not based on facts. The last two statements are valid because they allow for exceptions.

◆ **EXERCISE A: FAULTY AND VALID GENERALIZATIONS**

Following are ten statements. Decide which statements are valid generalizations and which statements are faulty generalizations. Write *V* for "valid" and *F* for "faulty" in the blank before each statement.

_____ 1. Short men feel inferior.

_____ 2. Fat people are happy.

_____ 3. Women experience discrimination.

_____ 4. Many people probably experience sexual harassment.

_____ 5. People need a college education to get a good job.

_____ 6. Gold is very expensive.

_____ 7. Mrs. Peppers is my favorite teacher.

_____ **8.** Blue birds fly.

_____ **9.** Money means power.

_____ **10.** Single people are unhappy.

Inductive Reasoning

As stated before, inductive reasoning moves from specific facts to a general conclusion. This process entails stating facts, making connections between the facts, and then moving from the facts available to a sound conclusion. Available facts may not necessarily lead to an absolute conclusion, but they do provide evidence that leads to a good conclusion. In other words, the conclusion may not be certain, but it will be valid.

Inductive Process

Fact: Paula has not answered her phone this week.

Fact: Paula has not returned the messages I left on her answering machine.

Fact: When I went to Paula's house, not only was it dark but also newspapers were piled beside her door.

Conclusion: Paula may be out of town or visiting friends.

The facts in this situation lead us to a logical conclusion, which is that Paula is away from home. However, other conclusions could be made. For example, Paula could be dead of a heart attack and lying on the bedroom floor, but this conclusion is not as logical as the first because there are no facts to back up this premise. On the other hand, the lack of response to the messages, the dark house, and piled newspapers indicate Paula's absence. The conclusion is not the only one possible, but it is valid.

◆ **EXERCISE B: INDUCTIVE REASONING**

After evaluating and integrating the following facts, write a sound conclusion for each situation in the space provided.

1. Fact: Temperature in the West has been colder than normal this year.

   Fact: Temperatures along the East Coast have been colder this year.

   Fact: Spring began late this year.

   Conclusion: _____

2. Fact: In Iran women wear veils.

   Fact: In Iran women do not work outside the home.

   Fact: In Iran women are not allowed to drive.

   Conclusion: _____

3. Fact: The job market is good in the Midwest.

   Fact: More people were hired in the Midwest than anywhere else in the United States.

   Fact: Unemployment is low in the Midwest.

   Conclusion: _____

4. Fact: Cats are content to be by themselves for long periods of time.

   Fact: Dogs need constant companionship.

   Fact: Dogs need daily exercise.

   Conclusion: _____

Deductive Reasoning

In contrast to inductive reasoning, deductive reasoning moves from a general principle to a specific idea or major premise, which may be true if the general principle is true. In deductive reasoning the conclusion follows from the premise if the method of reasoning is valid. Deductive reasoning is most clearly illustrated in a **syllogism**, a three-sentence chain of reasoning that includes a major and minor premise and conclusion.

Deductive Process (Syllogism)

Major premise: All persons die.
Minor premise: Elmer is a person.
Conclusion: Elmer will die.

◆ EXERCISE C: DEDUCTIVE REASONING

Complete the syllogisms in the following examples.

1. Major premise: All persons are created equal.

   Minor premise: Mary and Joe are people.

   Conclusion: _____

2. Major premise: All elephants eat peanuts.

Minor premise: _____

Conclusion: Dumbo eats peanuts.

3. Major premise: Students who do well on their SAT or ACT tests will earn high grades in college.

Minor premise: _____

Conclusion: _____

4. Major premise: If I pay my library fine, I'll be allowed to graduate.

Minor premise: _____

Conclusion: _____

5. Major premise: All students experience stress in their lives.

Minor premise: _____

Conclusion: _____

PERCEPTION

The way we look at situations, places, and things is the result of our personal **perception**, which reflects the way we view the world and influences the conclusions and decisions we make. As shown in Figure 2-4, perception begins by taking in information through the senses—hearing, seeing, feeling, tasting, and smelling. The senses then record and send messages to the brain, which processes the information by selecting, organizing, and interpreting the information sent.

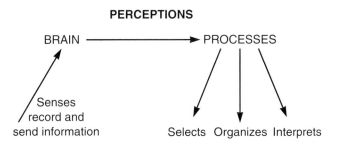

FIGURE 2-4 Perception process.

Perspective

We also view the world from our own orientation. We all perceive things differently because of varying interests, feelings, desires, and past experiences. Thus, our individual perspectives affect our perception. For instance, when children in elementary school discuss their teachers, they usually view their teachers as old. The reason for the children's perception is due to their own age, size, and limited world view. From the children's perspective, their teachers are old, no matter what the teacher's real age. So, although we take in information through our senses, it is really our mind that perceives by analyzing and integrating the information from our senses with what we already know and feel.

◆ EXERCISE D: PERSPECTIVE

Look at Figures 2-5–2-7. Each picture can be seen in two different ways. In the table that follows, write down the two different things you see in each picture. A description of the possible interpretations can be found on page 41.

	Perspective 1	*Perspective 2*
Figure 2-5		
Figure 2-6		
Figure 2-7		

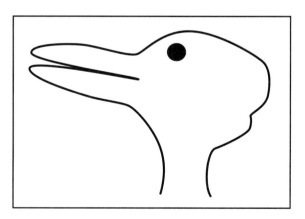

FIGURE 2-5

FIGURE 2-6

FIGURE 2-7

Errors of Perception

Because we tend to interpret information in our own unique way, from our own perspective, our perception can be distorted. Incomplete, inaccurate, and selective perceptions can result in a biased view. We often see what we want to see. If we are aware of our biases, however, we can adjust our thinking and recognize that our own perceptions and interpretations are not infallible. The following are some typical errors of perception:

1. **Stereotyping** expresses a belief about an entire group of people without recognizing the individual differences among members of the group. This type of thinking tends to be superficial because it is based on insufficient evidence.

   Examples: "All women are emotional."
   "Politicians are corrupt."
   "Teenagers are wild and irresponsible."

2. **Selective perception** takes place when a person selects only perceptions that attract his or her attention and blocks out others. With this type of faulty perception, people tend to focus on things that interest them or things they need rather than to look at the whole picture.

   Example: "Ann plays the piano beautifully and with ease because she has great talent." This statement is selective because practice and perseverance also contribute to Ann's playing.

3. **Resistance to change** occurs if decisions are inflexible and resistant to change.

   Example: Refusal to modify a route home even though another way is shown to be quicker and more pleasant.

4. **Either/Or thinking** is oversimplified thinking that perceives only two sides to an issue. It occurs when a person is confronted with complex issues.

   Example: "She loves me, she loves me not."
   "You are for me or against me."

5. **Ad hominem** is a type of faulty thinking in which a person attacks another person rather than deals with an issue

   Example: "I went to a feminist meeting last night. The speakers were about as homely a group of women as I have ever seen. No wonder they hate men. A man would have to be pretty desperate to have anything to do with them."

◆ **EXERCISE E: ERRORS OF PERCEPTION**

Read the following statements to determine which of the five types of errors of perception each statement illustrates. Identify the type in the space provided.

1. The literature courses here at the college are bad. My English teacher is a weak teacher; she does not know her material and is not interested in her students.

2. We can recognize that athletes who participate in major sports must be given special consideration within our grading system, or we can let the college sink into athletic limbo.

3. All computer experts are brilliant; therefore, James, who is a computer "freak," must be smart.

4. Teenagers are not mature enough to get married. They have the highest divorce rate of any age group. In fact, teenagers get into more trouble than other groups.

5. There is no use moving to a new place because one place is as good as another.

EVALUATION AND FLEXIBILITY

A critical thinker learns to look at things from all sides. This ability to see issues from someone else's viewpoint is important to understanding and evaluating situations, information, and people in order to make valid decisions. Passive thinkers tend to have narrow views, while active thinkers ask questions such as Who? What? Where? Not only do you need to ask questions, but you also need to see the situation from different points of view and to look for reasons and evidence to support various perceptions. A critical thinker should be open to modifying or changing his or her point of view when new evidence or information surfaces. You can become a critical thinker by using the following strategies:

- Think critically about your own perceptions.
- View situations from other points of view.
- Try to understand the reasons that support different perspectives.
- Develop your knowledge of the world.

The following exercise gives you an opportunity to practice enlarging your perspective and expanding your point of view.

◆ EXERCISE F: EVALUATION AND FLEXIBILITY

On a separate sheet of paper, write a one-page description of an event or a person that you and your parents (or your children, if you are a parent) view differently.

PROBLEM SOLVING

The ability to evaluate and be flexible in one's thinking is the underpinning of effective problem solving. When faced with an issue or a problem, a good thinker is willing to suspend his or her own belief long enough to consider other ideas or possible solutions, to evaluate those possible ideas and solutions based on new interpretations and information, and then to arrive at his or her own belief or solution. Some current national issues being considered are whether the government should institute a national health care program and whether doctor-assisted suicide and euthanasia of terminally ill patients who want to end their lives should be legalized. Before making decisions about major issues such as these, good thinkers first consider possible alternatives; next, they gather information and consider the consequences of each side of an issue. This critical thinking process of questioning and evaluating is illustrated in Figure 2-8.

By gathering information and considering the consequences of an opinion, you are developing evidence, or support, which can then be weighed and evaluated. This information may be found by reading and researching, by talking to experts as well as acquaintances, and by reasoning logically. Possible types of evidence include facts, examples, analogies, statistics, definitions, and cause-and-

FIGURE 2-8 Critical thinking process.

effect analysis. This evidence then becomes the reasons that lead to the decision either for or against a possible solution to a problem or position on a controversial issue. Listing reasons both for and against an idea or solution can help you come to a well-thought-out conclusion.

Problem solving isn't just reserved for national issues. It's a skill that each person uses in every aspect of life. Although the problems students meet in an academic setting are often intellectual ones, the same strategies can be applied to career choices, relationships, and a variety of everyday occurrences.

The first step in problem solving is to define, or understand, the problem. This involves being able to see what the problem entails. You need to separate facts from emotional responses to clarify the various components of the problem. To define an issue or problem means to look at the situation clearly and to set boundaries against a background of information. The second step is to gather facts and then generate alternative solutions, evaluating both the positive and negative elements of each solution. Finally, you need to select the best solution based on the problem-solving process.

The following five questions can be used in different situations to analyze a problem:

1. What is the problem?
2. What are some possible solutions or answers?
3. What are the pros and cons of each possible solution?
4. What other information is needed to reach a valid conclusion?
5. After weighing evidence, what is the best solution?

Use the five questions in analyzing the situations in Exercise G.

◆ EXERCISE G: PROBLEM SOLVING

In groups of three or four, consider the following issues and come to a conclusion about the best solution to each situation. You may want to write down how each step of the problem-solving process can be applied to the situations.

1. A student sees someone cheating on a test. What action should the student take?

_____

_____

_____

2. Do you think women should take their husbands' names when they marry?

_____

_____

_____

3. Is legalizing drugs an effective answer to America's growing drug problem?

_____

_____

_____

The process of defining the problem often involves examining a situation from different viewpoints or perspectives, as previously mentioned. An example of an issue with different viewpoints is illustrated in the article shown here by Jerry Adler with Brook Harrington. The issue involves membership rules for the Boy Scouts of America.

Fighting the Pack Mentality*

The Boy Scouts, long a bastion of tradition, face a series of legal challenges over membership rules.

It is the largest uniformed force in the nation, and in some ways the most exclusive. You can be female and a soldier in the United States Army; you can be an atheist and a police officer; you can be a homosexual and an Episcopal priest. But you can't be any of these things and a Boy Scout.

At least, not yet. These are times of turmoil for the Boy Scouts of America, as the unwelcome forces of liberalization let loose in the 1970s are knocking at the door with growing insistence. Micheal and William Randall, 9-year-old twins from Anaheim Hills, Calif., who were asked to leave their Cub Scout pack earlier this year for refusing to invoke God in their oath ("I [name], promise to do my best to do my duty to God and my country . . ."), are suing to win reinstatement. Just last week a U.S. district court in Chicago set a trial date for a suit by 8-year-old Mark Welsh, who is seeking to set aside the requirement for a "de-

claration of religious principle" from Scout families. "I was in Scouts for seven years and it never entered my mind that they could exclude people," said Welsh's father, Elliot, who in 1970 himself fought to the Supreme Court for the right to call himself a nonreligious conscientious objector. (He won.) "Scouts taught me about tolerance in the first place."

Gay Eagle: Predictably, the American Civil Liberties Union is in the forefront of the assault on the Scouts' right to set their own standards of admission. Local affiliates of the ACLU have agreed to represent the Randall twins and are considering bringing a case on behalf of five girls from Quincy, Calif., who sought to join a Cub Scout pack. Culminating a 10-year struggle, civil-liberties lawyers have gone to trial in the case of Tim Curran, a former Eagle Scout from Berkeley, who says he was told he couldn't be a troop leader because he was a homosexual. Last fall a California judge rejected the Boy Scouts' claim to be a private club exempt from state antidiscrimination laws.

In each case, the Boy Scouts respond that admitting gays, atheists or homosexuals would undermine their purposes. Although the Scouts have weathered several nasty scandals involving scout masters who abuse their charges, Scout spokesman Blake Lewis denies that the fear of molestation is behind the ban on gay scoutmasters. Homosexuals, he says, are "frankly not the traditional male role we are looking for." With respect to admitting girls, Donald York, a regional Scout executive based in Reno, Nev., points out that "most psychologists tell us that boys of scouting age (6 to 13) prefer to associate with other boys." And as for boys who do not believe in God, or America, or any of the other values enshrined in the Scouts' credo, Lewis observes that "if you start allowing people to choose the rules they want to obey, you start becoming a faceless organization." Which suggests that the real issue is what the Boy Scouts really are; uniformed forces for moral uplift, or, as the Randall twins' father, James, puts it: "This fun organization where you went camping and had a good time."

From the article it appears that the Randall twins and Mark Welsh felt discriminated against because of their religious beliefs, so one issue at stake is whether individuals' freedom is being violated. The Boy Scouts believe the integrity of their organization would be destroyed if atheists are admitted. So a second issue to consider is whether private clubs should be exempt from antidiscrimination laws. In fact, the *Newsweek* authors defined the problem as establishing the true nature of the organization. Eventually, the courts decided that the Boy Scouts had a right to exclude atheists from the organization. In effect, the courts upheld the nature of the Boy Scouts as a private club exempt from discrimination laws.

Although defining the problem is the first step, the ultimate goal is to find a solution. One method of discovering a solution is to list all possible solutions to the problem, using the brainstorming strategy in which all possibilities are considered without evaluation. Several feasible solutions may then become evident. Next, by considering the advantages and disadvantages of the most promising solutions, a person can decide on the most workable solution and then implement it. These problem-solving strategies can be applied to the content of your academic courses as well as to personal decisions and social issues. To gain experience in the problem-solving process, complete Exercise H.

◆ EXERCISE H: CRITICAL THINKING

After reading the following selection, answer the critical-thinking questions below. You may want to work with a partner.

1. What is the problem?

_____

_____

2. What are the possible solutions to the problems?

_____

_____

3. What are the pros and cons of each solution?

_____

_____

_____

4. What other information is needed to reach a valid conclusion or solution?

_____

_____

5. After weighing the evidence, what is the best solution?

_____

The Forgotten People*

The term endangered species *refers to plants and animals destroyed or threatened by habitat alteration. But, certain human populations—tribal peoples—are also threatened with extinction. About 1 of every 25 humans alive today is an Eskimo, Pygmy, Bushman, Indian, aborigine, or some other tribal member. These people live as their ancestors did, as hunters and gatherers or subsistence-level farmers.*

Tribal peoples have been uprooted in the name of progress to develop farms, mineral deposits, timber, dams, reservoirs, and wildlife parks. Often driven from their homelands, they are forced into areas unlike those in which they have lived for centuries. In Paraguay, for example, the remnants of the Toba-Maskoy tribe have been moved from their rain forest home to an arid region where their survival is in doubt.

Those native people who are allowed to remain in their homelands are susceptible to new diseases introduced by developers. Brazil's Indian population has shrunk from 6 million to 200,000 since the first Portuguese explorers arrived in the early 1500s. Although war was responsible for some deaths, diseases brought from foreign lands were, and still are, the greatest killers. Barbara Bentley, the director of Survival International (an organization dedicated to the protection of tribal people), says, "The easiest way to dispose of these isolated tribal people is by sneezing."

A government investigation in Brazil revealed that agents of a government bureau charged with protecting the native peoples actually practiced genocide by deliberately introducing smallpox, influenza, tuberculosis, and measles into Indian groups, which wiped out large numbers of native people. The same agents had joined with land speculators and white landowners in systematic murder and robbery of the native peoples.

Some tribes have been "assimilated" into the invading culture with disastrous results. Having been suddenly catapulted two or three centuries in time, they become lost, frightened, and confused by modern technology. Often, they returned to their homelands only to find them destroyed. Loss of homeland and

*From *Environmental Science,* Fourth Edition, by Daniel D. Chiras. Copyright © 1994 by The Benjamin/Cummings Publishing Company. Reprinted by permission.

traditional values can lead to fatal mental trauma. From Brazil to Australia, alcoholism, severe depression, and poverty take their toll. Once-skilled hunters are often reduced to begging.

The stories continue: Copper mining in Panama threatens thousands of Guaymi Indians; Kalinga tribes in the Philippines fight the construction of hydroelectric dams that would flood their rice terraces; 300,000 Chilean Mapuche Indians have recently been told that their land will be opened for timber cutting; in Peru, the long-isolated Amuesha Indians are threatened by a new highway that would link them to civilization.

The elimination of these cultures will put an end to age-old languages, myths, and social customs and result in the irreversible loss of knowledge, including information on medicinal plants, dyes, and diet. Tribal peoples are responsible for discovering more than 3000 plant species with antifertility properties, a potential boon for birth control research. Some of their plant materials give promising clues to cancer prevention and cure.

The very cultures modern civilization is systematically destroying also offer considerable guidance on sustainable practices. In fact, many goals of the sustainability movement, among them cooperative relationships and holistic thinking, are commonplace in ancient cultures. Thus, the question of whether we can afford to allow these tribal people a continued existence has become this: Can we afford to live without them?

CRITICAL THINKING

The critical-thinking components described in this chapter are crucial to implementing effective study strategies and comprehension of course material. Throughout the text, the critical-thinking elements are integrated so that you will be able to experience continual reinforcement of these skills. Learning to solve problems, to think logically, to see issues from different viewpoints, to analyze and evaluate ideas—in short, to become an active thinker—are cornerstones of academic success.

Answer to Figure 2-1, box of pearls

10 pearls in the box; 27 pearls on the string

Answers To Figure 2-2, brain teasers

1. Spiral notebook

2. Mental block

3. Blooming idiot

4. Homestretch

5. Broken promise

6. Spellbound

7. Bobolink

8. Zip code

9. Curly Qs

10. The plot thickens

11. String quartet

12. Jack-in-the-box

13. George Burns

14. Thumb screws

15. Sales tax

16. Melting pot

17. Disappearing act

Answers to Exercise D

Figure 2-5: A duck or a rabbit.

Figure 2-6: A vase or the profile of two faces.

Figure 2-7: An old woman or a young woman. (The necklace of the young woman becomes the mouth of the old woman.)

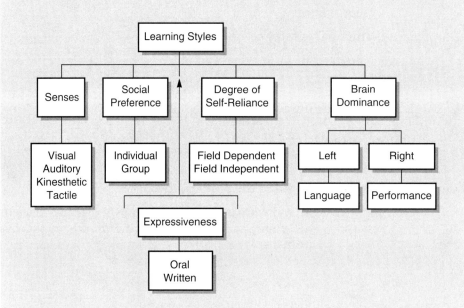

3

LEARNING STYLES

If a man does not keep pace with his companions, perhaps it
is because he hears a different drummer. Let him step to the
music which he hears, however measured or far away.
—*HENRY DAVID THOREAU,* Walden

Key Concepts

Auditory learning style   A way of learning in which the learner must hear what is to be learned.

Brain dominance   A theory that refers to the specialization of the functions by the left and right hemisphere of the brain.

Field dependent learning style   A way of learning in which learners prefer structure.

Field independent learning style   A way of learning in which learners like to direct their own learning.

Kinesthetic learning style   A way of learning in which the learner must work at and manipulate what is to be learned.

Metacognition   Knowing what you know and knowing what you do not know.

Tactile learning style   A way of learning in which the learner must touch what is to be learned.

Visual learning style   A way of learning in which the learner must see what is to be learned.

One factor that contributes to being a good student is knowing your-self and how you learn best. When you become aware of yourself as a learner, then you can make intelligent choices about how and when to study. Knowing what you know and knowing what you do not know is called **metacognition.** Having metacognition gives you the ability to make intelligent decisions about your learning. Since 85 percent of learning at the college level involves independent reading, "college students who are metacognitively unaware proba-bly will experience major academic problems." Therefore, one of the first things you might want to consider as you begin your col-lege career is what type of learning style you can best utilize. Just as people have different personalities, they have different learning styles. Knowing about learning styles is important because this in-formation will help you find the study strategies that work most ef-fectively for you.

Before you begin to read this chapter, complete the following learning styles inventory. Read the directions before beginning.

◆ LEARNING STYLE INVENTORY

Read each item carefully, and circle the number that best describes how you feel about the statement. The number *4* indicates the strongest agreement; the number *1* indicates the weakest agreement. After completing the inventory, transfer the number of each re-sponse to the score sheet. Then complete your total and score for each area.

Center for Innovative Teaching Experiences (C.I.T.E.)
Learning Styles Instrument

Question	*Most Like Me*		*Least Like Me*	
1. Making things for my studies helps me to remember what I have learned.	4	3	2	1
2. I can write about most of the things I know better than I can tell about them.	4	3	2	1
3. When I really want to understand what I have read, I read it softly to myself.	4	3	2	1
4. I get more done when I work alone.	4	3	2	1
5. I remember what I have read better than what I have heard.	4	3	2	1

Question	Most Like Me		Least Like Me	
6. When I answer questions, I can say the answer better than I can write it.	4	3	2	1
7. When I do math problems in my head, I say the numbers to myself.	4	3	2	1
8. I enjoy joining in on class discussions.	4	3	2	1
9. I understand a math problem that is written down better than one that I hear.	4	3	2	1
10. I do better when I can write the answer instead of having to say it.	4	3	2	1
11. I understand spoken directions better than written ones.	4	3	2	1
12. I like to work by myself.	4	3	2	1
13. I would rather read a story than listen to it read.	4	3	2	1
14. I would rather show and explain how a thing works than write about how it works.	4	3	2	1
15. If someone tells me three numbers to add, I can usually get the right answer without writing them down.	4	3	2	1
16. I prefer to work with a group when there is work to be done.	4	3	2	1
17. A graph or chart of numbers is easier for me to understand than hearing the numbers said.	4	3	2	1
18. Writing a spelling word several times helps me remember it better.	4	3	2	1
19. I learn better if someone reads a book to me than if I read it silently to myself.	4	3	2	1
20. I learn best when I study alone.	4	3	2	1
21. When I have a choice between reading and listening, I usually read.	4	3	2	1
22. I would rather tell a story than write it.	4	3	2	1

Question	Most Like Me		Least Like Me	
23. Saying the multiplication tables over and over helped me remember them better than writing them over and over.	4	3	2	1
24. I do my best work in a group.	4	3	2	1
25. I understand a math problem that is written down better than one I hear.	4	3	2	1
26. In a group project, I would rather make a chart or poster than gather the information to put on it.	4	3	2	1
27. Written assignments are easy for me to follow.	4	3	2	1
28. I remember more of what I learn if I learn it alone.	4	3	2	1
29. I do well in classes where most of the information has to be read.	4	3	2	1
30. I would enjoy giving an oral report to the class.	4	3	2	1
31. I learn math better from spoken explanations than written ones.	4	3	2	1
32. If I have to decide something, I ask other people for their opinions.	4	3	2	1
33. Written math problems are easier for me to do than oral ones.	4	3	2	1
34. I like to make things with my hands.	4	3	2	1
35. I don't mind doing written assignments.	4	3	2	1
36. I remember things I hear better than things I read.	4	3	2	1
37. I learn better by reading than by listening.	4	3	2	1
38. It is easy for me to tell about the things that I know.	4	3	2	1
39. I make it easier when I say the numbers of a problem to myself as I work it out.	4	3	2	1
40. If I understand a problem, I like to help someone else understand it too.	4	3	2	1

Question	*Most Like Me*		*Least Like Me*	
41. Seeing a number makes more sense to me than hearing a number.	4	3	2	1
42. I understand what I have learned better when I am involved in making something for the subject.	4	3	2	1
43. The things I write on paper sound better than when I say them.	4	3	2	1
44. I find it easier to remember what I have heard than what I have read.	4	3	2	1
45. It is fun to learn with classmates, but it is hard to study with them.	4	3	2	1

C.I.T.E. Learning Styles Instrument—Score Sheet

Visual Language	*Social—Individual*	*Auditory Numerical*
5. _____	4. _____	7. _____
13. _____	12. _____	15. _____
21. _____	20. _____	23. _____
29. _____	28. _____	31. _____
37. _____	45. _____	39. _____
Total _____	Total _____	Total _____
x 2 = _____ (Score)	x 2 = _____ (Score)	x 2 = _____ (Score)

Visual Numerical	*Social—Group*	*Kinesthetic/Tactile*
9. _____	8. _____	1. _____
17. _____	16. _____	18. _____
25. _____	24. _____	26. _____
33. _____	32. _____	34. _____
41. _____	40. _____	42. _____
Total _____	Total _____	Total _____
x 2 = _____ (Score)	x 2 = _____ (Score)	x 2 = _____ (Score)

		Expressiveness—
Auditory Language	*Expressiveness—Oral*	*Written*
3. _____	6. _____	2. _____
11. _____	14. _____	10. _____
19. _____	22. _____	27. _____
36. _____	30. _____	35. _____
44. _____	38. _____	43. _____
Total _____	Total _____	Total _____
x 2 = _____	x 2 = _____	x 2 = _____
(Score)	(Score)	(Score)

Score: 33–40 = Major Learning Style
20–32 = Minor Learning Style
5–20 = Negligible Use

(Used by permission of Wichita Public Schools.)

MAJOR LEARNING STYLES

The previous inventory can help you identify your unique learning style. There are five major learning modalities measured on the C.I.T.E. Learning Styles Instrument: visual, auditory, kinesthetic/tactile, social, and expressive. Although there are variations and areas of overlap within these styles, we will address each style separately. Read the following descriptions of learning styles, and then go back to the C.I.T.E. Learning Styles Instrument score sheet to analyze your results. Make a graph of your results to see your strengths and weaknesses clearly.

Visual

Having a strong **visual learning style** means that you need to see what you learn. Therefore, reading or seeing something is important because this is the way you learn. There are several factors that will contribute to your success if you tend to be visual. Reading textbooks is extremely important to your success, because it is when you read that you will comprehend the material best. Lectures are still important, but you need to use a written text to compensate for what you might have missed in lectures and to support your comprehension of the lecture's content. Note taking is also extremely important for you because it may be somewhat more difficult for you to follow the lecture than someone with an auditory learning style. Using reading handouts and completing written assignments are also necessary for your learning style.

A high score in the Visual Numerical area indicates that you need to see numbers in a book, on an overhead, or on the chalkboard in order to understand the concepts and complete the computations. You probably need to see the numbers in order to understand oral explanations of math concepts. Seeing how a problem is done without a great deal of oral explanation may be enough for you to understand how to do a problem.

Study Strategies

Because you are a visual learner, two strategies that you can use to support your learning style are highlighting and making marginal notes. These strategies will help reinforce your reading, which is a visual task, and review more effectively for tests. Developing cognitive maps and charts will be extremely helpful for you because people with this type of learning style tend to remember information when presented in some type of visual format. For further information on mapping and charting, see Chapter 7, which deals with many types of visual strategies. Writing is another learning mode that will assist you in remembering important information. Writing down information serves two purposes: it provides another visual aid and is also another mode of learning. You will probably do best with instructors who write on a chalkboard, use overheads or handouts, and give assignments in writing.

Auditory

Having a strong **auditory learning style** means that you learn best by hearing information. Auditory learners find lectures to be an important focal point. Missing lectures could be devastating for you since most of your understanding of a course's content is acquired from lecture. Although you still need to support attending lectures with reading, you may want to read some texts orally, since you learn the information more readily this way.

A high score in the Auditory Numerical area means that you need to hear math problems explained. You may remember phone numbers and other numbers easily when you hear them and may be able to do math computations easily in your head, especially if you verbalize them to yourself.

Study Strategies

Two study strategies that will benefit you and help you to retain information are hearing audiotapes and using oral practice. You will also learn a lot of information during class discussions, since the oral exchange of information will help you to remember what is important for tests. You may also benefit from using a tape recorder to make tapes to listen to. Taping lectures and listening to them will reinforce learning for you. Study groups, another auditory experience, will also help you learn the information more readily. Using index cards and verbally reciting the information from them is another excellent study strategy, especially when studying or reviewing for a test.

Kinesthetic and Tactile

Having a **kinesthetic learning style** requires that you experience and become physically involved in the learning experience for best results. The manipulation of material will aid the kinesthetic learner. If you have a **tactile learning style**, you learn best by touching what you are doing. Both styles tend to overlap. Because using several modes of learning is beneficial, the manipulation of material along with sight and sound will help you to retain what you are learning. You need to handle, touch, and work with what you are learning. Involvement with other students and participation in activities will also support your learning style.

Study Strategies

Use as many manipulative study strategies as possible. For example, writing, drawing visuals, and using demonstrations are productive ways for you to learn information. Index cards may be helpful, since you will not only be writing down the information but also manipulating the cards themselves. In conjunction with these strategies, pacing, moving around, and even chewing gum may create enough movement to enhance your learning. Movement such as tapping your foot or your pencil may help you concentrate more easily. Using your fingers to count off items you are reviewing or using your fingers to help you learn math will also be effective for you.

Social: Individual or Group

If your score in the Social—Individual area is above 30, you have a strong preference for studying alone. You probably think best and remember information most effectively after you have used either a visual, auditory, or kinesthetic study strategy that you have completed by yourself. If your score indicates a moderate preference for individual learning (20–29), you might profit from some group studying strategies, but you will probably also need to study the material for tests by yourself in order to remember and understand it successfully.

Study Strategies

If your score in the Social—Group area is above 30, finding a study partner or a study group to join will probably enhance your scores on tests because you show a strong preference for working and learning with other people. If you score in the moderate range (20–29), you may be able to profit from studying with other people. If your score in this area is below 20, then you can work in groups when it is required, but this method is not your strongest mode of understanding and remembering material.

Expressive: Oral or Written

Your expressive learning style indicates your preferred method of relating information to others, either socially or in a testing situation. If you scored above 30 in the Expressiveness—Oral area, you can probably easily tell people what you know and understand. People with this ability talk fluently and easily and seem to be able to say what they mean. Giving oral reports and participating in class discussions are activities that students who score high in oral expressiveness probably enjoy. Having to organize your thoughts and express yourself on essay tests and on assigned papers may seem a tedious task. Investing in a word processor may ease the writing task for you, because using a computer or word processor makes the writing process much faster and allows you to organize your thoughts after you get them down in written form. If you scored above 30 in the Expressiveness—Written area, you can probably organize and put your thoughts down on paper more readily than speaking them. You can learn to give oral reports and to speak effectively, but writing your thoughts down first or making notes to yourself during class discussions may make you more comfortable when speaking in public.

You may have scored moderately (20–29) in both of these groups, which indicates that you have no strong preferred method of relating information; you can convey information effectively in either way.

◆ **EXERCISE A: STUDY STRATEGIES**

Describe a school-related activity that you dislike. It might be writing papers, giving oral reports, participating in class discussions, completing math assignments, taking notes during lectures, or reading textbook assignments.

Then, using your scores on the C.I.T.I. Learning Styles Instrument, explain how you could make this task easier for yourself by using your strong learning modalities.

OTHER LEARNING STYLES

Another way to view yourself as a learner is to consider your reliance on yourself and others. If you prefer a **field dependent learning style**, you tend to rely on direction and structure; if you prefer a **field independent learning style**, you tend to prefer autonomy. Although many people are a mixture of both styles, most have a preference for one style or another. Each style has its disadvantages and advantages, but the important thing is to understand what works best for you.

Field Dependent

If you are a field dependent learner, you will do best with instructors who give explicit directions, assignments, and guidelines for projects, tests, and papers. If your instructor tends to be less structured, you may need to reinforce assignments by meeting with the instructor independently or finding a classmate who can reinforce the information about which you are not sure. Field dependent students tend to need emotional support, so it would be helpful to find an advisor, counselor, or instructor who can provide you with support when stress becomes overwhelming. A support system at home will also help you maintain your confidence and excel academically.

Field Independent

Field independent learners like to direct their own learning process. If you are field independent, you will prefer teachers whose style of teaching is not too structured and allows students many options. You may feel that you have a clear sense of direction and want to follow your own path; however, you need to be flexible enough to respond to suggestions and be open to change. Students who are field independent tend to have difficulty responding to explicit directions and end up doing things their own way, which can be a problem if assignments are not completed as required. Too much self-confidence can sometimes backfire, because you lose awareness of academic reality. If you have metacognition, then being field independent can be an advantage because you are a self-starter and need little support from others. Answer the questions on the following page to determine whether you are field dependent or field independent.

◆ **EXERCISE B: FIELD INDEPENDENT OR FIELD DEPENDENT**

Put a check mark next to each statement that describes you.

_____ 1. I like to study alone.

_____ 2. I study with friends or in a group.

_____ **3.** I like to study in a quiet place.

_____ **4.** I enjoy my studies and do not need any outside motivation to study.

_____ **5.** I am not overly motivated to study unless I have deadlines to meet.

_____ **6.** I tend to procrastinate.

_____ **7.** I am usually prepared.

_____ **8.** I prefer teachers who provide careful course outlines and objectives.

_____ **9.** I prefer teachers who encourage class discussion and activities.

_____ **10.** I prefer teachers who use lectures and textbook reading as a method of teaching.

_____ **11.** I enjoy classes that have class discussion and group activities.

Statements 1, 3, 4, 7, and 10 indicate field independent characteristics. The remaining statements indicate a dependent preference.

BRAIN DOMINANCE

Another area to be considered when analyzing how you learn has to do with whether your strengths lie in tasks demanding verbal ability or in tasks demanding creativity. The human brain is divided into two hemispheres, with each hemisphere controlling different functions. Although every task involves both sides of the brain, each side of the brain specializes in specific functions. Theories of **brain dominance** maintain that people often have a preference for one side of the brain over the other. The left brain is language centered, while the right brain focuses on creativity and intuitive processes. Most school tasks tend to demand left-brain ability because they tend to focus on highly structured language activities and sequential skills. This explains why creative people often do not like school and generally dislike the confines of academic tasks.

Students who tend to be left-brain dominant usually are quite verbal and may excel in written and oral presentations. Right-brain dominant students tend to enjoy more visual and creative endeavors, such as art and architecture. Look at Figure 3-1 to get a sense of the skills controlled by each side of the brain. Then take the following self-test to see whether you have a preferred dominance or tend to be balanced.

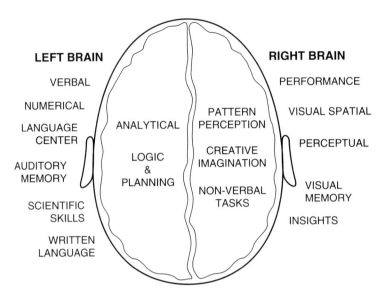

FIGURE 3-1   Brain.

◆ **TEST YOURSELF**

Do You Have a Right-Brain or Left-Brain Preference?
Different styles of learning or thinking are described by each item.
Put a check mark by the one that describes most accurately your
strength or preference.

_____ 1. a. Not good at remembering faces.

_____   b. Not good at remembering names.

_____   c. Equally good at remembering names and faces.

_____ 2. a. Respond best to verbal instructions.

_____   b. Respond best to instruction by example.

_____   c. Equally responsive to verbal instruction and instruc-
               tion by example.

_____ 3. a. Able to express feelings and emotions freely.

_____   b. Not easily able to express feelings and emotions.

_____ 4. a. Prefer classes where I have one assignment at a time.

_____   b. Prefer classes where I am studying many things at once.

_____   c. I have equal preference for the above type classes.

_____ **5. a.** Preference for multiple-choice tests.

_____   **b.** Preference for essay tests.

_____   **c.** Equal preference for multiple-choice, essay tests.

_____ **6. a.** Good at thinking up funny things to say and/or do.

_____   **b.** Poor at thinking up funny things to say and/or do.

_____   **c.** Moderately good at thinking up funny things to say and/or do. _____

_____ **7. a.** Prefer classes in which I am moving and doing things.

_____   **b.** Prefer classes in which I listen to others.

_____   **c.** Equal preference for above type of classes.

_____ **8. a.** Use factual, objective information in making judgments.

_____   **b.** Use personal experiences and feelings in making judgments.

_____   **c.** Make equal use of factual information and personal experiences.

_____ **9. a.** Almost always use whatever tools are available to get work done.

_____   **b.** At times am able to use whatever is available to get work done.

_____   **c.** Prefer working with proper materials for use they are intended for.

_____ **10. a.** Like classes or work to be planned, know exactly what I am to do.

_____   **b.** Like my classes or work to be open, flexible.

_____   **c.** Equal preference for structured work and activities open to change.

_____ **11. a.** Very inventive.

_____   **b.** Occasionally inventive.

_____   **c.** Never inventive.

_____ **12. a.** Preference for intuitive approach in solving problems.

_____   **b.** Preference for logical approach in solving problems.

_____   **c.** Equal preference for intuitive, logical approaches.

_____ **13. a.** Like classes where the work has clear and immediate applications (such as shop, mechanical drawing, home economics).

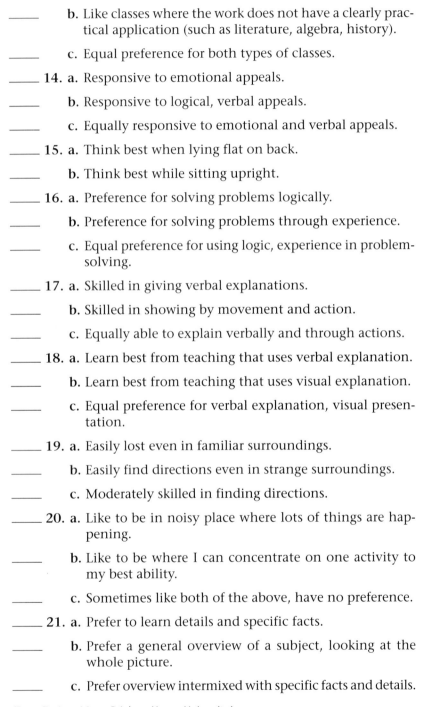

_____ **b.** Like classes where the work does not have a clearly practical application (such as literature, algebra, history).

_____ **c.** Equal preference for both types of classes.

_____ **14. a.** Responsive to emotional appeals.

_____ **b.** Responsive to logical, verbal appeals.

_____ **c.** Equally responsive to emotional and verbal appeals.

_____ **15. a.** Think best when lying flat on back.

_____ **b.** Think best while sitting upright.

_____ **16. a.** Preference for solving problems logically.

_____ **b.** Preference for solving problems through experience.

_____ **c.** Equal preference for using logic, experience in problem-solving.

_____ **17. a.** Skilled in giving verbal explanations.

_____ **b.** Skilled in showing by movement and action.

_____ **c.** Equally able to explain verbally and through actions.

_____ **18. a.** Learn best from teaching that uses verbal explanation.

_____ **b.** Learn best from teaching that uses visual explanation.

_____ **c.** Equal preference for verbal explanation, visual presentation.

_____ **19. a.** Easily lost even in familiar surroundings.

_____ **b.** Easily find directions even in strange surroundings.

_____ **c.** Moderately skilled in finding directions.

_____ **20. a.** Like to be in noisy place where lots of things are happening.

_____ **b.** Like to be where I can concentrate on one activity to my best ability.

_____ **c.** Sometimes like both of the above, have no preference.

_____ **21. a.** Prefer to learn details and specific facts.

_____ **b.** Prefer a general overview of a subject, looking at the whole picture.

_____ **c.** Prefer overview intermixed with specific facts and details.

(From Dr. Ivan Muse, Brigham Young University.)

Answer Key

R means right brain, *L* means left brain, and *I* means both sides are interactive.

1. A-L   B-R   C-I

2. A-L   B-R   C-I

3. A-R   B-L

4. A-L   B-R   C-I

5. A-R   B-L   C-I

6. A-R   B-L   C-I

7. A-R   B-L   C-I

8. A-L   B-R   C-I

9. A-R   B-I   C-L

10. A-L   B-R   C-I

11. A-R   B-I   C-L

12. A-R   B-L   C-I

13. A-R   B-L   C-I

14. A-R   B-L   C-I

15. A-R   B-L

16. A-L   B-R   C-I

17. A-L   B-R   C-I

18. A-L   B-R   C-I

19. A-L   B-R   C-I

20. A-R   B-L   C-I

21. A-L   B-R   C-I

Interpretation of Scores
Right Brain/Left Brain Survey

The higher the number, the stronger the cognitive style.

Example: 15 Is, 4 Ls, 2Rs = Interactive with strong left tendencies

Or

You need to have at least 12+ Rs, Ls, or Is to show a dominant preference.

Example: 12+ Rs = Right cognitive style
          12+ Ls = Left cognitive style
          12+ Is = Interactive cognitive style

Or

You can have a "mixed" processor.

Example: 10 Rs
          8 Is = Mixed with integrated tendencies
          3 Ls

Or

          10 Is
          8 Rs = Mixed with strong right tendencies
          3 Ls

◆ EXERCISE C

After scoring your answers to see whether you have a right- or left-brain preference, write a one- or two-page analysis of your learning styles. (Use a separate sheet of paper.) Be sure to consider your personal style in each of the categories described in the chapter: the five areas in the C.I.T.E. Learning Styles Instrument, field independence or dependence, and right- or left-brain preference.

CRITICAL THINKING

In groups of three, choose one person to be the spokesperson, one person to be the recorder, and one person to be the runner. (The runner checks to see that all needed information is recorded, collects material, and gives the material to the teacher.)

1. Each person should read his/her learning style description to the group.

2. As a group, choose one person's profile and use that *one* profile to develop the following:

    a. Describe the ideal teacher personality for this person.

    _____

    _____

    _____

b. Describe the ideal classroom structure (including the way assignments are given, papers assigned, kinds of tests and/or evaluations) for this person.

_____

_____

_____

c. Describe two study strategies this person could successfully use to study for a sociology or psychology test.

_____

_____

d. Describe one study strategy this person might use to study for a math test.

_____

e. Describe two courses this person might enjoy.

_____

f. Describe two time management (organizational) strategies this person might successfully use.

_____

_____

Use your insight and common sense as well as the information in Chapter 3 to develop strategies for this person.

REFERENCES

Center for Innovative Teaching Experience. Learning Styles Inventory. Wichita Public Schools. Wichita, Kansas.

Muse, Ivan. "Do You Have Right Brain or Left Brain Dominance?" Brigham Young University, Provo, Utah.

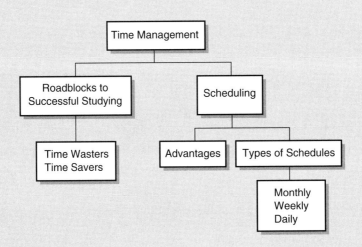

4

TIME MANAGEMENT

Dost thou love life? Then do not squander time,
for that is the stuff life is made of.
—BENJAMIN FRANKLIN

Key Concepts

Commitment   A promise to do something.

Perfectionist   One who has a tendency for setting extremely high standards and being displeased with anything less.

Prioritize   To arrange or deal with in order of importance.

Procrastinate   To postpone or delay needlessly.

Syllabus   The schedule of classes and assignments you receive in each course.

As Ben Franklin indicates, time is one of the most important elements of life. When you are young, there seems to be so much time, but as you grow older there never seems to be enough. Now that you are in college, you will be surprised at how fast time can fly. It is important to develop an awareness of how you use your time and to determine your own behavior in relationship to the time you have, because the way you spend your time is often related to your performance. Generally, students who are organized and manage their time wisely achieve their goals. The time-management techniques introduced in this chapter offer you tools to use to reach your objectives.

There are many types of schedules and organizational plans that you can use to keep on track with studying, classwork, leisure time, and work. Being familiar with these different options and types of schedules gives you choices about what techniques will work best for you. Since good time-management skills can often make the difference between poor academic and social adjustment or a successful college experience, examining common roadblocks to using time well is an important step toward academic achievement.

ROADBLOCKS TO SUCCESSFUL STUDYING

There are many roadblocks to successful studying. Since at least two hours of preparation should be allotted for each hour spent in class, effective time management is a necessity. Roadblocks are simply a lack of conscious planning. One roadblock to learning is a lack of goals and motivation. When students have not set priorities for themselves, it is usually an indication that they are not high achievers. Knowing where you are going and why is the beginning of a successful academic career.

A second roadblock to successful academic performance is not having a proper place to study. It is difficult to concentrate and learn when there are distractions and interruptions. A designated place that has everything you need helps you be more effective and encourages a mindset that is focused on studying.

A third roadblock has to do with personal behavior. Students who **procrastinate**, which is failing to recognize priorities and wasting time, will find studying difficult.

Some common time wasters are watching too much television and the inability to say no to nonacademic obligations and social events. Some time savers include removing distractions before you start a task, studying in the same place, and having all of your materials organized. Another time saver of "wasted" minutes between classes or waiting in line is reading or thinking about an assignment. Sometimes, having too much time stretched out before you can make it difficult to get started on a task.

Which time wasters and time savers do you use? Examining the way you use time now can open the way to making changes if you need to.

◆   **EXERCISE A: TIME WASTERS AND TIME SAVERS**

In groups of three or four, brainstorm time wasters and time savers that are not mentioned in the text.

Time Wasters	*Time Savers*
_____	_____
_____	_____
_____	_____
_____	_____
_____	_____
_____	_____
_____	_____
_____	_____
_____	_____
_____	_____
_____	_____
_____	_____
_____	_____
_____	_____
_____	_____

TIME COMMITMENTS

Identifying exactly how you currently spend time is another step toward using your time more effectively. The 168 hours in each week are the building blocks for constructing the kind of life you want. By identifying your essential **commitments,** you can see what choices you have, what decisions you need to make, and how you might re-arrange your activities.

Following are some ways other than studying that people spend their time:

Activities

- Sleep
- Breakfast
- Lunch
- Dinner
- Job (full or part time)
- Time spent in class
- Church, recreation, sports
- Socializing
- Household/family responsibilities
- Errands

◆ **EXERCISE B: YOUR TIME COMMITMENTS**

Complete the calendar in Figure 4-1 by writing your usual activity in the blanks. For example, if you usually eat dinner and socialize with friends from 6 P.M. to 8 P.M., write "dinner" and "socialize" in those two blanks. If you usually sleep from 11 P.M. to 7 A.M. during the week, write "sleep" in those time slots.

After you have completed the calendar, count the blank spaces to estimate the time left for studying. How many hours can you de-vote to study time?

COURSE GOALS

Before you adjust your weekly activities, you need to establish your goals and set your priorities. Plan on about two hours of study time for each hour in class; some classes may demand more, some less. By looking at the course **syllabus,** the schedule of classes and assign-ments you receive in each course, you can tell how many papers are due and approximate your time accordingly. The more papers and tests required, the more time the course will require. The volume of reading assignments and daily homework also will affect your preparation time. In addition, you need to set your own goals for the class. Are you going to work for an A in this course? Will you be satisfied with a C? Deciding realistically what you want to work for will also affect your time commitment, since getting As usually re-quires more time and effort than getting Cs.

Hours	Sunday	Monday	Tuesday	Wednesday	Thursday	Friday	Saturday
6–7							
7–8							
8–9							
9–10							
10–11							
11–12							
12–1							
1–2							
2–3							
3–4							
4–5							
5–6							
6–7							
7–8							
8–9							
9–10							
10–11							
11–12							
12–1							
1–2							
2–3							
3–4							
4–5							
5–6							

FIGURE 4-1   Weekly Commitments

◆ **EXERCISE C: SETTING GOALS FOR COURSES**

Complete the chart shown as Figure 4-2 on page 68 to set your goals in each course for the semester.

Putting Goals into Action

Setting both long- and short-term goals and deciding on study time are important in arranging and adjusting your schedule. First, you need to think of your other time commitments and the long-range goals you thought about in Chapter 1. Ask yourself which daily activities are necessary to achieve your long-range goals and **prioritize** them. Those daily activities that you identify need to become your first priority. For example, if becoming a teacher is one of your plans for the future, then the courses you take and the studying you do need to be among your top priorities. However, if your relationships are more important than your courses, then they should become a top priority. If both areas are important to you, you will have to arrange your schedule so that you can balance your time to fit in both areas.

Look again at the schedule in Exercise B, and observe how much time you spend on areas that are not of lasting value. Those areas can become lower priority items, and you can adjust your schedule accordingly. In adjusting your schedule, you may have difficult decisions to make. For example, you might find that working and taking classes occupy all of your daytime hours, that you have family obligations at night and on weekends, and that there are only a few hours left for studying. Then, some major realignments of your time and priorities may be necessary.

Examine what you can change by allowing others, such as roommates, spouses, or children, to assume responsibility for some tasks. In fact, you might find that redistributing responsibility will help them as much as it helps you. Although it is not easy to change your activities and reassign tasks, the rewards in the form of more personal satisfaction and enjoyment are great.

Complete the chart in Exercise D to reexamine areas where you might use your time differently.

◆ **EXERCISE D: DEFINING PRIORITIES**

1. What long-range goals do you have? List what matters most to you.

   a. _____

   b. _____

c. _____

d. _____

e. _____

2. What changes could you make in the way you use your time?

    a. _____

    b. _____

    c. _____

    d. _____

    e. _____

3. How can you enlist the support of others? In the space provided, list which tasks might be redistributed.

    a. _____

    b. _____

    c. _____

    d. _____

    e. _____

SCHEDULING

Use the goals and priorities you have established to decide how much time you wish to spend studying for each class. Then refer to the weekly commitments to work, family, and regular activities that you listed in Exercise B. Be sure you save time for some leisure. Now you are ready to devise a schedule that will be helpful to you.

Advantages

Having a schedule can have a positive effect on studying. Scheduling should be flexible so that changes can easily be made because studying time will vary as homework demands fluctuate. Although your biological clock should influence when you study, exceptions can be made. That is, although you should study when you feel most alert, the time does not necessarily have to be the same each day. There are many advantages to using a schedule, some of which are listed here:

- Helps you get more out of life.
- Makes your time more flexible.

Name of Course	Desired Grade	Major Assignments	Study Hours Needed Each Week

How much time will be needed to reach goals? _____

FIGURE 4-2   Chart

- Gets you started.
- Helps you not get behind.
- Prevents avoidance of disliked subjects.
- Eliminates the wrong type of studying (cramming).
- Promotes cumulative review rather than mass cramming.

Considerations

Allow Flexibility

Before using a schedule, though, remember that schedules are similar to rules: they are meant to be broken. Allow yourself the flexibility in your schedule to deal with unexpected events and emergencies, as well as varying homework demands. You also need to allow yourself the flexibility to change your schedule. If it isn't working, reexamine your priorities and commitments and then make the necessary changes.

Take Breaks

When making a schedule, remember that one of the best study strategies is to plan on taking regular breaks. According to many studies, most people can concentrate fully on one task for only about fifty minutes. After about an hour, you will need to take a break, if only for five or ten minutes to walk around or get a drink of water. So, when planning study time, remember that planning to study for many hours without a break is self-defeating. Also, many short review sessions are probably more productive than one long marathon study session.

Defeat Procrastination

All the schedules in the world won't help you if you never use them, so be aware of the ways in which you procrastinate before you begin making a schedule. Everyone procrastinates, but listening to the messages you give yourself can help to keep procrastination to a minimum. You may be telling yourself that you will not be able to do a good job; you may not be sure exactly what to do; you may be a **perfectionist** and have set up impossibly high standards for yourself. Maybe you feel angry about doing the work at all. Whatever the excuse, identify what you think and feel about the task. It may not make it easier, but you may be able to minimize your procrastination.

Following are some techniques to help you beat procrastination:

- *Ask for help.* If you realize that you're not sure exactly how to complete an assignment or to study for a test, talk to the professor, another student, or tutor about the task.

- *Use the salami technique.* Cut up large tasks into smaller segments, and list them on a piece of paper. Complete one of the tiny segments, and enjoy the feeling of accomplishment.
- *Try the thirty-minute plan.* Work on the task in thirty-minute segments.
- *Do the hardest part first.*
- *Talk to yourself.* Say aloud what you are going to do and when. Tell yourself you are capable of doing an adequate job.
- *Lower your standards.* Average is fine. You don't need to be brilliant. Just get the job done.

Types

There are many different kinds of calendars and organizers available in stores and in catalogs that you might want to use. The three basic kinds are monthly, weekly, and daily. Each has its advantage. The monthly calendar gives you an opportunity to plan ahead as you keep track of important exams and due dates. If you fill in the calendar with important events that are already scheduled, you can make adjustments in your weekly and daily schedules to accommodate times when several important events are scheduled closely together.

On the following pages are monthly, weekly, and daily planners for you to complete.

How to Use Monthly Planners

1. Fill out a sheet for each month of the semester.
2. Go through course outlines for each of your classes, and enter important information on the planner. Note dates for tests, papers, and projects.
3. Enter personal appointments.
4. If you wish, enter reading assignments for the month.

◆ EXERCISE E: MONTHLY PLANNER

Complete the monthly planner shown in Figure 4-3 for the current month. Look at your syllabi, and fill in assignments, tests, and all major obligations. With a partner, discuss how this schedule can help you manage your time. Identify one strength and one weakness of your schedule.

How to Use Weekly Planners

1. Using the goals and priorities you established, decide how much time you wish to spend studying for each class.

Month ____

Monday	Tuesday	Wednesday	Thursday	Friday	Saturday	Sunday

FIGURE 4-3   Monthly Planner

2. Figure out your weekly commitments.
3. Fill in the calendar with classes, work, and other commitments that are permanent.
4. Block out any appointments or obligations you have.
5. Be sure to save some time for leisure.

◆ **EXERCISE F: WEEKLY AND DAILY PLANNERS**

On the weekly and daily schedules shown in Figures 4-4 and 4-5, fill in your ideal schedules for a typical week and day. Then share your schedules with the group members. Identify one strength and one weakness of each schedule.

CRITICAL THINKING

After you have tried using a variety of planning formats for scheduling (Exercise F), evaluate the advantages and disadvantages of each. Then use the questions that follow to help you decide what types of time-management strategies work for you.

	Advantages	*Disadvantages*
Daily	_____	_____
	_____	_____
	_____	_____
Weekly	_____	_____
	_____	_____
	_____	_____
Monthly	_____	_____
	_____	_____
	_____	_____

1. Did you overestimate or underestimate the amount of time you needed for each course?

	Monday	Tuesday	Wednesday	Thursday	Friday	Saturday	Sunday
8:00							
9:00							
10:00							
11:00							
12:00							
1:00							
2:00							
3:00							
4:00							
5:00							
6:00							
7:00							
8:00							

FIGURE 4-4   Weekly Schedule

During especially busy times, it it sometimes helpful to establish a daily schedule. Below is an example of one daily schedule you might use. Making a "to do" list for the day, however, might be used in lieu of a schedule like this one, or you might use 3 x 5 cards to carry with you to list top priorities. Use this daily planner to schedule your busiest day of the week.

Morning

8:00
8:30
9:00
9:30
10:00
10:30
11:00
11:30

Afternoon

12:00
12:30
1:00
1:30
2:00
2:30
3:00
3:30
4:00
4:30
5:00
5:30

Evening

6:00
6:30
7:00
7:30
8:00
8:30

FIGURE 4-5   Daily Schedule

2. Did you find that you had time conflicts? What were they?

_____

_____

3. If you had time conflicts, can they be resolved? How?

_____

_____

_____

4. How does a study schedule help you organize your time better?

_____

5. How is a time schedule a helpful means for you to use? If you feel it is not, explain.

_____

_____

6. Did you stick to the time schedule, or did you decide not to use it? Explain why you decided on either course of action.

_____

_____

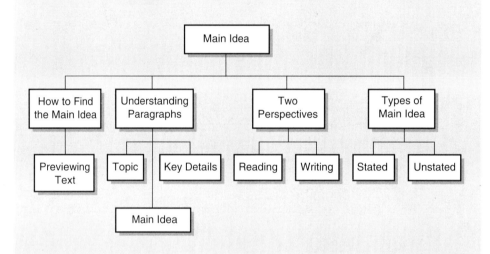

5

MAIN IDEA

Too much light often blinds gentlemen of this sort.
They cannot see the forest for the trees.
—CHRISTOPH MARTIN WIELUND

Key Concepts

Details   Those items that support the main idea.

Expository   Containing factual information.

Implied   Expressed indirectly.

Main idea   The central or most important thought in a paragraph.

Preview   To look over before reading.

Thesis   The major idea of an essay.

Topic   The unifying factor of the paragraph.

Students entering college are often overwhelmed with the amount of reading that has to be done. For example, if you take five classes, you may have to read as many as ten chapters a week, with each chapter containing about thirty pages. That adds to about 300 pages each week. Because of the amount of information you have to read, it is important that you find strategies to help you read effectively, efficiently, and to identify the most important material. In order to handle all this reading plus the new ideas and knowledge gained, you need to learn to separate the main ideas from the minor details. Finding the main idea in a reading selection or listening for the main idea in a lecture is essential for comprehension, effective studying, note taking, and the application of study strategies. Once the main idea becomes clear, then key **details** become easier to find and group. In all academic situations, understanding the main idea and recognizing the key details are paramount to comprehending material. Finding the main idea and key details is essential in reading, studying, writing, listening, and thinking.

MAIN IDEAS IN READING AND WRITING

Finding the main idea can be looked at from two different perspectives. One perspective is from the reader's viewpoint. When you read **expository** material, such as college texts, essays, and most factual material, you generally look for the main idea of the paragraph, chapter, or entire book. It is necessary to find the main idea in order to know what is important and what you need to learn.

The second perspective has to do with the writing process, since reading and writing are really different sides of the same process. When you write an essay or any kind of paper, you need to be sure that you include a main idea, or theme, around which your paper revolves. Without it, your paper will be merely a collection of ideas that will not blend together. During the reading process the reader searches for the writer's main idea to understand the writer's message and to learn the information the writer presents. As a writer, you need to focus and organize your writing so that your reader can find the main ideas in individual paragraphs and in the paper as a whole. Once you determine the main idea, you need to provide the details that support it. These details help make the main idea clear, so your message comes across clearly and completely. Your role as a writer is explored more completely in chapter 10, and you will also be given an opportunity to practice writing the main idea in the exercises at the end of this chapter.

Finding Main Ideas

Main ideas are found in many places. For instance, if we look at artwork or photographs, one idea or element of the work usually stands out. The artist or photographer makes a statement in the same way that a writer conveys a main idea. Of course, there are instances in which there is no directly stated or depicted main idea; rather, there are many details or much description. However, for our purposes, we will assume that most pictures and writing do contain a main idea. To begin the process of finding main ideas, looking at pictures and analyzing their focus will help you to grasp the concept of the main idea more easily.

◆ **EXERCISE A: MAIN IDEA**

Look at the pictures in Figures 5-1 and 5-2. Then answer the questions that follow.

1. What object provides the main idea in each of the illustrations?

   a. _____

   b. _____

FIGURE 5-1

FIGURE 5-2   Used by permission of Benjamin Gibson

2. Why did you choose the objects you did?

    a. _____

    b. _____

3. Compare your impressions with those of a fellow student.

4. Do you both agree on the main ideas? Why or why not?

_____

_____

UNDERSTANDING PARAGRAPHS

Now that you have experienced finding the overall main idea in pictures, let's look at how paragraphs are organized around a main idea. There are three essential elements of a paragraph: the topic, the main idea, and the key details. The **topic** is the subject of the paragraph. It is the one thing the paragraph is about—the unifying factor. For example, in an essay about families, the author might write one paragraph about parents and one paragraph about children of the family, so the topic of the entire essay would be families. The topic can usually be conveyed in one or two words.

The **main idea** is what the author wants to communicate about the topic. The main idea is the central, or most important, thought in the paragraph and may be contained in one or two sentences. There are two types of main ideas: stated and unstated (**implied**). The sentence that states the main idea is called the topic sentence. When the main idea is not directly stated in any one sentence, it is left up to the reader to infer, or reason out, the main point the author is making. The main idea is usually and most commonly located in the first sentence; the next most common location is in the last sentence. Sometimes the main idea is located in both places. In order to find the main idea, you will need to read the whole paragraph.

The **details** are proof, support, explanations, reasons, or examples that explain and support the paragraph's main idea. The key supporting details, which are statements that carry the primary supporting evidence needed to back up the main idea, are most important when studying for tests. Therefore, you must read to find both the main idea and the key supporting details. The following exercise will give you the opportunity to practice locating the main idea in a group of related sentences.

◆ **EXERCISE B: TOPICS AND MAIN IDEAS**

Underline the sentence in each set of related sentences that states the main idea. Then, in the space below the set of sentences, write the topic in your own words.

1. **a.** Moving to another part of the country rarely works for long since few places in the United States are entirely free of allergenic pollen.

   b. There are drawbacks to most remedies for relief of allergy symptoms, such as reactions to ragweed, tree pollen, and grass pollen.

   c. Most antihistamines cause drowsiness and lose their effectiveness after prolonged use.

   d. Injections are expensive and must be started months before the allergy season begins.

   e. To be fully effective, antihistamines must be taken before the onset of allergy symptoms and around the clock while symptoms persist.

   Topic: _____

2. a. An only child learns to be self-reliant at an early age.

b. The child receives the full attention of both parents.

c. Parents often include the child in their social plans and take him or her to "adult" places.

d. There are certain advantages to being an only child.

e. The only child learns to rely on his or her own imagination and creativity.

Topic: _____

3. a. The house displays a mastery of architecture.

b. It has skylights and is topped with a dome.

c. The library has more than 6,000 books, many in other languages.

d. A seven-day clock, driven by weights and pulleys, hangs above the front door.

e. Monticello, completed in 1809, displays many of Jefferson's interests.

Topic: _____

4. a. There are steps parents can take to encourage children to wear a helmet while riding a bike.

b. Let the child put on the helmet for biking.

c. When parents ride bikes, they should wear helmets, too.

d. Praise the child each time he wears the helmet.

e. Always insist your child wear the helmet each time he rides his or her bike.

Topic: _____

5. a. Christmas has become extremely commercialized in the last several decades.

b. Decorations are now displayed long before Thanksgiving.

c. Television and magazine advertising starts at the beginning of November.

d. Television commercials directed toward children increase in the fall just in time for children to begin harassing parents about presents.

e. As a result of the commercialization of Christmas, it has become a time of stress and guilt for many Americans.

Topic: _____

6. a. Many students enjoy soap operas.

   b. Even executives tune in to them during their lunch hour.

   c. Since soaps such as "Melrose Place" are now shown at night, viewers include those of all ages.

   d. Although most people believe the typical soap opera viewers are homemakers, people of all ages and occupations now view soap operas.

   e. Their interest, however, may be primarily in the advertisements during the programming.

   Topic: _____

7. a. Tornadoes are capable of causing millions of dollars of damage in just a short time.

   b. Hurricanes, a problem primarily in coastal areas, are feared by millions.

   c. A breeze on a summer's day is a relief, but some winds cause tremendous damage because of their speed and strength.

   d. A foehn is a warm dry wind, coming off the slopes of a mountain range, that can devastate crops in the plains.

   Topic: _____

8. a. Like cowboys, truckers are constantly on the move.

   b. The cowboy is no longer part of American life, but a new breed, the trucker, shares many characteristics with the cowboy.

   c. They travel thousands of miles a year and are seldom in one spot for long.

   d. Both the cowboy and the trucker are fiercely independent.

   e. A desk job, or any job perceived as not having a challenge, would repulse either group.

   Topic: _____

Finding Stated and Unstated Main Ideas

When organizing information, writers build paragraphs around a central point. Each paragraph becomes a subtopic of the major idea of the complete essay or the complete chapter. The central point of each paragraph can be stated in one sentence, which is usually referred to as the **topic sentence**, or the **stated main idea**.

The most common place for the topic sentence to appear is in the first sentence of the paragraph; the second most common place is the last sentence although the topic sentence can come in any place in the paragraph. Often, though, the main idea of the paragraph will not be stated directly in any one sentence. Rather, the main idea, or what the writer is saying about the topic, will depend on the reader's conclusion of the unifying idea of the paragraph. Even though the writer does not state the main idea of the paragraph directly, readers still need to be aware of this **unstated main idea** and to be able to state the main idea in their own words.

◆   **EXERCISE C: STATED MAIN IDEAS**

The following paragraphs have stated main ideas. Read each, and then underline the main idea.

1. *No element of the North American landscape was more basic to the development of the young republic than water. The earliest settlements on the Eastern seaboard were all at the ocean's edge, where they had ready access to transatlantic trade. Each major city in the new nation—Boston, New York, Philadelphia, Baltimore, Charleston, New Orleans—began life as a port. The interior trade of the continent concentrated almost entirely along natural watercourses. Water was the catalyst that made trade and settlement possible.* (Brinkley, Current, Freidel, & Williams, 1995, p. 299.)

2. *I have an increasing admiration for the teacher in the country school where we have a third-grade scholar in attendance. She not only undertakes to instruct her charges in all the subjects of the first three grades, but she manages to function quietly and effectively as a guardian of their health, their clothes, their habits, their mothers, and their snowball engagements. She has been doing this sort of Augean task for twenty years, and is both kind and wise. She cooks for the children on the stove that heats the room, and she can cool their passions or warm their soup with equal competence. She conceives their costumes, cleans up their messes, and shares their confidences. My boy already regards his teacher as his great friend, and I think tells her a great deal more than he tells us.* (White, 1991, p. 139)

3. *Maps are an essential tool for describing and revealing regions. If, as is often said, one picture is worth a thousand words, then a well-prepared map is worth at least ten thousand words to the geographer. No description in words can rival a map's descriptive force. Maps are valuable tools particularly because they so concisely portray spatial patterns in culture. Three types of regions are recognized by cultural geographers: formal, functional, and vernacular.* (Jordan, Domosh, & Rowntree, 1994, p. 7)

4. *I felt that I made them as uncomfortable as they made me. If I came into the room where they were, and they were talking together and my mother seemed cheerful, an anxious cloud would steal over her face from the moment of my entrance. If Mr. Murdstone were in his best humor, I checked him. If Miss Murdstone were in her worst, I intensified it. I had perception enough to know that my mother was the victim always: that she was afraid to speak to me, or be kind to me, lest she should give them some offense by her manner of doing so, and receive a lecture afterwards; that she was not only ceaselessly afraid of her own offending, but of my offending, and uneasily watched their looks if I only moved. Therefore I resolved to keep myself as much out of their way as I could and many a wintry hour did I hear the church clock strike, when I was sitting in my cheerless bedroom, wrapped in my little greatcoat, poring over a book.* (Dickens, p. 115)

5. *The Warsaw ghetto saw death in numbers that eclipsed even those in the pits at Babi Yar. People by the tens and hundreds and thousands starved or froze to death. Infants too weak to cry died by the hundreds, and old men died by the hundreds too weak to pray. Every morning the streets of the ghetto were strewn with new corpses. The sanitation teams walked through the streets with shovels and stacked the corpses onto pushcarts. Infants, children, women, men: piled up and wheeled off to the crematoriums to be burned.* (Uris, p. 120)

◆ **EXERCISE D: UNSTATED MAIN IDEAS**

In the following paragraphs, the main ideas are unstated. Read each, and then write a sentence stating the main idea.

1. *The women were both goodly height, Madame Ratignolle possessing the more feminine and matronly figure. The charm of Edna Pontellier's physique stole insensibly upon you. The lines of her body were long, clean and symmetrical; it was a body which occasionally fell into splendid poses; there was no suggestion of the trim, stereotyped fashion-plate about it. A casual and indiscriminating observer, in passing, might not cast a second glance upon the figure. But with more feeling and discernment he would have recognized the noble beauty of its modeling, and the graceful severity of poise and movement, which made Edna Pontellier different from the crowd.* (Chopin, 1976, p. 16)

   Main idea: _____

   _____

2. *Black shapes crouched, lay, sat between the trees leaning against the trunks, clinging to the earth, half coming out, half effaced within the dim light, in all the attitudes of pain, abandonment, and despair. Another mine on the cliff went off, followed by a slight shudder of the soil under my feet. The work was going on. The work! And this was the place where some of the helpers had withdrawn to die.* (Conrad, 1978, p. 82)

   Main idea: _____

   _____

3. *I do not wish to give the impression that men in office are incapable of governing wisely and well. Occasionally, the exception appears, rising in heroic size above the rest, a tower visible down the centuries. Greece had her Pericles, who ruled with authority, moderation, sound judgment, and a certain nobility that imposes natural dominion over others. Rome had Caesar, a man of remarkable governing talents, although it must be said that a ruler who arouses opponents to resort to assassination is probably not as smart as he ought to be. Later, under Marcus Aurelius and the other Antonines, Roman citizens enjoyed good government, prosperity, and respect for about a century. Charlemagne was able to impose order upon a mass of contending elements, to foster the arts of civilization no less than those of war, and to earn a prestige supreme in the Middle Ages—probably not equaled in the eyes of contemporaries until the appearance of George Washington.* (Tuchman, 1991, p. 277)

   Main idea: _____

   _____

4. *The sky was full then and the coming of spring was a religious event. I would awaken to the sound of garage doors creaking open and know without thinking that it was Friday and that my father was on his way to six-thirty mass. I saw, without bothering to notice, statues at home and at school of the Virgin and of Christ. I would write at the top of my arithmetic or history homework the initials Jesus, Mary, and Joseph. (All my homework was thus dedicated.) I felt the air was different, somehow still and more silent on Sundays and high feast-days. I felt lightened, transparent as sky, after confessing my sins to a priest. Schooldays were routinely divided by prayers said with class-mates. I would not have forgotten to say grace before eating. And I would not have turned off the light next to my bed or fallen asleep without praying to God.* (Rodriguez, 1991, p. 178)

Main Idea: _____

_____

5. *It starts with people drinking to relieve tension or to get rid of fears. A few drinks make them feel better because they cannot manage with-out some type of coping strategy. But often, these few drinks lead to a drinking spree, which can lead to negative physical effects or illness. If one continues to drink it becomes difficult to discontinue the use of alcohol. In the final stages of the disease, permanent damage to both mental and physical faculties occur.* (*Original*, Laskey/Gibson)

Main idea: _____

_____

◆ EXERCISE E: DISTINGUISHING BETWEEN STATED AND UNSTATED MAIN IDEAS

Now that you have had experience finding both stated and unstated main ideas separately, read the following passages to decide which paragraphs contain a stated main idea and which contain an unstated one. Underline the stated main ideas, and write the unstated main ideas in the margins beside the paragraph.

1. *Friendship is a school for character, allowing us the chance to study in great detail and over time temperaments very different from our own. These charming quirks, these contradictions, these nobilities, these blind spots of our friends we track not out of disinterested*

curiosity: we must have this information before knowing how far we may relax our guard, how much we may rely on them in crises. The learning curve of friendship involves, to no small extent, filling out this picture of the other's limitations and making peace with the results. (With one's own limitations there may never be peace.) Each time I hit up against a friend's inflexibility I am relieved as well as disappointed: I can begin to predict, and arm myself in advance against repeated bruises. I have one friend who is always late, so I bring a book along when I am to meet her. If I give her a manuscript to read and she promises to look at it over the weekend, I start preparing myself for a month-long wait. (Lopate, 1989, p. 136.)

2. *The husband shall have all the pigs, the wife the sheep. The husband shall have all the horses and mares, the oxen and cows, bullocks and heifers; the wife shall have the goats . . . All the vessels for milk, except one pail, are the wife's; all the dishes, except one meat dish, are the husband's. One cart and yoke are the wife's. All the jars and drinking vessels are the husband's. Of the bedding, the husband shall have all the bedclothes which are beneath, the wife those which are above. The husband shall have the cauldron, the pillow, the winnowing sheet, the coulter, the wood axe, the gimlet (hole-borer), the fire dog, all the sickles except one, and the gridiron. The wife shall have the pan and the tripod, the broadaxe and the sieve, the ploughshare, the flax and the seed of the flax, and the precious things except gold and silver. If there are any of these (gold or silver) they are to be divided in two equal parts. The products of the loom shall be divided in two equal parts, both linens and woolens. The husband shall have the barn and the grain and whatever is above or in the ground, and the hens and the geese and one cat. The wife shall have the meat that is salted and the cheese that is fresh . . . and the vessel of butter . . . and the ham . . . and as much of the flour as she can carry. Each of them shall have his or her personal clothing, except the cloaks which shall be divided.* (Fletcher, 1986, pp. 58–59.)

3. *You were not allowed to sing. Operators would have liked to have sung, because they, too, had the same thing to do and weren't allowed to sing. We weren't allowed to talk to each other. Oh, no, they would sneak up behind if you were found talking to your next colleague. You*

were admonished: "If you keep on you'll be fired." If you went to the toilet and you were there longer than the floor lady thought you should be, you would be laid off for half a day and sent home. And, of course, that meant no pay. You were not allowed to have your lunch on the fire escape in the summer-time. The door was locked to keep us in. That's why so many people were trapped when the fire broke out. . . . (Newman, 1993, p. 653)

4. *Your feelings and thoughts, your beliefs and dreams, your plans and actions are all the product of activity in your central nervous system, of which the brain is the main component. The human brain weighs less than three pounds when fully grown. It is composed largely of water and a host of chemical elements and compounds, assembled into billions of neurons and glial cells. This complex mass is responsible for all the phenomena that psychologists seek to explain.* (Wortman & Loftus, 1988, p. 65)

5. *Who really knows what the average businessman is trying to say in the average business letter? What member of an insurance or medical plan can decipher the brochure that tells him what his costs and benefits are? What father or mother can put together a child's toy—on Christmas Eve or any other eve—from the instructions on the box? Our national tendency is to inflate and thereby sound important. The airline pilot who wakes us to announce that he is presently anticipating experiencing considerable weather wouldn't dream of saying that there's a storm ahead and it may get bumpy. The sentence is too simple—there must be something wrong with it.* (Zinsser, 1985, p. 29.)

Finding Key Details

The central idea of a paragraph, whether stated directly in a topic sentence or unstated, is always explained and made clear to the reader by the details in the paragraph. These details give the reader added information about the main idea of that paragraph. However, some details are more important than others in how directly they illustrate the main idea. The key details, or major details, are most important because they explain the main idea and give direct evidence of it. Minor details provide additional information about the key details and indirectly support the main idea.

◆ **EXERCISE F: IMPORTANT DETAILS**

Each of the following numbered statements could function as the topic sentence of a paragraph. After each statement are sentences containing details that may relate to the main idea. Read each sentence, and make a check mark beside those with details that can be considered primary support for the main idea.

1. Many young people feel that once a person begins working in a certain vocation, it is impossible to change into another field.

_____ **a.** Making a difficult but needed change can prevent physical and mental disorders.

_____ **b.** No matter how old one is or what vocation one chooses, one can always change to a job that is more suitable or more desirable.

_____ **c.** There is no such thing as one perfect job for an individual.

_____ **d.** Often there will be several careers for which any individual is qualified.

2. There are no formal rites of passage for adolescents in American society, but several traditions serve as initiations into the adult world.

_____ **a.** A teenager's first date can be considered a step into the adult world.

_____ **b.** A new job also serves as an informal rite of passage.

_____ **c.** A driver's license also serves as a bridge to independence and freedom.

_____ **d.** Parents often view a driver's license as the teenager's pulling away from the family and developing an independent life.

_____ **e.** There are no ceremonies or celebrations surrounding these milestones, but both parents and teenagers sense a change in the relationship to the rest of the family unit.

3. Many American writers chose to live in Europe during the 1920s for many reasons.

_____ **a.** After World War I many intellectuals were disillusioned, and Europe offered a more interesting intellectual community.

_____ **b.** Fitzgerald and Hemingway were two famous writers who spent much of their time in France and Spain.

_____ **c.** Many European nations were less conservative than the United States and allowed more artistic freedom.

_____ **d.** Censorship was prevalent in the United States during the 1920s.

_____ **e.** Prohibition in the United States added to the atmosphere of repression, while in Europe there were no restrictions on alcohol.

4. College life demands more self-reliance than does high school.

_____ **a.** No one is around to remind the student to get to appointments or to make needed phone calls.

_____ **b.** Students can no longer depend on parents to wake them up and push them out the door in the morning.

_____ **c.** New freedoms require new independence and responsibility.

_____ **d.** Managing money and time is left entirely to the college student.

_____ **e.** Some of the new freedoms are exhilarating; others demand organization and responsibility.

5. Although often seen as a phenomenon that burst suddenly into the music scene, rock and roll really had roots in the blues and the youth culture of the 1950s.

_____ **a.** The name *rock and roll* was taken from an old blues lyric, "My baby rocks me with a steady roll."

_____ **b.** Rock and roll was basically dance music, aimed at the burgeoning population of young people born after World War II.

_____ **c.** Among the most distinctive features of rock and roll was the electric guitar.

_____ **d.** Soul music, in essence, black-based folk music, contributed greatly to the development of rock and roll.

6. Humans have studied other primates for centuries.

_____ **a.** Because apes were considered evil during the Middle Ages, no scientific study was done during that time.

_____ **b.** Early civilizations in Asia and Africa even worshipped monkeys, and some religious statues of them date as far back as 3500 B.C.

_____ **c.** Instead of worshipping monkeys and apes, the ancient Greeks and Romans tried to study them from a scientific point of view.

_____ **d.** Aristotle, the Greek philosopher and naturalist, was the first to write a detailed description of primates.

_____ **e.** Darwin used a large amount of primate research in *The Descent of Man.*

7. As soon as a person experiences the emotion of fear, he or she also experiences many physiological changes.

_____ **a.** Increase in adrenaline to the blood stream causes deeper breathing.

_____ **b.** Anxiety reactions become acute.

_____ **c.** No saliva flows into the mouth, and the throat becomes dry.

_____ **d.** The increase in oxygen gives muscles greater energy and strength.

_____ **e.** All digestive action stops.

8. The Inca Empire, which stretched from Ecuador to Argentina by the fifteenth century, was an extremely prosperous, efficient society.

_____ **a.** Although the Incas did not know how to write, they developed a useful method of record keeping by tying knots into cords, which were then attached to a large rope.

_____ **b.** The Incas were successful, dedicated farmers who built terraces into the side of the mountains so water would not run off the land.

_____ **c.** The Incas built miles of roads, paved with huge flat stones or carved out of solid rock, with bridges of rope and poles hung over canyons.

_____ **d.** Part of the crops were stored in a giant warehouse so if any part of the empire needed food, it was readily available.

_____ **e.** The Spaniards took the Incas' land by deceit and brutality and made slaves of the Incas.

USING TOPIC SENTENCES AND
DETAILS IN WRITING

Applying the concepts discussed about topic sentences and details can strengthen your own writing. Each paragraph in your writing should be centered around one idea, and although you do not have to state that idea directly in a topic sentence, doing so can improve the effectiveness of your writing. Using topic sentences can help you organize your thoughts and make your ideas clearer to the reader. It is also important to develop your ideas fully by including specific details and explanations. These techniques will help the reader understand the central idea of the paragraph.

◆ **EXERCISE G: THE MAIN IDEA AND SUPPORTING DETAILS**

Listed below are five sentences that could work as topic sentences. Choose one sentence, and write a paragraph using the sentence as the main idea of the paragraph. Remember to support the main idea with relevant key details.

1. Fast food restaurants lack an attractive physical atmosphere.
2. Public transportation eliminates parking problems.
3. The physical condition of animals in zoos is often deplorable.
4. Small, compact automobiles have distinct advantages.
5. My roommate has an irritating nervous habit.

THE OVERALL MAIN IDEA

The main ideas of each paragraph contribute to the overall main ideas of an essay or a textbook chapter. In an essay, this overall main idea is called a **thesis**, and it most commonly occurs in the introductory paragraph of an essay. In the chapter of a book, the thesis may be stated in the first paragraph or introduced in the title or heading of the chapter. Looking for the overall main ideas is not only important in reading assignments but is also important for active listening and note taking, which is explained in chapter 6.

◆ **EXERCISE H: THE MAIN IDEA**

Read the following essay entitled "A Black Athlete Looks at Education" by Arthur Ashe, and underline the overall main idea, or thesis, of the entire essay. Then, in the space provided at the end of the selection, express the thesis in your own words.

*A Black Athlete Looks at Education**

Since my sophomore year at UCLA, I have become convinced that we blacks spend too much time on the playing fields and too little time in the libraries. Consider these facts: for the major professional sports of hockey, football, basketball, baseball, golf, tennis and boxing, there are roughly only 3170 major league positions available (attributing 200 positions to golf, 200 to tennis and 100 to boxing). And the annual turnover is small.

There must be some way to assure that those who try but don't make it to pro sports don't wind up on street corners or in unemployment lines. Unfortunately, our most widely recognized role models are athletes and entertainers—"runnin' " and "jumpin' " and "singin' " and "dancin'."

Our greatest heroes of the century have been athletes—Jack Johnson, Joe Louis, and Muhammad Ali. Racial and economic discrimination forced us to channel our energies into athletics and entertainment. These were the ways out of the ghetto, the way to get that Cadillac, those regular shoes, that cashmere sport coat.

Somehow, parents must instill a desire for learning alongside the desire to be Walt Frazier. Why not start by sending black professional athletes into high schools to explain the facts of life?

I have often addressed high school audiences and my message is always the same: "For every hour you spend on the athletic field, spend two in the library. Even if you make it as a pro athlete, your career will be over by the time you are 35. You will need that diploma."

Have these pro athletes explain what happens if you break a leg, get a sore arm, have one bad year or don't make the cut for five or six tournaments. Explain to them the star system, wherein for every star earning millions there are six or seven others making $15,000 or $20,000 or $30,000. Invite a bench-warmer or a guy who didn't make it. Ask him if he sleeps every night. Ask him whether he was graduated. Ask him what he would do if he became disabled tomorrow. Ask him where his old high school athletic buddies are.

We have been on the same roads—sports and entertainment—too long. We need to pull over, fill up at the library and speed away to Congress and the Supreme Court, the unions and the business world.

I'll never forget how proud my grandmother was when I graduated from UCLA. Never mind the Davis Cup. Never mind the Wimbledon title. To this day, she still doesn't know what those names mean. What mattered to her was that of her more than thirty children and grandchildren, I was the first to be graduated from college, and a famous college at that. Somehow, that made up for all those floors she scrubbed all those years.

———————————————————

———————————————————

———————————————————

Finding Overall Main Ideas

Now that you have had practice in finding the main idea in paragraphs, you need to transfer the process to finding the overall main ideas contained in textbook chapters. You can find the overall main idea by **previewing** a chapter. The format itself, such as headings, titles, subtitles, and boldfaced print, will be a clue to what the author thinks is most important. Before you begin the actual reading, look at the chapter's title and headings. Also, be sure to look at the **boldfaced** print. This is another way that the author conveys what is important to the reader. Reading the first paragraph of each section will also help you to key in on the main idea, because in textbooks the overall main idea is often introduced in the first paragraph. In addition, you should look at the graphic aids, such as charts, diagrams, and pictures, that are included in the text, since often they present the important information in a visual form. They will not only help you focus on the main idea but will also clarify the ideas presented. Finally, you should read the summary and questions at the end of the chapter before you begin reading. The summary is a collection of the main ideas, and the questions usually refer back to the main ideas. Previewing the summary and questions, will help direct the reader's eye to the main idea while reading the chapter. Therefore, focusing on the key elements the author is emphasizing and using these previewing strategies will help you to find the main idea.

◆ EXERCISE I: TEXT PREVIEWING

Use one of your textbooks to practice the previewing strategies described in the preceding paragraph. Use the chart shown here to indicate the previewing aids you identified by placing a check mark in the appropriate box.

Previewing Aids	*Included*	*Not Included*
Introductory Material		
Title	_____	_____
Subtitle	_____	_____
Preface	_____	_____
Introduction	_____	_____
Boldface Print		
Chapter title	_____	_____
Chapter heads	_____	_____
Phrases	_____	_____
Key words	_____	_____
Graphic Aids		
Graphs	_____	_____
Maps	_____	_____
Charts	_____	_____
Pictures	_____	_____
Chapter Summary	_____	_____
Chapter Questions	_____	_____

Previewing Aids	*Included*	*Not Included*
Vocabulary Lists		
Appendix	_____	_____
Glossary	_____	_____
Index	_____	_____

◆ EXERCISE J: MAIN IDEA IN TEXTBOOK CHAPTERS

Read the following selection from a sociology textbook,* and write the main ideas from each paragraph in the spaces provided at the end of the selection. Some ideas are stated directly, while others are implied. Once you have found the main ideas in each paragraph, state the overall main idea of the selection in the space after the selection.

> *In the late 1970's, many Americans were deeply moved by Alex Haley's successful quest for his family tree, which was documented in his book* Roots *and later popularized on network television. Beginning with stories passed down by his grandmother, Haley was able to trace his heritage back to Africa—to a man named Kunta Kinte who lived in a village in Gambia, West Africa, and who was brought to the United States in chains by slave traders.*
>
> *Many of us, like Alex Haley, have retraced our roots by listening to elderly family members tell us about their lives—and about the lives of ancestors who died long before we were even born. Yet a person's lineage is more than simply a personal history; it also reflects societal patterns that govern descent. In every culture, children are introduced to relatives to whom they are expected to show an emotional attachment. The state of being related to others is called* **kinship.** *Kinship is culturally learned and is not totally determined by biological or marital ties. For example, adoption creates a kinship tie which is legally acknowledged and socially approved.*
>
> *The family and the kin group are not necessarily the same. While the family is a household unit, kin do not always live together or function as a collective body on a daily basis. Kin groups include aunts, uncles, cousins, in-laws, and so forth. In a society such as the United States, the kinship group may come*

*Richard T. Schaefer, Sociology, McGraw-Hill, 1989. Printed with permission of The McGraw-Hill Companies.

together only rarely as for a marriage or funeral. However, kinship ties frequently create obligations and responsibilities. We may feel compelled to assist our kin and feel free to call upon relatives for many types of aid, including loans and baby-sitting.

*How are kinship groups identified? The principle of descent assigns people to kinship groups according to their relationships to an individual's mother or father. There are three principal ways of determining descent. In the United States, the system of **bilateral descent** is followed, which means that both sides of a person's family are regarded as equally important. No higher value is given to the brothers of one's father as opposed to the brothers of one's mother.*

*Most societies—according to Murdock, 64 percent—give preference to one side of the family or the other in tracing descent. **Patrilineal** (from Latin pater, "father") **descent** indicates that only the father's relatives are important in terms of property, inheritance, and the establishment of emotional ties. Conversely, in societies which favor **matrilineal** (from Latin mater, "mother") **descent**, only the mother's relatives are significant; the relatives of the father are considered unimportant.*

Main Ideas

Paragraph 1 _____

Paragraph 2 _____

Paragraph 3 _____

Paragraph 4 _____

Paragraph 5 _____

Overall Main Idea:

_____

_____

_____

_____

_____

◆ **EXERCISE K: MAIN IDEA OF A TEXTBOOK SELECTION**

Read the following selection from an American history book, and find the main ideas of each paragraph. Some ideas are stated directly; others are implied. Then write the overall main idea of the selection in the space provided.

*Recovering the Past**

Popular Music

One way to recover the past is through music. Popular songs not only provide insight into attitudes and beliefs but also quickly convey the mood and feelings of an era. Through their lyrics, songwriters express the hopes and fears of a people and the emotional tone of an age. Consider, for example, the powerful message conveyed in the Democratic party adoption of "Happy Days Are Here Again" as a campaign theme during the Great Depression. The decline of pop music and the rise of rock and roll in the 1950s tells historians a great deal about social moods and changes in that decade.

The pop music style of romantic ballads and novelty numbers with smooth singing and a quiet beat dominated the early 1950s. Popular songs such as "I Believe," "Young at Heart," and "Tennessee Waltz," sung by Frankie Laine, Frank Sinatra, and Patti Page, respectively, typified the musical tastes of young adults eager to establish a secure suburban family life in the aftermath of the upheavals of the Depression and World War II. The lyrics of these songs are bland, homey, and overly sentimental.

Contrasting with these syrupy ballads was the rhythm and blues performed by black artists for black audiences. A strong beat and mournful tone were the distinguishing marks of this music. The two styles not only had different beats and rhythms but also treated common themes, like love, in different ways. Pop artists sang of sentimental love, while rhythm and blues singers expressed emotional and physical love.

In the 1950s, the first baby boom teenagers emerged with a distinctive musical taste and enough discretionary income to influence the growth of the popular music industry. No longer children and not yet adults, these affluent teenagers struggled to define themselves in the Eisenhower age of suburban conformity. At first they were drawn to the beat of rhythm and blues

*From THE AMERICAN PEOPLE: CREATING A NATION AND A SOCIETY, 3rd Edition by Gary B. Nash and Julie Roy Jeffrey. Copyright © 1994 by Harper Collins College Publishers. Reprinted by permission.

as a rebellion against the mellow pop music of their parents. As the teenage market grew, white groups began to imitate black rhythm and blues songs, as in the 1954 song "Sh-Boom," done originally by the Chords and remade by the Crew Cuts.

But teenage listeners became increasingly dissatisfied with these imitations and looked for a livelier type of music. They found it in rock and roll (the name referred to descriptions of sex in black music). One of the first rock hits was "Rock Around the Clock" by Bill Haley and the Comets, used in the soundtrack of a controversial movie about an urban high school, Blackboard Jungle *(1955). Parents worried about the effect this music would have on their children. Some thought rock music caused juvenile delinquency, while others worried about its origins in "race music" and its sexual suggestiveness.*

It took a truck driver from Memphis, Elvis Presley, to turn rock and roll into virtually a teenage religion, giving it a preeminence in teenage culture it has yet to relinquish. Presley's sexy voice, gyrating hips, and other techniques borrowed from black singers helped make him the undisputed "king of rock and roll." A multimedia blitz of movies, television, and radio helped to make songs like "Heartbreak Hotel," "Don't Be Cruel," and "Hound Dog" smash singles. Eighteen Presley hits sold more than a million copies in the last four years of the 1950s. Almost alone, Presley mobilized a whole new teenage record market, making himself a millionaire in the process. In 1956, teenagers bought 50 percent of all records, and in two years that figure had risen to 70 percent. The popularity of Presley's rhythm and blues-inspired music helped bring black singers like Fats Domino and Chuck Berry into the mainstream as well.

Pop music died a rapid death as rock and roll swept the nation. "Your Hit Parade," a popular television show featuring top pop hits in the early 1950s, was canceled in 1957 because its singers looked ridiculous singing rock songs. In that same year, "American Bandstand" attracted teenage viewers with 90 minutes of dancing and rock music every day after school. The clean-looking young host, Dick Clark, gave rock and roll a better image with parents. In addition, many black artists toned down the sexual references and softened the hard beat of their songs in hopes of appealing to the larger white audience.

As rock and roll developed in the late 1950s, it focused on topics that appealed to the teenage market. Favorite themes were dances ("At the Hop"), love ("A Teenager in Love"), and the fear of parental punishment for teenage romance ("Wake Up, Little Susie"). Adults, then as now, were slow to understand the appeal of such music, reflecting a wide gap in generational perspective, as the lyrics of the song "Teen-Age Crush" suggest.

The 1950s saw a revolution in music that reflected a larger demographic shift and changing social values in the United States. How did popular music reflect the changes that occurred in the 1960s and 1970s, decades featuring the Beatles, Bob Dylan, the Rolling Stones, Simon and Garfunkel, the Doors, Stevie Wonder, the Eagles, Elton John, Neil Young, Michael Jackson, and others? What changes in the younger generation might account for these continuing musical shifts? What historical forces brought about changes in rock music? What music is popular today, and what does it say about the beliefs, values, and concerns of contemporary American Youth?

Main idea of entire selection: _____

_____

_____

_____

_____

CRITICAL THINKING

Being able to apply your knowledge and opinions to new situations is one mark of a good thinker. In this chapter you learned about topic sentences and key details. Applying your skills in using these concepts can help you become a more effective thinker. The exercise below gives you an opportunity to use these concepts in analyzing situations that affect our society.

In groups of three, select a problem of national or global significance either from the list below or from topics suggested by group members.

The homeless
Illegal immigrants
Teenage pregnancy
High divorce rate
Terrorist attacks
Gun control

Violence on television
Sex-role stereotyping

Choose a recorder to write your responses as members of your group share associations, beliefs, and opinions about the topic. Include all responses, even though some may seem more pertinent than others. The group next needs to analyze and evaluate the presented ideas to choose one viewpoint, association, or response that would work as a topic sentence. Then, as a group, write a 100–150-word paragraph supporting that topic sentence with relevant, convincing details. Choose a spokesperson to read the group's paragraph to the class.

REFERENCES

Ashe, A. (Feb. 6, 1977). A Black Athlete Looks at Education. *New York Times.*

Brinkley, A., Current, R., Freidel, F., Williams, T. (1995). *American History: A Survey, Vol. 1: to 1877.* New York: McGraw-Hill, Inc.

Chopin, K. (1976). *The Awakening.* New York: W. W. Norton & Company.

Conrad, J. (1910). *Heart of Darkness.* New York: Signet Classic.

Dickens, C. (1965). *David Copperfield.* Boston: Houghton Mifflin.

Fletcher, I., ed. and trans. (1986). *Latin Redaction A of the Law of Hywel.* Aberystwyth, Wales. Center for Advanced Welsh and Celtic Studies.

Jordan, T., Domosh, M., Rowntree, L. (1994). *The Human Mosaic: A Thematic Introduction to Cultural Geography,* Harper Collins.

Lopate, P. (1989). Modern Friendship. *Against Joie De Vivre.* New York: Poseidon Press, pp. 131–142.

Nash, G., Jeffrey, J., Howe, J., Davis, A., Frederick, P., Winkler, F. (1994). Recovering the Past: Popular Music. *The American People.* Harper & Row.

Newman, P. (1993). Working for the Shirtwaist Company. In Henretta, J., Brownlee, W., Brody, D., Ware, S. *America's History.* New York: Worth Publishers.

Rodriguez, R. (1991) Credo. In G. Muller. *The McGraw-Hill Reader,* New York: McGraw Hill, pp. 178–185.

Schaefer, R. (1989). *Sociology.* New York: McGraw-Hill.

Tuchman, B. (1991). An Inquiry into the Persistence of Unwisdom in Government. In G. Muller. *The McGraw-Hill Reader,* New York: McGraw Hill, pp. 274–286.

Uris, L. (1958). *Exodus.* New York: Bantam Books.

White, E. (1991). Education. In G. Muller. *The McGraw-Hill Reader.* New York: McGraw-Hill, pp. 139–141.

Wortman, C. & Loftus, E. (1988). *Psychology.* New York: Knopf.

Zinsser, W. (1985). *On Writing Well: an Informal Guide to Writing Nonfiction.* New York: Harper & Row.

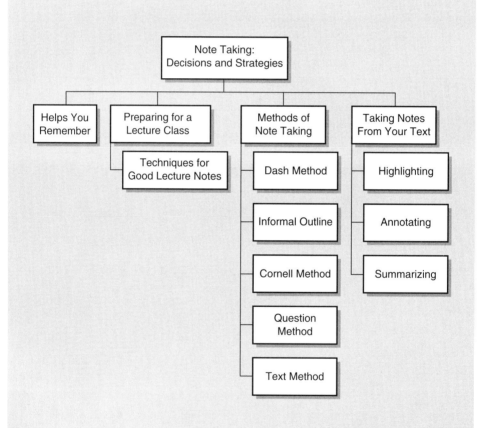

6

NOTE TAKING: DECISIONS AND STRATEGIES

He listens well who takes notes.
—DANTE, Divine Comedy

Key Concepts

Active listening   Hearing with thoughtful attention.

Annotate   Marginal notes.

Concentration   Focusing one's attention on one thing.

Discrepancy   Difference or disagreement.

Distractions   Things that divert the mind or attention.

Retention curve   The percent of information remembered over a period of time.

Summarizing   Condensing information into a brief paragraph containing key points.

The average full-time student takes five courses and spends about fifteen hours each week in classes. Although some of that class time may be spent in small-group discussions or projects, much of a student's time in the traditional college classroom is spent listening to lectures, directions, or interpretations of assigned readings.

WHY NOTE TAKING IS IMPORTANT

You can make the best use of your time in class by taking notes that are organized, accurate, and complete. The notes provide a record of the information presented in the lecture.

Without good notes, you will also deprive yourself of the only source of material presented in class. The act of writing down information makes the information easier to remember, especially for visual learners. Because you will forget about 60% of a lecture within an hour after class, notes become a valuable record to use for review and studying for tests. Figure 6-1 illustrates a **retention curve** so you can see how easily information is forgotten.

If the information presented in class is not in your textbook, the lecture may be the only place to find it. Teachers' lectures generally are more than a summary of the textbook so, if you do not have a good note-taking system, you may lose much information and not know what the professor considers important. You may not even be aware what information you missed until the exam, when it is too late.

You need to use your critical thinking skills to make decisions about what information to record. In the beginning you may have a difficult time taking notes because you are unsure of what needs to be included or you may try to write down every word that is uttered by your professor. Once you know how to listen (see the next section) and evaluate the material presented, it will be easier to take effective notes and to highlight the important concepts needed for learning and good test taking. Reviewing these notes continuously can increase your understanding and critical evaluation of new concepts, which in turn will improve your test scores and your involvement with the subjects you are studying.

In addition to serving as a record of lecture content, the physical act of writing down information acts as reinforcement and forms a bridge between new ideas and your recalling those ideas. This reinforcement is needed because much of the information you hear is forgotten quickly. As the chart in Figure 6-1 indicates, without the aid of notes you will remember only 23% of information in a lecture less than a week after hearing it.

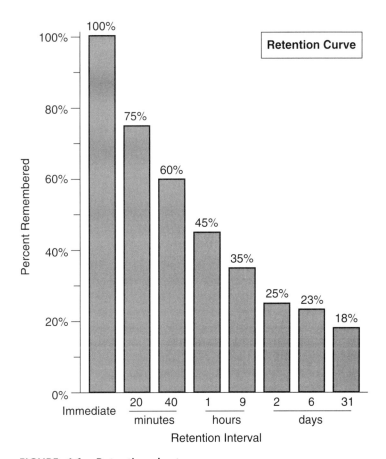

FIGURE 6-1   Retention chart.

ACTIVE LISTENING

You must be an active listener to take good notes. **Active listening** is hearing with thoughtful attention. It is an active process during which the student needs to be alert to the lecturer. There is a difference between hearing and active listening. Attentive listening means you register the lecture's message; merely hearing means the lecture is not the main focus of your attention. You might be thinking about other things or day dreaming, so you aren't really tuned into the lecture. Some behaviors that indicate ineffective listening include doodling, whispering to a neighbor, daydreaming, and watching the clock.

It also takes **concentration** to listen effectively, and concentration requires that you think about the task you are engaged in. You have to block out external **distractions**, such as your neighbor at the next desk or the noise outside the classroom. You also need to block out your own internal distractions, such as planning what to wear to a party that night or worrying about what your friend told you before class. In fact, concentrating on the task you're faced with can be relaxing because you are totally absorbed and can leave your worries behind. Psychologists refer to this absorption as "flow," and some believe it provides a state of true contentment.The following exercise will help you to evaluate your ability to listen effectively.

◆ **EXERCISE A: IMPROVING YOUR LISTENING SKILLS**

With a partner, take turns talking to one another about your feelings toward the classes you are taking this semester. You may wish to focus on a particular idea about your classes. For instance, you may wish to talk about how easy or hard a subject is. You might wish to discuss your attitude toward the work involved. First, one person should talk for approximately one minute. Then, the partner should repeat back what he or she heard. When one person is talking, the listener should not speak, interrupt, or ask questions. He or she should simply listen. The original speaker should either confirm or reject the accuracy of the message the listener received. Next, switch roles and repeat the process. Continue alternating roles as speaker and listener until each has had several turns.

PREPARATION FOR A LECTURE CLASS

Read Assigned Chapter

One thing you can do to prepare for a lecture is to read the assigned chapter before class. This builds your background knowledge about the subject, which leads to better note taking and improved understanding of the lecture.

Even if you are unable to read the assigned chapter carefully, skim the chapter to get a general overview of the material presented. Another alternative is to read the chapter summary for the main ideas or to review previous notes. These strategies will help to build a bridge from old information to the new information presented in class.

Form Questions

You also need to anticipate lecture content by forming questions you have based on the assigned reading. This strategy will help you to tune into the lecture more easily and will help you listen for the answers to the questions you have formulated while taking notes.

Identify Note-Taking Goals

Another activity that will help you prepare for a lecture class is to be aware of your note-taking goals. Do you want to take down the main ideas, the factual information, the details, the examples, the instructor's anecdotes, and/or the questions of other students? In a class that combines a short lecture with discussion, a good strategy might be to include in your notes the discussion topics for later reviews. After you have attended the class several times, choose to take the kind of notes that will be most helpful for you. Generally, students find that writing down the main ideas presented is the most beneficial note-taking approach for successful test results. Depending on how fast the lecturer speaks and how much material is covered in a class session, adding some relevant details and examples of the main idea is also a worthwhile approach.

In the following exercise, practice your concentration and listening skills. Try to block out all internal and external distractions so you can listen with full concentration.

TAKING GOOD LECTURE NOTES

Positive Listening Strategies

If you are an active listener, you can develop positive listening strategies. Since there is a **discrepancy** between how fast a person can talk (an average of 125 words per minute) and how fast we can process what we hear (400 to 600 words per minute), the listener tends to get bored and can easily tune out the lecture unless positive listening strategies are employed. These strategies help a person stay focused on the lecture during the gap in time between the speaking time and the time it takes to process what is heard.

Some positive listening strategies include consciously concentrating on the lecture and maintaining eye contact with the lecturer. Becoming involved with the material by thinking about the lecture will also help you stay focused on the content. Other strategies include writing down questions in the margin of your notes to ask later and listening for the major ideas. You might also think about how the content of the lecture is related to other subjects or previous lectures.

◆ **EXERCISE B: LISTENING DRILL**

Write the numbers *1* through *10* on a piece of paper. Your instructor will give you a task to complete for each number. The task will be stated once and only once. You will have limited time to complete each task. Listen carefully and work quickly.

◆ **EXERCISE C: SELF-EVALUATION OF YOUR POSITIVE LISTENING STRATEGIES**

Write a paragraph describing your skills as a listener. How well do you listen? What strategies do you plan to use to improve your listening skills?

_____

_____

_____

_____

_____

_____

_____

_____

Techniques for Taking Good Lecture Notes

- *Sit near the lecturer.* Sitting as close to the lecturer as possible makes it easier for you to hear the lecture, read material on the chalkboard or overhead, and concentrate on what's being said. Sitting in the back row won't prevent your taking good notes, but this position is certainly more conducive to daydreaming and doodling.
- *Keep notes in a loose-leaf notebook.* The loose-leaf notebook allows you to rearrange and add to your notes more easily than a spiral-bound notebook does. In the loose-leaf notebook, handouts and your own reading notes can be placed next to the corresponding lecture material, so when you're reviewing your notes or studying for a test, the material is organized and readily available.
- *Format notes clearly.* Begin each set of notes with the proper identification: the date, course title, subject of lecture, page number. Make your handwriting as legible as possible, or print the notes so you can read them easily. Leaving wide margins and blank lines between paragraphs and lists makes the notes easier to read. Blank space is also useful because if you miss an important point, you will have space in which to add it later.
- *Use your own shorthand.* Devising your own shorthand makes the recording process faster and less tedious. Use an abbreviated, or

shortened, form of any words that are used often. Here are some possible abbreviations:

Some Suggested Abbreviations
and—+ or +
with—w/
example—i.e. or ex.
literature—lit
different—diff
discussion—disc
organization—org
Old Testament—OT

- *Listen actively and selectively.* Don't try to write down every word that's spoken. Instead listen actively, and write notes selectively. Use the following questions to help you identify important information.

  1. What is the main point?
  2. What are the major divisions?
  3. Which details are essential?

- *Listen to the lecturer's clues.* Being sensitive to the lecturer's clues will help you realize what is important. Some phrases that indicate main ideas are ones such as "Three causes are . . ."; "An important point is . . ."; "Six characteristics are. . . ." When you hear phrases such as these, be sure to include in your notes the information that follows.
- *Take notes in your own words.* Putting the information in your own words helps you to understand the material. Some information, however, such as definitions, formulas, quotations, and technical language, probably should be written down verbatim because minor variations may radically change the meaning of the original idea.
- *Edit your notes.* After class, review your notes to make any changes that are necessary. Make sure the notes are complete, and add additional information to clarify them if necessary. Correct spelling of important terms. Do *not* merely recopy notes, since this is generally a rote exercise and not a learning experience.

Methods of Note Taking

It is important to use a consistent note-taking method because then you will tend to take more organized notes and reading them will be easier. First, you need to listen for the main ideas. Every lecture has several main ideas supplemented by details. In order to decide what the main ideas are and what important details need to be recorded, you will need to use your critical-thinking skills. While you are taking notes, you should be making decisions and sorting out the important material that needs to be remembered for learning the concept and successfully completing tests and other required course work. The following are five suggested note-taking methods:

- Dash Method
- Informal Outline
- Cornell Method
- Question Method
- Text Method

After reading about and practicing each method, decide which method will work best for you.

The Dash Method

The dash method of note taking (a schematic of which is given in Figure 6-2) emphasizes main ideas and groups examples and details underneath the main idea. The exact placement of dashes is an individual's choice.

Figure 6-3 shows actual notes taken in a biology lecture using the dash method.

◆ **EXERCISE D: USING THE DASH METHOD**

Read the following paragraph, and organize the material using the dash method.

The 1890s in America were a decade of social tension. The depression of 1893–1896 accentuated *class divisions, and urbanization and industrialization were beginning to change traditional ways of life. The World's Columbian Exposition in Chicago in 1893 announced the fact of the machine age in a dramatic, public fashion.* Darwinism *and higher criticism*

Dash Method

Main Idea	or	—Main Idea I
—Details		Details
—Details		Details
Main Idea		—Main Idea II
—Details		Details
—Details		Details

FIGURE 6-2   Dash system structure.

of the Bible were threatening traditional ways of thinking about human origins and destiny. It is not surprising that in such a period the particular Puritan-American brand of Victorian morality became an especially rigified stronghold against social and intellectual ferment. (Calley, 1976, p. 117)

_____

_____

_____

_____

_____

_____

_____

_____

_____

_____

Chapter 9 - Nervous System

3 functions of nervous system:
— Sensory function
— Integrative function
— Motor function

Sensory function
— Involves sensory receptors area of peripheral nerves
— Info gathered is converted into signals in the form of nerve impulses, which are transmitted to ins

Integrative Function
— Signals are integrated creating sensations (perceptions) to memory and helping to produce thoughts
—— Conscious or unconscious decisions are made and then often acted upon by _____ of motor function

Motor Functions
— Use peripheral nerves that carry impulses to effectors, which are outside the nervous system
— Effectors are muscles or glands

FIGURE 6-3   Dash system model.

The Informal Outline

Although trying to write a formal outline while taking notes can be confusing, structuring an informal outline is helpful because it keeps your notes organized and helps you to sort out the main ideas from the details. Figure 6-4 illustrates how to use this method.

Informal Outline

> *Main Idea*
> 1. Detail
> 2. Detail

FIGURE 6-4   Informal outline structure.

Figure 6-5 shows actual notes taken in a biology lecture using the informal outline.

Anatomy: structure, morphology

Physiology: function of body parts

Needs of Organisms:
1. Water
   Most abundant substance in the body
   Transports substances
   Needed for metabolic processes
2. Food
   Provides body with necessary chemicals used as energy sources, as new material for new matter
3. Oxygen
   Used for releasing energy from food
   Energy then used for metabolic process
4. Heat
   A flow of energy
   Product of metabolic activity
   Rate of retention depends on amount of heat present
5. Pressure: The application of force to something
   Atmospheric pressure—a role in breathing
   Hydrostatic pressure—heat action creates blood pressure

FIGURE 6-5   Informal outline model.

◆ EXERCISE E: USING THE INFORMAL OUTLINE

Read the following selection, and take notes using the informal outline method.

> *Movies often reflect attitudes Americans hold. For example, in the 1950's, when Americans enjoyed* immense *economic pros-*

perity and domestic tranquility, *many Westerns were made. John Wayne, the* archetypal *western hero, portrayed a strong, moral, silent man who always held high principles. In his films, Wayne usually won the love of a beautiful girl, but she was not his goal throughout the movie. Instead, he saved ranchers from evil bankers who threatened to foreclose and settlers from ma-rauding bands of* belligerent *Indians. In sharp contrast, films from the mid-Sixties to the late Seventies offered heroes who seemed tortured by the political turmoil of the times. This was not seen in the 1942 film* Casablanca. *In the film* The Deer Hunter, *the* protagonist *Nick enlisted in the Army to fight in Vietnam. Instead of the glorious military victory he anticipated, he found that the war, filled with death and destruction, lingered on long after the last American assault. War films in the 1940's always showed the Americans as victors. In the 1980's, however, America has returned to a stronger economy and is led by a pres-ident who advocates self-reliance and strength. Ronald Reagan won by a landslide in the 1984 election. These beliefs are evident in our movies. For instance, in the* Rocky *series, Rocky Balboa moves from the underdog in a championship fight to the heavy-weight champion of the world through his determination and* per-severance. *In the* Rambo *movies, Sylvester Stallone creates a Vietnam vet, trained in guerrilla warfare, who single-handedly de-stroys a town in* First Blood *and who rescues American prisoners of war from Southeast Asian communists in the second* Rambo *film. Hence, American attitudes toward ourselves and our country are often apparent in our films.*(Fitzpatrick, 1989, p. 89)

Recall	Lecture Notes
Key Words and Phrases	

FIGURE 6-6   Cornell Method

Cornell Method

The Cornell note-taking system is a note-taking method that was developed by Walter Pauk, a well-known study skills expert, forty years ago at Cornell University. This system was developed to help students become more organized when taking notes (Pauk, 1988). The Cornell Method involves dividing your notes into two sections. One section is used for taking notes in class, and the other section is used for review after the lecture.

The basic format of the Cornell Method is shown in Figure 6-6 and outlined here.

1. Record during the lecture.
2. Reduce—that is, summarize in the left column.
3. Recite—that is, transfer information into memory.
4. Reflect—that is, think about what you have learned.
5. Review to help retention of information.

The advantages of the Cornell Method are that (1) it offers simple efficiency, (2) there is no need for rewriting, and (3) it is completely logical.

Using this method involves three steps, which may be summarized as follows:

Step 1: Before the Lecture

a. Use a large loose-leaf notebook.
b. Take notes only on one side of the page.
c. Draw a vertical line about 2½ inches from the left edge of each sheet. Classroom notes will be recorded in the space to the right of this line. After the lecture, key words and phrases will be written to the left of this line.
d. Before each lecture, read over the previous day's lecture notes. This practice will help you understand the progress of the course.

Step 2: During the Lecture

a. Record notes in simple paragraph form. Be sure to make notes clear and complete enough so that they will have meaning later.

b. It is not necessary to make an elaborate outline of notes.

c. Try to capture general ideas rather than illustrative details. You can get names and dates from the textbook.

d. Skip lines to show the end of one idea and the start of another.

e. Learn to use abbreviations effectively.

f. Write legibly.

Step 3: After the Lecture

a. Read notes as soon as possible.

(1). Make scribbles legible.

(2). Fill in places where you missed words or ideas.

(3). Underline or draw a box around words containing the main ideas.

b. In the recall column (left side), jot down key words and phrases that will stand as cues for the ideas and facts on the right. Use your own words to write a brief summary phrase. This will help you to organize and structure the lecture.

c. Cover up the right side of the sheet, and recite the information you have jotted down in the left column. Uncover the right column to verify what you have said. The procedure of reciting is a powerful learning technique. Be sure to consistently review so that you will retain the information you have learned.

Figure 6-7 shows actual notes from a psychology lecture using the Cornell method.

Recall	Principles of Gestalt Psychology
Gestalt not as influential today as earlier. Ex: See pairs of ball and a block, not pairs of blocks and pairs of balls.	Assumptions of Gestalt psychology have less influence today. Some principles still are accepted. 1. *Proximity* means that elements close together seem to organize into units of perception. 2. *Similarity* means that objects that appear to be the same area are more naturally grouped together. 3. *Good continuation* identifies properties that appear as logical extensions of others. 4. *Closure* is the tendency to complete shapes that are incomplete. 5. *Symmetry* suggests that balanced objects are a more pleasing perception than unbalanced objects.

FIGURE 6-7   Model of the Cornell method.

The Question Method

The question method is similar to the Cornell method, but rather than putting recall words in the left column you look at your lecture notes and develop questions based on the material. (See Figure 6-8.) These questions are used for review and studying for tests. When you begin to study, you can cover the lecture notes with your hand or a sheet of paper. Then try to answer the questions without looking at your notes. You can check your notes to see whether the information is correct. If you are successful in answering your questions, you can move on. If you have difficulty, you need to repeat the process.

The Text Method

The text method integrates information from the textbook with the lecture notes. You begin by reviewing lecture notes and then reading the text. As you read, you take notes from the text that correspond to the lecture and add them to the left column. (See Figure 6-9.) The advantage of this method is that the information gathered is in one place, which makes studying easier.

Questions	Lecture Notes

FIGURE 6-8   Question Method

Text Notes	Lecture Notes

FIGURE 6-9   Text Method

TAKING NOTES FROM YOUR TEXT

Another type of note taking is done when you read your text. You should not only take notes from lectures but also from your text, because note taking from your text will aid your concentration and memory, just as it does when you take notes from a lecture. Notes from textbooks can consist of highlighting, marginal annotations, and summary systems. Just as students forget lecture material if not written in notes, they do not remember reading material as readily if they do not mark their texts. These textbook notes can then be used when studying for a test.

When you highlight, annotate, or summarize, you select the main ideas and important terms more efficiently. You will be more likely to understand and remember what you have read if you are actively involved with the reading material. Strategies such as writing questions or summaries in the margin help you organize facts and ideas and serve as a first step in weighing and evaluating information.

Employing such a study system will make you an active learner. If you do nothing with textbook material, you will find it difficult to remember what you have read. Furthermore, when you mark your text, you will have something to go back to when reviewing for a test.

Highlight

Highlighting is one study strategy that is very popular with students. However, you need to highlight correctly for it to be effective. Highlighting can easily become a rote exercise. Some students have a habit of highlighting too much, and some students don't highlight enough. Care needs to be taken when using this strategy. The first step to effective highlighting is thinking about your purpose for highlighting. Generally, students highlight to distinguish the main idea and important details from superfluous material. Another reason for highlighting is to aid studying. When you come back to review the information in your text, you will only have to focus on the highlighted portion of your text, thus saving yourself from having to reread the entire chapter. You will be able to zoom in on the important information you need to learn.

An efficient way to highlight is to read a paragraph before you begin to highlight. After you have read the paragraph, then you will be able to go back and highlight the important points because you will be able to see the organization of the paragraph and identify the main ideas. It is difficult to decide what to highlight when you don't read the material beforehand.

Highlighting can be done with a marker, or you can use a pencil to underline. If you decide to use a marker, then it is a good idea to use a light, bright marker such as yellow or orange. When you use a dark color, it is much harder to read when you go back to review. Another option is to use two different colors to distinguish between main points and details.

Highlighting may be difficult at first because you need practice highlighting the right amount of information—not too much and not too little. You need to determine whether you wish to highlight important phrases or complete sentences. It is not always necessary to underline complete sentences, and highlighting a complete paragraph accomplishes little. Generally, do not highlight examples, case studies, or information too detailed to assist memory and understanding. In order to determine whether your highlighting is effective, read over your highlighting and ask yourself whether the material highlighted makes sense and helps you to understand the main thrust of the text. Figures 6-10 through 6-12 illustrate ineffective and effective highlighting.

Daydreaming is another form of consciousness that involves a low level of conscious effort. *Daydreaming lies somewhere between active consciousness and dreaming while we are asleep. It is a little like dreaming when we are awake. What are daydreams like? English poet/essayist Samuel Johnson said they are "airy notions of hope or fear beyond the sober limits of probability." Daydreams usually start spontaneously when what we are doing requires less than our full attention. Mindwandering is probably the most obvious type of daydreaming. We regularly take brief side trips into our own imagery and memory, even as we read, listen, or work. Occasionally the side trip goes on and on. Sometimes daydreaming is triggered by sensations from the world around us, but often its origins seem internal. When we daydream, we often drift into a world of fantasy. We imagine ourselves on dates, at parties, on television, at faraway places, at another time in our lives. At other times, our daydreams are about ordinary, everyday events, such as paying the rent, getting our hair done, dealing with someone at work, solving a problem with a friend or spouse. This type of semiautomatic thoughtflow can be very functional. Even though daydreams occur while you are shaving, ironing, or walking to the store, planning and problem solving naturally occur in the daydreams. They can remind us of important things ahead. Daydreaming keeps our mind active while helping us cope, create, and fantasize (Klinger, 1987).*

*When we sleep and dream, our awareness level is lower than when we daydream, but remember that we no longer think of sleep as the complete absence of consciousness. Sleep and dreams, though, are at very low levels of consciousness. How is being asleep different from being in a coma? Sleep is periodic, natural, and reversible. (*Santrock J. (1989). Psychology of Mind and Behavior. p. 130.)

FIGURE 6-10   Too little highlighting.

Daydreaming is another form of consciousness that involves a low level of conscious effort. *Daydreaming lies somewhere between active consciousness and dreaming while we are asleep. It is a little like dreaming when we are awake. What are daydreams like? English poet/essayist Samuel Johnson said they are "airy notions of hope or fear beyond the sober limits of probability." Daydreams usually start spontaneously when what we are doing requires less than our full attention. Mindwandering is probably the most obvious type of daydreaming. We regularly take brief side trips into our own imagery and memory, even as we read, listen, or work. Occasionally the side trip goes on and on. Sometimes daydreaming is triggered by sensations from the world around us, but often its origins seem internal. When we daydream, we often drift into a world of fantasy. We imagine ourselves on dates, at parties, on television, at faraway places, at another time in our lives. At other times, our daydreams are about ordinary, everyday events, such as paying the rent, getting our hair done, dealing with someone at work, solving a problem with a friend or spouse. This type of semiautomatic thoughtflow can be very functional. Even though daydreams occur while you are shaving, ironing, or walking to the store, planning and problem solving naturally occur in the daydreams. They can remind us of important things ahead. Daydreaming keeps our mind active while helping us cope, create, and fantasize (Klinger, 1987).*
 When we sleep and dream, our awareness level is lower than when we daydream, but remember that we no longer think of sleep as the complete absence of consciousness. Sleep and dreams, though, are at very low levels of consciousness. How is being asleep different from being in a coma? Sleep is periodic, natural, and reversible.

FIGURE 6-11 Too much highlighting.

Daydreaming is another form of consciousness that involves a low level of conscious effort. *Daydreaming lies somewhere between active consciousness and dreaming while we are asleep. It is a little like dreaming when we are awake. What are daydreams like? English poet/essayist Samuel Johnson said they are "airy notions of hope or fear beyond the sober limits of probability." Daydreams usually start spontaneously when what we are doing requires less than our full attention. Mindwandering is probably the most obvious type of daydreaming. We regularly take brief side trips into our own imagery and memory, even as we read, listen, or work. Occasionally the side trip goes on and on. Sometimes daydreaming is triggered by sensations from the world around us, but often its origins seem internal. When we daydream, we often drift into a world of fantasy. We imagine ourselves on dates, at parties, on television, at faraway places, at another time in our lives. At other times, our daydreams are about ordinary, everyday events, such as paying the rent, getting our hair done, dealing with someone at work, solving a problem with a friend or spouse. This type of semiautomatic thoughtflow can be very functional. Even though daydreams occur while you are shaving, ironing, or walking to the store, planning and problem solving naturally occur in the daydreams. They can remind us of important things ahead. Daydreaming keeps our mind active while helping us cope, create, and fantasize (Klinger, 1987).*
 When we sleep and dream, our awareness level is lower than when we daydream, but remember that we no longer think of sleep as the complete absence of consciousness. Sleep and dreams, though, are at very low levels of consciousness. How is being asleep different from being in a coma? Sleep is periodic, natural, and reversible.

FIGURE 6-12 Effective highlighting.

Now you're ready to complete Exercise F.

◆ **EXERCISE F: HIGHLIGHTING**

Read the following paragraph, and highlight the main idea and important details.

Creoles are the descendants of French or Spanish, born in Louisiana. Incorrectly the term is applied to any one born and living in New Orleans or its vicinity. Indeed there is a broader misapplication common in some parts of the state, where fresh eggs, Louisiana cows, horses, and chickens are called creole eggs, creole ponies, etc.

New Orleans, in reality, is two cities, the dividing line being a broad, tree-bordered avenue, running east and west from Lake Pontchartrain to the Mississippi River. "Up town," or the south side of this avenue, which is called Canal Street, is the home of the American population, while "down town," the north side, is the French or Creole Quarter. Up town the streets and the houses and many of the residents are new. It is a progressive, a self-made, a new city. Down town is the old town, with little improvement since the days when the houses were first built. Occasionally a creole family crosses the line, as it were, and goes to live up town, but they rarely become Americanized, for, above all things the creole is conservative. (Shaffer, 1892, p. 346)

Annotate

There are many ways to **annotate**, or mark, your text. Often annotating is used in conjunction with highlighting because some information is too complex to highlight. It is a good way to emphasize and sort out important information. As with highlighting, annotating is an excellent study strategy because it keeps you actively involved with the text material.

One method of annotating is to read a paragraph or a section of a text and then to briefly summarize the main idea or important points found in the material. Another technique is to put key words in the margin while reading and then to summarize based on these margin notes.

You can use notations such as question marks to indicate that clarification of this material is needed and stars to show which items were emphasized during the lecture. Circling words you don't know can help you learn vocabulary.

Other techniques include numbering lists described in the text or putting an asterisk after results, characteristics, or causes. You can also write questions in the margin that need clarification by your instructor. Such annotations will help you remember these items for tests.

Be careful not to make so many marks that you will be unable to focus on the important ideas.

Figure 6-13 demonstrates some of these marking strategies.

effects
psych

Marijuana, <u>a milder hallucinogen than LSD, comes from the hemp plant,</u> *Cannabis sativa,* which originated in Asia but <u>is now grown in most parts of the world.</u> *Marijuana is made of the hemp plant's dry leaves; its dried resin is <u>known as hashish.</u> The active ingredient in marijuana is THC, which stands for the chemical delta-9-tetrahydrocannabinol. This ingredient does not resemble the chemicals of other psychoactive drugs, and the <u>brain processes affected by marijuana for the most part, remain uncharted. Because marijuana is metabolized slowly, its effects may be present over the course of several days.</u>*

The <u>physical effects of marijuana</u> include increases in pulse rate and blood pressure, reddening of the eyes, coughing, and dryness of the mouth. <u>Psychological effects</u> include a mixture of excitatory, depressive, and hallucinatory characteristics, making it difficult to classify the drug. The <u>drug can produce spontaneous unrelated ideas;</u> distorted perceptions of time and place can occur; verbal behavior may increase or cease to occur at all; and increased sensitivity to sounds and colors might appear. <u>Marijuana</u> also can impair <u>attention</u> and <u>memory,</u> suggesting that smoking marijuana <u>is not conducive to optimal school performance.</u> When marijuana is used daily in heavy amounts, it also can <u>impair the human reproductive system</u> and may be involved in some birth defects. A downturn in marijuana use occurred in the 1980's (Johnston, O'Malley, Bachman, 1990).(Santrock, J. p. 153).

Behaviors
affected

impairs
marijuana
can cause
many
negative
behaviors
& effects

FIGURE 6-13   Combining highlighting and annotating.

Exercises G and H will give you the opportunity to practice the strategies of annotating and highlighting.

◆   **EXERCISE G: HIGHLIGHTING AND ANNOTATING**

Highlight the main ideas and key details in this following passage. Use marginal markings and annotations to clarify underlining.

Behavior Chains

*Operant behavior is not usually a matter of isolated acts. Rather, most operant behavior is a chain, or series of events. One event acts as a cue for the chain. **Behavior chains** that are taught by means of operant conditioning must be learned one link at a time. The case of Barnabus, a laboratory rat at Columbia University, suggests just how long these chains can be even among nonhumans.*

At the signal of a flashing light, Barnabus would dash up a circular path to a landing. Here he would cross a moat and climb a ladder to a second landing. He then got into a wagon and pedaled to the bottom of a stairway, which he climbed to a third platform. There he squeezed through a tube and entered an elevator. As the elevator descended, he pulled a chain, which raised the university flag. When he finally reached the floor of his cage, Barnabus pressed a bar and was rewarded with food (Pierrel & Sherman, 1963). Every step of this complicated behavior chain was taught by **shaping.** *Each reaction was rewarded, and each reward triggered the next link in the chain.*

Behavior chains are most readily learned if they are taught backward, with the last part of the chain learned first. The best way to teach someone to hit a baseball is to tie the ball to a string that is suspended from a tree, so that the learner can first try hitting the ball when it is not moving. After this has been learned, the person can then go backward in the chain and learn to hit a ball thrown by a pitcher—how to judge its speed and direction, when to swing and when to wait. (Morris, 1982, p. 155)

◆ **EXERCISE H: HIGHLIGHTING AND ANNOTATING**

Highlight and make marginal notes for this selection.

*Gender Identity and Gender Roles**

There are obvious biological differences between the sexes. Most important, women have the capacity to bear children, whereas men do not. These biological differences contribute to the development of gender identity, which refers to the self-concept of a person as being male or female. Gender identity is one of the first and most far-reaching identities that a human being learns. Typically, a child learns that she is a girl or he is a boy between the ages of 18 months and 3 years (Cahill, 1986).

Many societies have established social distinctions between the sexes which do not inevitably result from biological differences. This largely reflects the impact of conventional gender-role socialization. In Chapter 4, gender roles were defined as "expectations regarding the proper behavior, attitudes, and activities of males and females." The application of traditional gender roles leads to many forms of differentiation between women and men. Both sexes are physically capable of learning to cook and type, yet most societies determine that these tasks should be performed by women. Both men and women are capable of learning to weld and fly airplanes, but these functions are generally assigned to males.

It is important to stress that gender identity and gender roles are distinct concepts. Gender identity is based on a sense of one-

*From Richard T. Schaefer, *Sociology,* pp. 271–272. Reproduced with permission of The McGraw-Hill Companies.

self as male or female; gender roles involve socialization into norms regarding masculinity and femininity. Yet being male does not necessarily mean being "masculine" in a traditional sense; being female does not necessarily mean being "feminine." Thus, a woman who enters a historically male occupation such as welding, and who displays such traditionally masculine qualities as physical strength and assertiveness, may have a positive and highly secure gender identity. She may feel quite comfortable about being female—and, in fact, proud to be a woman—without feeling feminine as femininity has conventionally been defined. Similarly, a gentle, sensitive man who rejects the traditional view of masculinity may be quite secure in his gender identity as a man (Bem, 1978:20–21; L. Hoffman, 1977).

Gender Roles in the United States

Gender-Role Socialization *All of us can describe the traditional gender-role patterns which have been influential in the socialization of American children. Male babies get blue blankets, while females get pink ones. Boys are expected to play with trucks, blocks, and toy soldiers; girls are given dolls and kitchen goods. Boys must be masculine—active, aggressive, tough, daring, and dominant—whereas girls must be feminine—soft, emotional, sweet, and submissive.*

It is adults, of course, who play a critical role in guiding children into those gender roles deemed appropriate in a society. Parents are normally the first and most crucial agents of socialization (see Chapter 4). But other adults, older siblings, the mass media, and religious and educational institutions also exert an important influence on gender-role socialization in the United States.

Psychologist Shirley Weitz (1977:60–110) has pointed to two mechanisms which are primarily responsible for gender-role socialization: differential treatment and identification. In an illuminating study of differential treatment, a baby was sometimes dressed in pink and called "Beth" and at other times dressed in blue and called "Adam." Adults who played with the baby indicated that, without question, they knew whether the child was male or female from its behavior. They remarked on how sweet and feminine she had been, and on how sturdy and vigorous he had been. Clearly, these adults perceived the baby's behavior on the basis of their understanding of its sex. Such gender-related assumptions commonly lead to differential treatment of girls and boys (Will et al., 1976).

The process of identification noted by Weitz is more complex. How does a boy come to develop a masculine self-image whereas a girl develops one that is feminine? In part, they do so by identifying with females and males in their families and neighborhoods and in the media. If a young girl regularly sees female characters on television working as defense attorneys and judges, she may believe that she herself can become a lawyer. And it will not hurt if women that she knows—her mother, sister, parents' friends, or neighbors—are lawyers. By contrast, if this young girl sees women portrayed in the media only as models, nurses, and secretaries, her identification and self-image will be quite different.

The portrayal of women and men on television has tended to reinforce conventional gender stereotypes. In the past, women were presented most frequently as homemakers, nurses, and household workers—positions which reflect stereotyped notions of "women's work" (Commission on Civil Rights, 1977, 1979). However, by the 1980s, women had achieved a better image on prime-time network programs. A study by the National Commission on Working Women (1984a) found that 76 percent of the women portrayed on these shows were employed outside the home; only 8 percent were full-time homemakers. In an important change, more women are being seen in roles that display "leadership, authority, and courage." At the same time, the report noted that television is increasingly showing men as "nurturers" who care for others, primarily children. These changes, if maintained over time, will influence the identification and self-images of young girls and boys.

Females have been most severely restricted by traditional American gender roles. Throughout this chapter, we will see how women have been confined to subordinate roles within American political and economic institutions.

How to Summarize

Summarizing, or condensing information into a shorter form containing the key points or main ideas, is an important skill that can be used for many purposes. It can be used for marginal annotations, for note taking, for study purposes, and for required class work. In a sense, when you take lecture notes, you are summarizing what has been said.

When studying text material, you might choose to summarize the main idea of each paragraph, each section, or the whole chapter. Alternatively, you might just use marginal summary words. The same principles apply to whatever you decide to summarize. The following guidelines will help you with this process:

- Remember to look for main ideas.
- Read or skim a passage.
- Select main points, and number them in logical order.
- Write points into sentences in the numbered order.

◆ EXERCISE I: SUMMARIZING

Read the following selection, and highlight the main ideas.

Language

Language tells us a great deal about a culture. In the old west, words such as gelding, mare, piebald, sorrel, *and* stallion *were all used to describe one animal—the horse. Even if we knew little of this period of American history, we could conclude from the list of terms that horses were quite important in this culture. As a result, they received an unusual degree of linguistic attention.*

In contemporary American culture, the terms convertible, dune buggy, van, four-wheel drive, sedan, *and* station wagon *are all employed to describe the same mechanical form of transportation. Perhaps the car is as important to us as the horse was to residents of the old west. Similarly, the Paipai Indians of Baja, California, have two words for the desert. They can distinguish between two general types of desert, whereas our culture has only one word that is applicable (Berreman et al., 1971, pp. 409–410; Carrol, 1956).*

(From Richard T. Schaefer, *Sociology*, p. 69. Reproduced with permission of The McGraw-Hill Companies.)

Now that you have read the selection above, list the main points to summarize the ideas presented.

_____

_____

_____

_____

◆ EXERCISE J: SUMMARIZING

Circle the key words as you read the following two textbook selections. After you have finished each selection, scan the key words and then write a brief summary (one or two sentences) of each selection.

Medieval Times*

In medieval times (the sixth through the fifteenth centuries), little importance was placed on childhood as a separate phase of

*Berk, 1993, p. 6.

*the life cycle. The idea accepted by many theories today, that the child's nature is unique and different from that of youths and adults, was much less common then. Instead, once children emerged from infancy, they were regarded as miniature, already-formed adults, a view called **preformationism.** This attitude is reflected in the art, language, and everyday entertainment of the times. If you look carefully at medieval paintings, you will see that children are depicted in dress and expression as immature adults. Before the sixteenth century, toys and games were not designed to occupy and amuse children but were for all people. And consider age, so important an aspect of modern personal identity that today's children can recite how old they are almost as soon as they can talk. Age was unimportant in medieval custom and usage. People did not refer to it in everyday conversation, and it was not even recorded in family and civil records until the fifteen and sixteenth centuries (Aries, 1962).*

Nevertheless, faint glimmerings of the idea that children are unique emerged during medieval times. The church defended the innocence of children and encouraged parents to provide spiritual training. Medical works had sections acknowledging the fragility of infants and children and providing special instruction for their care. And some laws recognized that children needed protection from adults who might mistreat or take advantage of them. But even though in a practical sense there was some awareness of the smallness and vulnerability of children, as yet there were no theories about the uniqueness of childhood or separate developmental periods (Berk, 1993, p. 6; Borstelmann, 1983; Sommerville, 1982).

Summary: _____

_____

The Search for Asylum*

In the decade after World War II, some 45 million people relocated under pressure. And the flow continues unchecked. Between 1977 and 1987, 750,000 people sought asylum in Western Europe—200,000 in 1986 alone. To the political and cultural refugees in Europe must be added the economic immigrants. These amounted to 70% of all immigration into Europe during the 1960s and 1970s.

According to the Geneva conventions on the subject, refugees are people who leave their own country, unable to return for fear of persecution on racial, religious, ethnic, or political grounds. Asy-

*Fellman, J., Getis A., Getis, J., 1985, *Human Geography.* 4th Ed. W. C. Brown Publishers, p. 87.

lum seekers *are refugees asking a different country to take them. The petitioned state is under no obligation to agree. Among European countries, the policy in the late 1980s was to discourage applicants. Border controls were tightened across Western Europe. Formerly accessible Sweden began to refuse entry to applicants with unsubstantiated claims for asylum; Belgian police turned back petitioners of doubtful merit or improper papers.*

A basic question concerns an individual's right to free movement. In Western culture that right has traditionally been considered absolute within a country's borders and for departing emigrants, though international free movement into countries is everywhere controlled. In other cultures a different view may hold—one in which the emigrant is considered a traitor. For those societies and others, the state—not the individual—has the human right to determine place of residence, including residence within the state itself.

Summary: _____

_____

CHECKLIST FOR NOTE-TAKING

Use this checklist to evaluate your note-taking efficiency. Write the number (and letter or letters where appropriate) in the applicable column. Discuss your self-evaluation in groups. Which strategies received the most endorsements? Which received the least?

I Have Used This Strategy	*I Plan to Use This Strategy*	
		Before Lecture
_____	_____	1. Read the related textbook material.
_____	_____	2. Look at course outlines and objectives.
_____	_____	3. Review previous notes.
_____	_____	4. Anticipate lecture content.
_____	_____	5. Discuss ideas with classmates.
		During the Lecture
_____	_____	1. Attend the lecture.
_____	_____	2. Sit where you can see and hear.

I Have Used This Strategy	*I Plan to Use This Strategy*	

_____	_____	3. Have mind set to listen.
_____	_____	4. Listen actively for main ideas. **a.** Use title for headings. **b.** Note speaker's pattern of ideas. **c.** Be alert to speaker's voice and gestures. **d.** Copy down material written on the chalkboard.
_____	_____	5. Record notes in organized form. **a.** Write legibly. **b.** Leave margin on left. **c.** Leave space between ideas. **d.** Write in sentence form.

After the Lecture

_____	_____	1. Revise and review notes immediately after class.
_____	_____	2. Reflect on notes; relate them to the textbook.
_____	_____	3. Review notes frequently to retain information.

CRITICAL THINKING

Good listeners interact with the ideas presented to them—whatever the topic. They build their response based on previous knowledge of the subject and on the information provided, continuously asking questions and predicting what will be said next. Effective listeners are active listeners who form questions and express their beliefs about a subject.

The first aspect of active listening is to be able to separate what is actually being said from the listener's own response and beliefs. After receiving an accurate message, the active listener forms a question or opinion based on that information. Of course, during a lecture or conversation, this process takes place very quickly, but practicing the art of active listening can improve a student's performance in both situations.

1. Either as a class or individually, listen to an interview on a television program such as *60 Minutes, 20/20,* or by TV journalists such as Barbara Walters or Bill Moyers. First, take notes using one of the note-taking systems discussed in this chapter. Next, write a brief summary of the interview. Then, list two questions that come to your mind. Finally, state your opinion about the interview.
2. Select one person in the news today whom you would like to interview. Read one article about this person. Describe the person you chose to a classmate. Have the listener repeat your message about this person. Were your opinions restated accurately? Then have the listener ask questions or state his or her belief about the person. Reverse the listener and speaker roles.

Following are some questions you might use to form your explanation of the personality you chose:

a. Why is this person interesting to you?
b. What information did you learn from reading?
c. What is your opinion of this person?

REFERENCES

Berk, L. (1993). *Infants, Children, and Adolescents.* Boston: Allyn and Bacon.

Calley, M. (1976). The Context of the Awakening. *A Norton Critical Edition: The Awakening.* New York: Norton & Company, Inc.

Fellman, J., Getis, A., Getis, J. (1985). *Human Geography.* Dubuque, IA: W. C. Brown Publishers.

Fitzpatrick, R. (1989). *The Complete Paragraph Workout Book.* Lexington, MA: D. C. Heath.

Morris, C. (1982). *Psychology, An Introduction.* Englewood Cliffs, NJ: Prentice-Hall.

Santrock, J. (1986). *Psychology: The Science of Mind and Behavior.* Dubuque: W. C. Brown Publishers.

Schaefer, R. (1989). *Sociology.* New York: McGraw-Hill.

Shaffer, M. (June, 1892). Creole Women. *The Chautauguan VX,* 346. In M. Calley, ed. *Kate Chopin: The Awakening: An Authoritative Text, Contexts, Criticism.* New York: W. W. Norton & Company, 119–121.

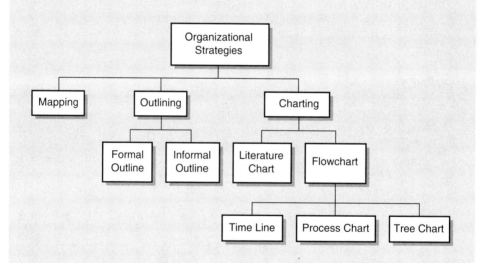

7

ORGANIZATIONAL STRATEGIES

One picture is worth more than ten thousand words.
—CHINESE PROVERB

Key Concepts

Charting   A strategy that creates a structure that organizes information into categories.

Mapping   A strategy that creates a visual picture of main ideas and important details and their relationship.

Outlining   A strategy that creates an arrangement showing the relationship between ideas and concepts.

In an earlier chapter we examined learning styles and discovered that there is a visual mode of learning. Using organizational strategies can be very helpful when you need to remember information. They help you to organize, condense, and visualize the information you are learning. Use of these strategies will help to clarify the text material and to involve you in the studying process. The more active you are in learning information, the better you will be in retaining it.

Although the strategies you use for different types of material will vary, organizational strategies can be used when you need to understand a concept, wish to remember a process, or need to know a series of steps or specific sequences of information. **Mapping, charting** and **outlining** are the three major organizational strategies presented in this chapter. Because these strategies provide a visual picture of the information you want to understand and remember, use of these strategies will help you increase retention and will provide a framework for adding other knowledge related to the information you organize.

Knowledge of outlines, maps, and charts will provide a springboard for you to create your own unique style of organizing materials. You may choose to use one or more of these strategies when you take notes during a lecture, review your notes after class, review textbook reading, or study for a test. You can use them when you preread or skim a chapter, or when you are doing the actual reading. The ideal way to use any of these organizational strategies is to preread the chapter; make your structure; and then, as you read, fill in the structure. You can also go back and make your structure after you have read the material.

◆ **EXERCISE A: ADVANTAGES OF ORGANIZATIONAL STRATEGIES**

List below the six positive results of using organizational strategies described in the previous paragraphs.

1. _____

2. _____

3. _____

4. _____

5. _____

6. _____

MAPPING

The following map models illustrate some of the different types of maps that are possible to construct. Figure 7-1 illustrates a type of map for which there is only one major idea with several key details to remember. Although this material might be presented on several different pages in a textbook, it can be condensed into this small but efficient map. You can then use the map to help you remember the material for a test.

The map shown in Figure 7-2 covers an entire section in a psychology text. It is more complex than Map Model 1, but, nevertheless, it presents the information clearly and in a condensed form. This information would be hard to remember if just highlighted. In a map form, however, the material is easier to remember.

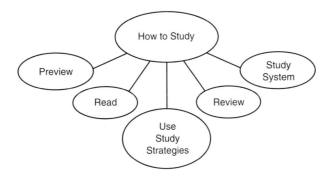

FIGURE 7-1   Map Model 1.

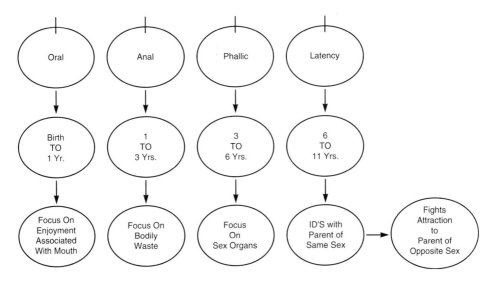

FIGURE 7-2   Map Model 2—Freud's psychosexual stages.

Figure 7-3 presents a more complex map. Even though it deals with information from a geology text that is more detailed, it presents a clear picture of the two types of minerals. This map gives you the opportunity to see the whole picture, as well as to see the differences and similarities between the two types of minerals.

The map model shown in Figure 7-4 deals with an entire literature lesson or chapter and is more detailed than any of the other models. Nevertheless, the map clearly organizes and categorizes the various concepts presented.

As you can see, mapping is a series of major concepts and important details joined together by various lines. Major concepts are usually boxed or circled. The beauty of this strategy is that you learn as you gather the information and begin to understand and clearly see the relationship between ideas while creating the map. Another advantage of this strategy is that you can clearly see the entire picture after your map is formed. Mapping provides a visual picture that helps you remember the information for tests and exams.

To construct your map, follow the procedure listed here:

1. Write the title, using a box or a circle to give it importance.
2. After selecting the major ideas and supporting details that you want to remember, write them on lines that connect with the title.
3. Attach subpoints to major points to show their relative importance.

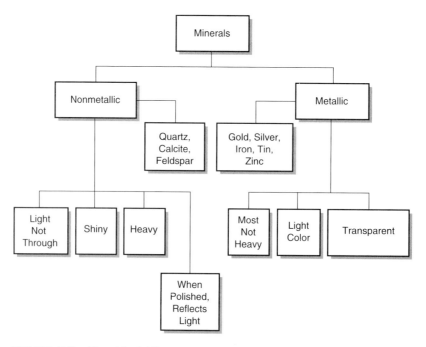

FIGURE 7-3   Map Model 3.

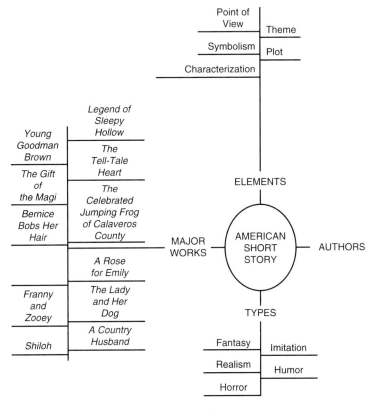

FIGURE 7-4   Map Model 4—web idea map.

◆   **EXERCISE B: MAPPING**

As a class, develop a map for the following selection.

Felonies and Misdemeanors
Crimes are divided into two general categories, felonies and misde-
meanors. Felonies are serious criminal offenses. Felonies are purposely
committed and are heinous in nature. When a person is caught and con-
victed of a felony, he or she is imprisoned and may even be sentenced to
death. Common felonies include murder and robbery. Once you commit a
felony, you are no longer eligible for public office or other types of govern-
ment jobs.

Misdemeanors are much less serious than felonies. Misdemeanors,
unlike felonies, are not generally committed with any intent. For example,
violation of traffic rules or drunkenness are classified as misdemeanors.
Usually the punishment for this type of crime is a fine, or imprisonment
in a county jail. Misdemeanors do not affect your ability to hold a public
office and generally do not cause you to lose your job.

◆   **EXERCISE C: MAPPING**

Create your own map for the following selection. In small groups share your maps and decide which is the most effective.

Humanistic Therapies*

In the **humanistic psychotherapies,** *clients are encouraged to understand themselves and to grow personally. In contrast to psychodynamic therapies, humanistic therapies emphasize conscious thoughts rather than unconscious thoughts, the present rather than the past, and growth and fulfillment rather than curing an illness. The two main forms of the humanistic psychotherapies are person-centered therapy and Gestalt therapy.*

Person-Centered Therapy

Person-centered therapy *is a form of humanistic therapy, developed by Carl Rogers (1961, 1980), in which a therapist provides a warm, supportive atmosphere to improve a client's self-concept and to encourage the client to gain insight into problems. Roger's therapy was initially called client-centered therapy, but he more recently rechristened it person-centered to underscore his deep belief that all persons have the ability to grow. The relationship between a therapist and another person is an important aspect of Roger's therapy. The therapist must enter into an* *intensely personal relationship with the client, not as a physician diagnoses a disease, but as one human being relates to another.*

Rogers believed that each of us grew up in a world filled with conditions of worth; the positive regard we received from others had strings attached. We usually did not receive love and praise unless we conformed to the standards and demands of others. This causes us to be unhappy and have low self-esteem as adults; rarely do we feel that we measure up to such standards or feel that we are as good as others expect us to be.

To free a person from worry about the demands of society, a therapist creates a warm and caring environment. A Rogerian therapist never disapproves of what a client says or does. Rogers believed that such unconditional positive regard improves a person's self-esteem. Therapists deliberately follow a course of action that is nondirective and facilitative, hoping to encourage clients to understand themselves and to engage in independent self-appraisal and decision making.

Rogers advocated other techniques in addition to providing unconditional positive regard. **Genuineness** is the Rogerian concept that describes the importance of a therapist being genuine and not hiding behind a facade. Therapists must let clients know their feelings. **Accurate empathy** is the Rogerian concept that describes a therapist's identification with a client. Rogers believed that therapists must sense what it is like to be the client at any moment in the client-therapist relationship. **Active listening** is the Rogerian concept that describes the importance of active listening skills as a client and therapist interact. Active listening is improved when the therapist restates and supports what the client has said and done.

Gestalt Therapy

Gestalt therapy is a humanistic therapy, developed by Frederick (Fritz) Perls (1893–1970), in which therapists question and challenge clients to help them become more aware of their feelings and face their problems. Perls was trained in Europe as a Freudian psychoanalyst, but, as his career developed, his ideas became noticeably different from Freud's. Perls agreed with Freud that psychological problems originate in unresolved past conflicts and that these conflicts need to be acknowledged and worked through. Also like Freud, Perls stressed that interpretation of dreams is an important aspect of therapy.

In other ways, however, Perls and Freud were miles apart. Perls believed that unresolved conflicts should be brought to bear on the here and now of an individual's life. A therapist should *push clients into deciding whether they will continue to allow the past to control their future or whether they will choose right now what they want to be in the future. To this end, Perls confronted individuals and encouraged them to actively control their lives and to be open about their feelings.*

Gestalt therapists use a number of techniques to encourage individuals to be open about their feelings, to develop self-awareness, and to actively control their lives. A therapist sets examples, encourages congruence between verbal and nonverbal behavior, and uses role playing (Harmon, 1990; Korb, Gorrell, & Van De Riet, 1990). To demonstrate an important point to a client, a Gestalt therapist might exaggerate or overportray a characteristic exhibited by the client. Often a therapist will openly confront a client to stimulate change. Consider a young woman who comes to a Gestalt therapist. She slouches back with one leg across the arm of her chair and strokes her leg with her hand. She tells the therapist she is not interested in men and denies that she ever tries to act sexy. The Gestalt therapist imitates her behavior in an exaggerated manner and remarks, "Come on, you've got to be kidding. What a joke. Look at what you are doing with your leg and arm. I've never seen anyone who is more seductive than you are!" (Kendall & Norton-Ford, 1982).

Another technique of Gestalt therapy is role playing, either by a client, a therapist, or both. For example, if an individual is bothered by conflict with her mother, the therapist might play the role of the mother and reopen the quarrel. The therapist may encourage the individual to act out her hostile feelings toward her mother by yelling, swearing, or kicking the couch, for example. Perls believes that this technique encourages clients to confront their feelings. In this way, Gestalt therapists hope to help people better manage their feelings instead of letting their feelings control them.

As you probably have noticed, a Gestalt therapist is much more directive than is a person-centered therapist. By being more directive, a Gestalt therapist provides more interpretation and feedback. Nonetheless, both of these humanistic therapies encourage people to take responsibility for their feelings and actions, to be truly themselves, to understand themselves, to develop a sense of freedom, and to look at what they are doing with their lives.

Behavior Therapies

Behavior therapies *use principles of learning to reduce or eliminate maladaptive behavior. Behavior therapies are based on the* *behavioral and social learning theories of learning and personality. Behavior therapists do not search for unconscious conflicts like psychodynamic therapists or encourage individuals to develop accurate perceptions of their feelings and self like humanistic therapists. Insight and self-awareness are not the keys to helping individuals develop more adaptive behavior patterns, say the behavior therapists. The insight therapies—psychodynamic and humanistic—treat maladaptive symptoms as signs of underlying, internal problems. Behavior therapists, however, assume that the overt maladaptive symptoms are the problem: people can become aware of why they are depressed and still be depressed, for example. Behavior therapists try to eliminate the symptoms or behaviors rather than search for insight into their underlying causes.*

The behavior therapies were initially based almost exclusively on the learning principles of classical and operant conditioning, but behavior therapies have become more diverse in recent years. As social learning theory grew in popularity and the cognitive approach became more prominent in psychology, behavior therapists have increasingly included cognitive factors in their therapy. First we will discuss the classical and operant conditioning approaches and then turn to the cognitive behavior therapies.

OUTLINING

Outlining is another strategy that you can use to organize material. Although formal outlines can become cumbersome, knowing how to outline is helpful because you may be asked to use this method in some of your classes. As with mapping, outlining can help you see the overall picture of what you are learning. For example, if you look at the table of contents in your text, you will see an outline of the overall picture presented.

As when learning any information, the first thing you need to do when creating an outline is to find the most important, or key, ideas. Second, you must discover how the information is organized; in other words, how the material is sequenced. These are important steps because if you don't know the main ideas and the organizational pattern, you will not be able to develop an effective outline. The third step is to discover the important details and relate them to the main point. Ideas of equal importance should have equal identification on the outline. For example, in the formal outline structure, topics identified by roman numerals are those of equal importance.

The topics identified by capital letters that are subordinate to the roman numerals are the main ideas. You then add details. You can have as many categories as you like, but you must have at least two of each. For example, if you have a *I*, then you must have a *II;* if an *A*, then you need a *B*. To construct an outline, follow the procedure listed here:

1. Find the most important, or key, ideas.
2. Discover the important details, and relate them to the main points.
3. Remember that ideas having equal importance should have equal identification.
4. Look for relationships of ideas.

Following is a model for a formal outline:

I.   Central Theme of Introduction

    A. State purpose
    B. How you will accomplish your purpose

       1. Details
       2. Details

II. Main point

    A. Examples
    B. Supporting evidence

III. Main point

    A. Important detail
    B. Important detail

IV. Conclusion

Following is a model for an informal outline. Notice that you do not need to use roman numerals or be as concerned about subdivisions as in a formal outline.

Main Idea

  1. Important details
  2. Important details

Main Idea

  1. Important details or points
  2. Important details or points
  3. Important details or points

(See Chapter 6, page 114, for a model of an informal outline.)

◆   **EXERCISE D: FORMAL OUTLINING**

As a class, write a formal outline of the following paragraph in the space provided.

Shopping Centers

There are three basic types of shopping centers. The convenience center, the neighborhood shopping center and the large mall center. The convenience centers are located in heavily traveled areas. They are fairly small and may contain as few as 3 to 5 stores. Grocery stores, drug stores, hardware stores, and laundromats usually populate this type of center. The neighborhood shopping center is larger and can have as many as 10–15 stores. The location is generally situated in an area that is convenient to the neighborhood or general surrounding area. Small department stores, travel agencies, dry cleaners, shoe repair shops and bookstores are some of the stores located in this type of center. Finally large malls can be located just about anywhere but tend to serve a very large area. These malls can contain anywhere from 40–100 stores. They usually contain several large department stores, specialty shops, restaurants, music stores, banks and just about any type of store that consumers need for shopping.

_____

_____

_____

_____

_____

_____

_____

_____

_____

_____

◆ **EXERCISE E: FORMAL OUTLINING**

Individually or in pairs, write a formal outline of the following selection.

Gender Makes a Difference

There are both physical and physiological differences (differences in physical processes) between the genders. Physically, boys tend to be superior in gross motor skills while girls exhibit skill in fine eye to hand coordination. After boys reach the age of six, they tend to be stronger than girls.

Physiological differences include a propensity for males to be color blind because color blindness is a sex-linked recessive gene which means the gene is recessive in females and dominant in males. Female's sensory perception tends to be much more sensitive than males, especially perception of taste, odor, and high pitched sounds. Male infants are more likely to have brain damage than females because females are better able to tolerate changes in oxygen during the birth process. Boys also tend to experience hyperactivity syndromes more often than girls because of minimal brain damage which suggests that girls are able to tolerate environmental fluctuations better than males. (Original, Laskey/Gibson)

_____

_____

_____

_____

_____

_____

_____

_____

_____

_____

_____

◆ **EXERCISE F: INFORMAL OUTLINING**

Reread the two preceding selections in Exercises D and E, and make an informal outline for each.

_____

_____

_____

_____

_____

_____

_____

_____

_____

_____

CHARTING

Charting is similar to mapping because both are visual strategies. However, the main emphasis of charting is classifying information into specific categories while mapping tends to focus more on the relationship between concepts. As you chart information, the similarities and differences between categories become clearer and are therefore easier to remember.

One example of when you might use a charting strategy is for a psychology textbook chapter that includes information on psychologists' birth places, theories, and influences. It is easier to understand and remember this type of material when you have organized it into some kind of organized chunk. The material then becomes condensed, makes sense, and is easier to remember. Another positive result is that you will have created an excellent study guide. You can develop a chart as you read, or you can go back after you have completed a reading assignment to make your chart.

The most difficult element of charting is developing the categories for your structure. Once you have determined your categories, you will only have to fill in the information about the specific categories from the text. The following steps should be followed when you develop your chart.

1. Preview chapter information.
2. Determine the main ideas and important details.
3. Decide which categories to use.
4. Arrange words and ideas (concepts) in a diagram or structure that shows relationships.
5. Fill in structure as you read.

Figures 7-5 and 7-6 illustrate two different models, one for literature and one for history.

History and other social science courses are difficult to study for because they cover a great deal of material. Developing a chart will help you to visualize and retain important information. Both the details and the whole picture become clear after using this organizational strategy. An overview for war might look like this: (Yours might include several pages.)

War	Dates	Causes	Major Leaders	Major Battles	Outcomes	Implications for Future

FIGURE 7-5   History Chart—an overview of wars.

Name of Literary Work	Setting	Major Characters	Major Events	Theme	Literary Devices Used (If Applicable)

FIGURE 7-6   Literature Chart. If you are studying novels and plays, you might organize your information into a chart.*

*The headings you choose are determined by the content of what you are reading.

There are four kinds of charts that you will find useful in your studies. Flowcharts are used to show sequences, process charts picture a process horizontally, time lines illustrate chronological order, and tree charts illustrate relationships.

A flowchart is shown in Figure 7-7. Flowcharts combine elements from both charts and maps. Flowcharts are diagrams that illustrate steps in a process. They are particularly effective in science and business classes.

Process charts are similar to flowcharts, but they illustrate the material horizontally rather than vertically. The process chart in Figure 7-8 illustrates the process of gas combustion.

How to Make Maple Syrup

In spring, drill hole into maple tree.

↓

Put metal spout in hole.

↓

Hang bucket from spout.

↓

Collect sap each day.

↓

Boil sap until small amount of water remains.

↓

Strain syrup.

↓

Bottle.

FIGURE 7-7   Flowchart

FIGURE 7-8   Process chart.

Great Composers

FIGURE 7-9   Time line chart.

Time lines, like the one shown in Figure 7-9, are chronological charts that facilitate visualization of a sequence of events. They are especially useful for history and government courses.

Tree charts show structures and relationships. Like the ones shown in Figure 7-10, they are often used to show family relationships and business structures. This type of chart is particularly useful for history and business courses.

◆   **EXERCISE G: CHARTING**

As a class, develop a chart for the following selection.

You have already developed a map for this selection. After you have completed your chart, compare the map with the chart to see which method works best for you.

Felonies and Misdemeanors

Crimes are divided into two general categories, felonies and misdemeanors. Felonies are serious criminal offenses. Felonies are purposely committed and are heinous in nature. When a person is caught and convicted of a felony, he or she is imprisoned and may even be sentenced to death. Common felonies include, murder and robbery. Once you commit a felony you are no longer eligible for public office or other types of government jobs.

Misdemeanors are much less serious than felonies. Misdemeanors, unlike felonies, are not generally committed with any intent. For example, violation of traffic rules or drunkenness are classified as misdemeanors. Usually the punishment for this type of crime, is a fine, or imprisonment in a county jail. Misdemeanors do not affect your ability to hold a public office and generally do not cause you to lose your job.

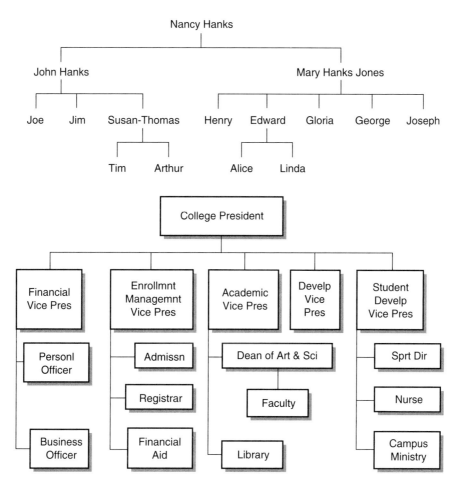

FIGURE 7-10   Tree charts.

◆   **EXERCISE H: CHARTING**

Read the following selection, and then develop your own chart. Share the results in small groups.

Woman Suffrage*

Because women seemed to be more easily aroused against temperance than men, temperance advocates very generally favored the "emancipation of woman," particularly with respect to conferring upon them the right to vote. The woman suffrage movement like the temperance movement, had attracted attention long before the

*From John Hicks, *American Nation,* 3rd edition. Copyright ©1958 by Houghton Mifflin Company.

Civil War, but the attainment of suffrage by the illiterate freedmen of the South had spurred the woman reformers on to renewed activity. Surely women were as fit to cast their ballot as ex-slaves. Led by such intrepid workers as Susan B. Anthony and Elizabeth Cady Stanton, and joined by a host of professional reformers who before the Civil War had centered their attack upon slavery, the suffragists made a little progress. A few states reluctantly conceded to women the right to vote in school elections, and far out in the West the two territories of Utah and Wyoming established complete political equality. Eventual victory for the suffragists was forecast by the increasing freedom with which women attended college, entered such professions as the ministry, the law, and medicine, and organized Women's clubs.

That the zeal for reform, so characteristic of Americans during the generation preceding the Civil War had been eclipsed rather than destroyed by the struggle was apparent in a majority of ways. Dorothea L. Dix, to mention a single name, laid down her war work only to resume her earlier efforts for the improvement of conditions among criminals, paupers, and the insane. In state after state boards of charities were set up to deal with the problem of relief. State schools for the deaf and the blind were established, and occasional efforts were made to deal separately with the problem of juvenile delinquency. In Massachusetts, for example, an industrial school for delinquent girls was opened during the seventies at Lancaster. Even the humane treatment of animals was demanded, and an American Society for the Prevention of Cruelty to Animals, founded in 1866 by Henry Bergh on the model of the British Royal Society for the same purpose, made rapid progress. Through its efforts American children by the million read the well-told tale, Black Beauty (1877), by Anna Sewell, an English writer; more important still, the Society interested itself in the well-being of children as well as animals, and did much to rescue the unfortunate from conditions that were sure to drag them down. All such efforts, however, were at best only piecemeal and comparatively little thought was given to the underlying causes of insanity, poverty, and crime. Some light was shed on the subject by the work of R. L. Dugdale, The Jukes: A Study in Crime, Pauperism, Heredity, and Disease (1877), which traced the history of a feeble-minded and diseased family that had cost the state of New York a million dollars since 1800.

◆ **EXERCISE I: CHARTING**

Read the following selection, and apply the most effective graphic organizer to create a map, a chart, or an outline. Alternatively, divide into small groups with each group using one of the three organizing strategies.

Personality Disorders*

There are certain types of mental disorders that are not neurotic disorders, nor are they classified among the more serious psychotic disorders. DSM-III refers to them as personality disorders. In these cases, a personality trait is so exaggerated and inflexible that it causes serious social problems. These people attribute the source of their problems to others; thus, they see no reason to change, and as a result they cause the same problems to recur, even though they are not happy about the results. It follows that they seldom seek therapy.

*A **schizoid personality** is characterized by a persistent inability and little desire to form social relationships and the absence of warm or tender feelings for others. Such "loners" cannot express their feelings and are perceived by others as cold, distant, and unfeeling. Moreover, they often appear vague, absent-minded, indecisive, or "in a fog." Because their withdrawal is so complete, schizoids seldom marry and may have trouble holding a job that requires them to work with or relate to others (APA, 1980)*

*   **Paranoid personalities** also appear to be "odd." They are suspicious and mistrustful even when there is no reason to be, and are hypersensitive to any possible threat or trick. They refuse to accept blame or criticism even when it is deserved. They are guarded, secretive, devious, scheming, and argumentative, though they often see themselves as rational and objective.*

*   Persons suffering from an **antisocial personality disorder** used to be called "sociopaths" or "psychopaths." They lie, steal, cheat, and show little or no sense of responsibility, although they are often intelligent and charming on first acquaintance. The "con man" exemplifies many of the features of the antisocial personality. Other examples might include: the man who compulsively cheats his business partners because he knows their weak points; the imposters who appear in the papers after their deceit is discovered; and various criminals who show no guilt. The antisocial personality rarely shows the slightest traces of anxiety or guilt over his or her behavior. Indeed, these people blame society or their victims for the antisocial actions that they themselves commit.*

*   Some psychologists feel that antisocial behavior is the result of emotional deprivation in early childhood. Respect for others is the basis of our social code, but if you cannot see things from the other person's perspective, rules about what you can and cannot do will seem to be only an assertion of adult power, to be broken as soon as possible. The child for whom no one cares, say psychologists, cares for no one. The child whose problems no one*

*From Morris, Charles G., PSYCHOLOGY: An Introduction, 4th ed. © 1982, pp. 424–425. Reprinted by permission of Prentice Hall, Upper Saddle River, NJ.

identifies with can identify with no one else's problems. Other psychologists feel that inconsistent parental behavior may explain many antisocial personality disorders. Sometimes the parents of these people punished them for being bad, sometimes they did not. Sometimes the parents worried over them and lavished attention on them, sometimes they ignored them and forced them to be prematurely independent. Thus, these children felt that their actions had no influence on how others behaved toward them.

Borderline personality disorders *are less clearcut than other disorders. The basic characteristic is "instability"—of mood, behavior, attitude, or emotion. The person is noticeably unpredictable or impulsive, particularly in areas that are potentially self-damaging, such as alcohol or drug abuse, sexual hyperactivity, gambling, suicide, overeating, or shoplifting (APA, 1980). They continually question their self-image, wondering who they are and why they behave as they do. Unlike antisocial people, they are often beset by anxiety and guilt over their life choices. The personal relationships of people with this kind of disorder are extremely turbulent, and they may have no tolerance for frustration.*

Narcissism, *or the total love of oneself, has been the subject of much recent clinical interest and research. The word narcissism comes form a character in Greek mythology named Narcissus, who fell in love with his own reflection in a pool, and pined away because he could not reach the beautiful face he saw before him.*

While we all love ourselves to some extent, a person with a narcissistic personality disorder has near total self-absorption, a grandiose sense of self-importance, a preoccupation with fantasies of unlimited success, a need for constant attention and admiration, and an inability to love or really care for anyone else (APA, 1980). But Otto Kernberg, who has devoted considerable study to narcissism, observes that the self-esteem of the narcissistic person is really very fragile: "The pathological narcissist cannot sustain his or her self-regard without having it fed constantly by the attentions of others" (Wolfe, 1978).

Many psychologists believe that narcissism begins early in life. While all infants tend to be narcissistic, most grow out of it. But for reasons that we do not yet understand, the narcissistic person never makes the change. Some social critics assert that certain tendencies in modern American society—such as our worship of youth and beauty, and our disregard for old age—have contributed to an apparent "boom" in narcissistic personality disorders (Lasch, 1979). Clinical data, however, do not support this speculation. While acknowledging that our society stimulates narcis-

sism, Kernberg argues that this cannot be the root of the disorder: "The most I would be willing to say is that society can make serious psychological abnormalities, which already exist in some percentage of the population, seem to be at least superficially appropriate" (Wolfe, 1978).

CRITICAL THINKING

One step in the critical-thinking process is evaluating evidence as support for decision making. Find an article from a newspaper or news magazine about a moral dilemma or a controversial issue. Create a map or chart that illustrates the evidence supporting each side of the issue. After you have created the map or chart, write a paragraph explaining which evidence is most convincing to you.

_____

_____

_____

_____

_____

_____

_____

_____

_____

_____

REFERENCES

Hicks, J. (1971). *American Nation.* Boston: Houghton Mifflin.
Morris, G. (1982). *Psychology: An Introduction.* Englewood Cliffs, NJ: Prentice-Hall.
Santrock, J. (1991). *Psychology: The Science of Mind and Behavior.* Dubuque, IA: W. C. Brown Publishers.

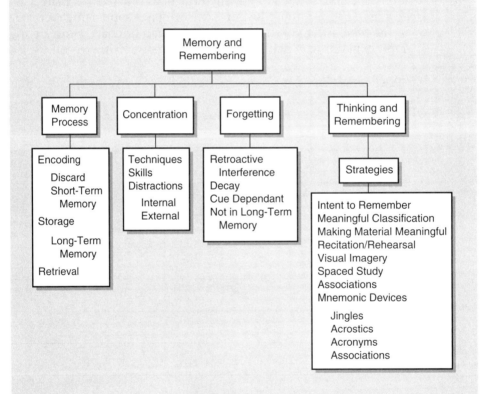

8

MEMORY AND REMEMBERING

Key Concepts

Encoding   The first stage of remembering in which stimuli are transferred into a form that can be placed in memory.

Exclusion   The ability to block out all stimuli not related to the immediate task.

External Distractions   Distractions that occur from outside sources.

Focusing   The ability to center attention on the task.

Forgetting   The inability to retrieve information stored in long-term memory or the lack of transferring information from short-term memory to long-term memory.

Internal Distractions   Distractions or emotional upsets that emanate from inside a person.

Learning   The process of storing information so that it can be pulled from long-term memory.

Long-term memory   A memory system with a large capacity in which information is retained for a long time.

Memory   The storing of things learned and retained through recall and recognition, a process of reproducing or recalling what has been learned and retained.

Mnemonic devices   Memory tricks designed to help one remember information.

Recitation   Saying aloud and repeating ideas for the purpose of remembering.

Rehearsal   Repetition of information.

Retrieval   The third stage of remembering in which information is located and put into use.

Short-term memory   A memory system with a limited capacity in which information is retained for as long as thirty seconds.

Storage   The second stage of remembering in which information is held in memory for later use.

Memory is vital to learning. Without memory you could not pass tests, relate ideas, or function effectively. In fact, without memory you would not be able to think critically because it is the information you have stored that is sorted and used to make decisions. Since memory is connected to every mental process, developing good techniques for remembering is essential to doing well in school. Using memory techniques to increase your ability to remember can make test taking, reading, and note taking easier.

In order to remember, students need to understand the material; therefore, both remembering and understanding play an important role in learning new material and enable you to apply information to new learning situations. There are many factors that contribute to memory, but for our purposes this chapter focuses on the memory process itself, ways to remember, concentration, and memory strategies.

THE MEMORY PROCESS

Memory is the storing of things learned and retained through recall and recognition, a process of reproducing or recalling what has been learned and retained. Memory can be short term or long term and can last a lifetime. Memory involves three stages: **encoding** (entrance), **storage**, and **retrieval.**

The first stage of memory, encoding, involves sending information from the senses to the brain. As illustrated in Figure 8-1, memory begins at the sensory level—seeing (reading), listening (hearing), feeling, smelling, and tasting. In this stage sensory stimuli are changed into a form that can be placed in memory. For example, if you touch something hot, a message is sent to the brain where the information is processed and the response is sent from the brain to your hand, which you will then quickly remove from the heat. Sensory memory lasts for about two seconds. After the brain registers the sensory information, it is then sent to **short-term memory**, which is "a limited capacity memory system in which information is retained for as long as 30 seconds". For example, if you look in the phone book for a telephone number and only use it once, this information will be discarded. However, if you use the telephone number many times, it will then be stored in your long-term memory. This is the next step in the memory process, moving data from short-term memory into **long-term memory.** Long-term memory is "a relatively permanent memory system that holds huge amounts of information for a long period of time." The information that is not sent to long-term memory is discarded. If you want to use the information that is stored in long-term memory, you need to retrieve it and raise it to consciousness. This is what study strategies accomplish. They provide the cues that enable you to bring the stored information back to the conscious level.

Recall and recognition are part of memory. Recall occurs when you must retrieve previously learned information. Recognition occurs when you only need to identify previously learned items. Thus, when studying, students need different strategies to implement recall and recognition. For example, when taking a multiple-choice test, one needs only to recognize the material, so index cards are an effective study strategy. However, if one needs to recall information for an essay test, outlining or using the study sheet system that will be discussed in Chapter 9 would be more productive.

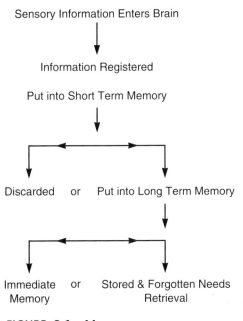

FIGURE 8-1   Memory process.

◆ **EXERCISE A: LONG-TERM MEMORY**

Practice activating your long-term memory by writing a detailed description of the house or apartment you lived in when you were five years old. Spend about fifteen minutes writing the description. Begin your description by pretending that you are walking toward the house. How does it look? Continue your description by giving the details you see as you move through the front door and then through each room in the house. How many details can you remember? How good is your long-term memory? Share your description with another classmate to see whether your partner's long-term memory is as active as yours.

_____

_____

_____

_____

_____

_____

_____

_____

_____

_____

_____

_____

_____

_____

_____

_____

CONCENTRATION

The first step in remembering is being able to concentrate on the material well enough to commit it to memory. Concentration is the ability to keep your mind on what you are doing. In order to achieve this state, you need to find ways to immerse yourself fully into the material that is being presented.

Techniques

Having a positive attitude toward studying greatly increases concentration, because if you have the desire to study, your attention will only be focused on learning the material. Focusing on what you are studying includes using study strategies, questions, and as many modes of learning as possible. The more learning modes you are able to utilize, the more effective your studying will be. Also, the more involved you are with the material, the better your concentration will be. Oral and silent reading, writing, and using visuals help students become part of the flow. Of course, it is difficult to concentrate when you are physically or emotionally fatigued, so make sure you eat and sleep properly and try to study when you are most alert. It also helps to reward yourself after a successful session. For instance, take a break or eat a treat.

Skills Needed

Two behaviors are needed in order to achieve good concentration. The first is **exclusion**, the ability to block out all stimuli not related to your immediate task. Exclusion involves blocking out **external distractions** that come from sources outside your domain, such as noise, loud music, telephones, people, and tempting aromas. The following items are strategies that will help you eliminate external distractions:

- Control noise level.
- Have necessary materials handy.
- Study in a quiet, secluded area.
- Set short-term goals.

In addition to excluding outside factors, you also need to focus your attention on the task you wish to achieve. **Focusing** requires that you fully direct your attention to the task of studying. It is better to set a reachable goal for yourself than attempt a marathon study day. You also need to have a positive mind set. If you feel that you will be bored or you just want to complete your studying quickly, you will not focus as well as when your attitude is, "I am ready, willing, and able to learn!"

Not only do you have to deal with external distractions, but you may also have **internal distractions**. These include personal and emotional problems, anxiety, and family pressures. Internal distractions involve your emotions and thoughts. They can keep you from focusing on the task at hand. So, when you study, you need to clear your mind of all thoughts and only think about what you need to learn.

Once you begin to concentrate, you need to make sure that you retain what you are learning. **Forgetting** is the inability to retrieve information stored in long-term memory or the lack of transferring information from short-term memory to long-term memory. Although you may be concentrating, it is possible to forget if you have not developed a method for remembering, because the greatest amount of forgetting occurs directly after finishing the learning task. Using study strategies and reviewing the material regularly are both effective strategies for improving memory.

◆ **EXERCISE B: CONCENTRATION**

Spend ten seconds looking at the picture shown in Figure 8-2. Cover up the picture, and list as many details about the picture as you can. Now look back at the picture with a classmate, and decide how many details are included in the picture. Were you able to remember at least ten of them? What factors aided or impeded your ability to concentrate on the picture? If you were able to remember at least ten specific details, you were probably concentrating well on the picture.

_____

_____

_____

_____

_____

FORGETTING

Retroactive interference is new learning that interferes with recall of old learning. For instance, retroactive interference can occur when you study the evening before a test but subsequently attend two lecture classes in the morning before the test. The information from the two classes may interfere with your recall of the information and may cause you to do poorly on the test. Thus, the ideal situation is to review the material as near to the test as possible. Another reason for forgetting is the process of decay. **Decay** is the passing of time that

FIGURE 8-2   Used by permission of Benjamin Gibson

causes memory loss; however, decay lessens with review and with constant repetition of information. An example of decay would be meeting someone you knew five years ago and recognizing the face but not the name. The passage of time has caused you to forget. **Cue dependent forgetting** is a form of forgetting because of a failure to use effective retrieval cues. For instance, you think you know the title of a song you are listening to, but you don't have any cues to use to help you remember it. However, if you can associate the song to a vocalist, group, or movie, you may find the cues needed for remembering. That's what study methods and strategies can do; they provide a cue system to help you remember. Failure to commit information to long-term memory is also another reason why people can't remember what they have read. However, as stated before, repetition and constant review help to overcome this.

LEARNING

Now that you know what causes memory difficulties, you need to concentrate on how to remember important information. First, let's begin with defining ***learning,*** which is the process of storing information so that it can be returned, or pulled, from long-term memory. In order to store information in long-term memory, you need to learn the material. Once you have learned something and it is stored in long-term memory, the process or skill learned is relatively permanent. For example, once you learn to ride a bike, the knowledge of how to do it is stored in your long-term memory. Even if you haven't ridden a bike in many years, you will quickly remember this skill because you are retrieving information already learned. This definition of learning applies only to the context of memory, but this is exactly what you have to do when you prepare for tests, exams, oral presentations and when you engage in class participation. You are constantly required to pull information from long-term memory in order to respond to various academic requirements.

THINKING AND REMEMBERING

Another important element of memory is thinking. How could we think if we didn't have memory? Without memory we would have a difficult time learning because we would not be able to draw from previous experiences. We do not just have one thought but accumulate our thoughts; one thought builds on another. Every thought has the potential to connect with another thought, which creates more new thoughts, which then becomes part of the critical thinking process. When you put all of your thoughts together, you will have a body of knowledge that will help you to achieve your academic goals. Thinking depends on how much and how well we can remember (Kirby & Goodpaster, 1995), because without memory there wouldn't be a past, only present existence.

STRATEGIES THAT AID MEMORY

You need to ask yourself, "What can I do to remember the information that I need to perform well in school and in the workplace?" The following are strategies and exercises that will aid you in storing and retrieving information.

Intent to Remember

In order for you to remember information, the material needs to be important enough for you to want to remember. If the desire to retain the information is lacking, then memory will be weak. For example, people generally remember debts owed to them but forget details in other areas where motivation to remember is absent.

◆ **EXERCISE C: INTENT TO REMEMBER**

Try to describe the color of the dishes you used when eating breakfast this morning.

Try to remember what color clothes you wore two days ago.

Try to remember the day and time your boyfriend or girlfriend last called you.

Which of these questions was the easiest for you to remember? Why?

Meaningful Classification

Materials that are clear and easy to understand are usually organized in some meaningful way. It is difficult to remember information that is randomly collected or presented. However, if the information is put into categories, it is much easier to remember. For example, if you were to go to a pharmacy and needed the items shown in Exercise D, it would be difficult to remember the things on the list. However, if you organized them in some meaningful manner, you would remember them more easily. This is true for any information you want to remember.

◆ **EXERCISE D: MEANINGFUL CLASSIFICATION**

Suppose you had to go to a pharmacy to buy the following items. Categorize them into a meaningful structure so that you can remember them more easily.

toothpaste	mousse	tissue	dental floss	curling iron
mouthwash	shampoo	aspirin	hair spray	cough medicine
milk of magnesia				

_____   _____   _____

_____   _____   _____

_____   _____   _____

_____   _____   _____

◆ **EXERCISE E: MEANINGFUL CLASSIFICATION**

Read the following paragraphs, and organize the information into meaningful groups.

Intimacy is key in a world of connection where individuals negotiate complex networks of friendship, minimize differences, try to reach consensus, and avoid the appearance of superiority, which would highlight differences. In a world of status, independence is key, because a primary means of establishing status is to tell others what to do, and taking orders is a marker of low status. Though all humans need both intimacy and independence, women tend to focus on the first and men on the second. It is as if their lifeblood ran in different directions.

Group A	*Group B*
_____	_____
_____	_____
_____	_____
_____	_____

Many women feel it is natural to consult with their partners at every turn, while many men automatically make more decisions without consulting their partners. This may reflect a broad difference in conceptions of decision making. Women expect decisions to be discussed first and made by consensus. They appreciate the discussion itself as evidence of involvement and communication. But many men feel oppressed by lengthy discussions about what they see as minor decisions, and they feel hemmed in if they can't just act without talking first. When women try to initiate a freewheeling discussion by asking, "What do you think?" men often think they are being asked to decide. (Tanner, 1990, pp. 26–27)

Group A	*Group B*
_____	_____
_____	_____
_____	_____
_____	_____

Making Material Meaningful

Materials that make sense are easy to remember. In contrast, information that seems random or confusing is hard to remember. If your assignment is difficult and confusing, reading something easier first may help to clear your confusion. For example, if you are reading a difficult chapter in your history text, reading the same material in a high school version first will clarify the information and make your college text more meaningful.

◆ **EXERCISE F: RANDOM INFORMATION**

Can you remember the following letters in fifteen seconds?

PML   JRB   GRM   WTZ   PDB   LZA

◆ **EXERCISE G: MEANINGFUL INFORMATION**

Try to remember the following letters in fifteen seconds. Why are these letters easier to remember than those in Exercise F?

ABC   AT&T   ASAP   RSVP   BLT

◆ **EXERCISE H: EASY VERSUS DIFFICULT MATERIAL**

Read both of the following poems. Which one is easier to understand? Why?

Poem 1

'Twas brillig, and the slithy toves
  Did gyre and gimble in the wabe:
All mimsy were the borogoves,
  And the mome raths outgrabe.

from "Jabberwocky" by Lewis Carroll

Poem 2

O, my love is like a red, red rose,
  That's newly sprung in June.
O, my love is like the melodie,
  That's sweetly played in tune.

from "Oh, My Love is Like a Red, Red Rose" by Robert Burns

Recitation and Rehearsal

Two more strategies that aid memory are **recitation,** which involves saying aloud the ideas that you want to remember, and **rehearsal,** the repetition of information. Recitation is important because it helps to transfer information from short-term memory to long-term memory. It works because it helps you understand the material, thereby strengthening memory.

Rehearsal is also important because the more you repeat something, the more likely you are to remember it. Rehearsal involves:

1. Reciting
2. Writing
3. Rereading

◆ **EXERCISE I: RECITATION**

Recite once the following paragraph from the Preamble of the Constitution. Can you repeat what you recited without looking back at the text? Now recite the paragraph four times. How much can you remember now?

> *We the people of the United States, in order to form a more perfect union, establish justice, insure domestic tranquility, provide for the common defense, promote the general welfare, and secure blessings of liberty to ourselves and our posterity, do ordain and establish this Constitution for the United States of America.*

The more times you recite this paragraph the easier it will be to remember.

◆ **EXERCISE J: RECITATION**

In groups, memorize the following passage from the Gettysburg Address. Keep track of the number of recitations it takes to memorize it.

> *Four score and seven years ago our fathers brought forth on this continent, a new nation, conceived in Liberty, and dedicated to the proposition that all men are created equal.*
>
> *Now that we are engaged in a great civil war, testing whether that nation, or any nation, so conceived, and so dedicated, can long endure. We are met here on a great battle-field of that*

war. We have come to dedicate a portion of it as a final rest-ing place for those who here gave their lives that that nation might live. It is altogether fitting and proper that we should do this.

Visual Imagery

Forming a visual picture of details you want to remember is another aid to memory. Visualization can be thought of in two ways. One is to visualize ideas and thoughts in your mind. For example, using visual imagery for remembering that President Lincoln was born in 1809 could involve remembering a picture of President Lincoln's log cabin with the date 1809 carved over the door. The second is to use strategies such as mapping and charting to form a visual picture. (Refer to Chapter 7 for a review of mapping and charting.)

◆ **EXERCISE K: VISUAL IMAGERY**

Draw a visual image to help you remember the following items and their relationships.

1. Short-term memory
2. Long-term memory
3. Storage
4. Retrieval

Spaced Study

The length of time and spacing between reading and studying different subjects affects learning. Most experts believe that fifty minutes should be the maximum time for study, with ten-minute breaks interspersed at fifty-minute intervals. However, you need to find the time frame that works best for you.

Use the following chart to record the time you begin a study session and the time you complete your session. Note how long you can concentrate. Stop studying when you lose your focus. Watch for the following signs, which indicate loss of concentration:

1. Lack of comprehension
2. Staring into space, that is, daydreaming
3. Glazed eyes
4. Feeling of fatigue
5. Inability to remember what you have read

Sessions	Time Began	Time Ended	Total Time
1			
2			
3			

Because research has shown that students remember more from several short study sessions than from one long marathon session, short, usually wasted periods of time can be put to effective use by studying three to five pages of material. If you find it hard to concentrate, studying time will have to be adjusted. Once you are aware of your individual attention span, you can work on lengthening it.

◆ **EXERCISE L: FINDING USABLE TIME**

In groups or as a class, brainstorm to determine where you waste short periods of time that could be used to read or study.

Making Connections

New information is easier to learn and remember if you connect it with previously learned or familiar material. For example, if you read a chapter on the Holocaust and you had family members who were involved either as soldiers or prisoners, you would probably remember the information more easily than someone who had no personal associations to make. The more associations you can make, the easier it will be to remember important information.

◆ **EXERCISE M: ASSOCIATIONS**

Following is a list of words that may be unfamiliar to you. Read the definitions of each word. Then cover up the definitions. Can you remember the definitions of each word? Now, in order to commit these words to long-term memory, think of associations for each.

Word	*Definitions*	*Associations*
Morose	sad, gloomy	_____
Emaciated	extremely thin, almost to point of starving	_____
Machinations	act of plotting	_____
Vicarious	experienced indirectly	_____
Cygnet	baby swan	_____
Altruistic	truth	_____

Mnemonic Devices

Mnemonic devices are memory tricks that help you to recall information. The emphasis is on memorization, not learning. For example, "Thirty days have September, April, June, and November. All the rest have thirty-one except February alone" is a mnemonic device.

The following are different types of mnemonic devices that are often used to remember or memorize information.

- Jingles
- Acrostics
- Acronyms
- Associations

Jingles are simple, repetitive, catchy rhymes. For example, "*I* before *E* except after *C*" is a rhyme that people use to remember the correct spelling of words such as *receive* and *receipt*.

Acrostics consist of phrases or sentences created from the first letter or first few letters on the list you need to remember. One example of an acrostic is the sentence "*M*en *v*ery *e*asily *m*ake *j*ugs serving *u*seful *a*nd *n*umerous *p*urposes." This phrase will enable you to remember the order of the planets in our solar system: Mercury, Venus, Earth, Mars, Jupiter, Saturn, Uranus, Neptune, and Pluto. The first letter of each word (except *and*) corresponds to the first letter of the planets.

Acronyms consist of a word formed from the first letters of a name or nouns. For instance, in order to remember how to prevent heart attacks, remember the acronym *SWEAR*.

S = give up *s*moking
W = lose *w*eight
E = *e*xercise regularly
A = at the *a*ge of forty get a check up every year
R = get sufficient *r*est every night

Associations are mental connections or relationships between thoughts or ideas. For example, if you are at a party and are introduced to a lot of people whose names you wish to remember, you can use association by assigning each person an animal's name. A tall person named Gordon could be associated with a giraffe, and a short person with curly hair named Polly could be associated with a poodle.

◆ **EXERCISE N: MNEMONIC DEVICES**

1. Imagine you are at a party and meet people with the following names. Devise a mnemonic device to help you remember each person's name. You might use a concrete substitute for a name, you might associate the name with someone or something you already know, or you might make up a simple rhyme for the person's name.

    1. Jane Johnson
    2. Richard Green
    3. Bonnie Smith
    4. Benji Abbott
    5. Karen Carpenter

2. Imagine that you are in a geography class and have been asked to learn the names of the Great Lakes (Michigan, Ontario, Erie, Huron, and Superior). Make up four different mnemonic devices using rhymes, first letters, a sentence, and a story to help you remember the names of the Great Lakes.

3. Think of an acronym that will help you remember the colors of the spectrum: red, orange, yellow, green, blue, indigo, and violet. Remember that an acronym is a word that is made up of the first letter of each word in the series you want to learn.

4. Think of a mnemonic sentence that will help you remember the first five presidents of the United States: Washington, Adams, Jefferson, Madison, and Monroe.

5. The psychologist Eric Erikson described eight developmental stages that humans progress through. The eight stages are infancy, early childhood, play age, school age, adolescents, young adult, adulthood, and old age. Develop a mnemonic device that will help you remember these stages.

CRITICAL THINKING

Critical thinking depends on an effective memory; the more information you store, the better you will be able to think. Without stored information, you will not have a good foundation for making decisions or forming ideas. The facts, experiences, and ideas that you remember from your background knowledge or schema will become a part of your thinking apparatus. By developing and strengthening memory skills, you are, therefore, strengthening your thinking ability because you are gathering and employing the information needed to form valid ideas and to make good decisions.

◆ EXERCISE: CRITICAL THINKING

Analyze the following statements by listing the pros and cons of each one. Next, decide how each situation should be handled. Then below the statements, write the facts, experiences, or ideas you recalled in order to make your decision.

1. A hospital should treat anyone needing help, regardless of whether he/she has health insurance.

2. There should be smoking sections available in restaurants and public buildings.

3. Longer prison terms for convicted criminals is an effective answer for reducing crime.

REFERENCES

Tannen, D. (1990). *Women and Men in Conversation.* New York: Ballantine Books.

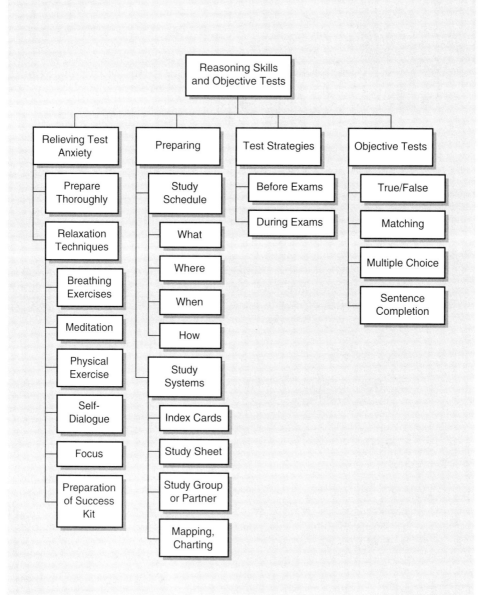

Reasoning Skills and Objective Tests

Relieving Test Anxiety
- Prepare Thoroughly
- Relaxation Techniques
  - Breathing Exercises
  - Meditation
  - Physical Exercise
  - Self-Dialogue
  - Focus
  - Preparation of Success Kit

Preparing
- Study Schedule
  - What
  - Where
  - When
  - How
- Study Systems
  - Index Cards
  - Study Sheet
  - Study Group or Partner
  - Mapping, Charting

Test Strategies
- Before Exams
- During Exams

Objective Tests
- True/False
- Matching
- Multiple Choice
- Sentence Completion

9

REASONING SKILLS FOR OBJECTIVE TESTS

From contemplation one may become wise, but knowledge comes only from study.
—A. EDWARD NEWTON,
A Magnificent Farce

Key Concepts

Objective tests   Tests that focus on recognition of information and include multiple-choice, true-false, matching, and sentence completion questions.

Study system   A specific method for studying for tests.

Test anxiety   Unreasonable fear manifested by physical and/or emotional responses at the thought of taking a test or during a testing situation.

Students who receive good test scores do not simply review the materials covered in the text and lecture. Instead they depend on using effective self-awareness, critical-thinking skills, and metacognition (which, you'll recall from Chapter 3, is knowing what you know and don't know). In fact, a student who achieves high scores on tests not only knows the material thoroughly but also has developed effective study strategies and an efficient study system that help to ensure top scores.

Before the test, you need to activate your own self-assessment. What parts of the material covered on the test do you understand? What areas are difficult for you to understand? Which information do you need to memorize? What questions can you anticipate being on the test? Successful test takers generally have the ability to answer these questions. If you can determine these answers, you will be able to decide what information you need to memorize and to anticipate what probable questions will be on the test. In other words, you need a good grasp of what you know and what you don't know; this is metacognition.

Another important factor in receiving good test results involves the critical-thinking process. Students who are able to apply logical, critical-thinking skills to test taking achieve the best results on exams. In addition to memorizing facts, you need to use logical reasoning to answer the questions. Often you can figure out an answer you are unsure of by using deductive reasoning. Your reasoning might be patterned after the following example:

If you know that A = B

and B = C,

then you can conclude that A = C.

The same process occurs with content material:

DNA contains genes.

Genes determine inherited traits.

Therefore, one could draw the conclusion that the composition of DNA determines hereditary factors.

By employing this kind of logical reasoning, you can improve your test scores and feel more confident and relaxed during the test. Using critical thinking and applying metacognition will help you study and take tests more effectively. The study systems and test-taking strategies described in this chapter provide the basic tools to assist you in becoming a skilled test taker. They will help you become active learners and approach exams with confidence.

RELIEVING TEST ANXIETY

Test anxiety can lower test scores. Many students suffer anxiety at the mere thought of taking a test. For those students, school becomes an ordeal, since tests are an integral part of college life. Learning test-taking strategies is one way of alleviating the problem. They include relaxation techniques and positive self-dialogue.

Part of being a good test taker is knowing your strengths and weaknesses, including your ability to perform under stressful situations such as tests. Therefore, it is important to explore your anxiety level in order to be able to deal with test anxiety. Following is a test anxiety evaluation tool. Follow the directions to determine your level of anxiety.

◆ EXERCISE A: TEST ANXIETY CHECKLIST

Fill in the blanks on this list according to whether you experience any of the symptoms described. Completing the checklist will give you some idea about your emotional response to test taking.

Physical Symptoms	*Yes*	*No*
1. Headaches before or during tests	_____	_____
2. Nausea before or during tests	_____	_____
3. Heavy perspiration	_____	_____
4. Heart beating fast or pounding	_____	_____
5. Shakiness and trembling during test	_____	_____
6. Stomachache, change in eating habits	_____	_____
Cognitive Symptoms		
7. "Blankness" or difficulty remembering answers	_____	_____
8. Difficulty in making a choice or decision on an answer	_____	_____
9. Difficulty concentrating or paying attention to the test questions	_____	_____

	Yes	*No*
10. Problems in thinking clearly or reasoning out the answers	_____	_____
11. Inability to comprehend and remember the sentences	_____	_____
12. Thinking very slowly and laboriously	_____	_____

Emotional Symptoms

13. Feeling scared and panicky about needing more time	_____	_____
14. Feeling worried about doing poorly	_____	_____
15. Feeling overwhelmed	_____	_____

If you frequently experience many of the symptoms described in Exercise A, then learning to control your anxiety is an important step toward improving your test results. Test anxiety symptoms can lower your performance because they interfere with your ability to think clearly and to concentrate on the task before you.

Adequate Preparation

Students who don't prepare well for tests often experience panicky feelings simply because they do not know the subject thoroughly. They have crammed right before the test or have not allowed enough time in their schedules to prepare for the test adequately. Since fear feeds on itself, once students experience several episodes of test anxiety, they are more likely to associate test taking with anxiety whether they are well prepared or not. Therefore, being well prepared for the test is a must for reducing test anxiety. Since anxiety is basically fear, students can develop confidence and extinguish excessive anxiety by overlearning the material. Be sure you *do* understand the material. Be sure you *have* read the required material. Use the memory techniques described in the book until you know the material backwards and forwards.

As part of preparing for tests, a student needs to be in good physical condition by getting plenty of sleep and eating regularly. Plan your study schedule realistically, so you will have time to eat regular meals, get enough sleep, and exercise regularly. Setting up a schedule such as the one described in Chapter 4 will help you to feel in control of yourself and the situation. It will also help you feel well physically.

Six Strategies

In addition to feeling adequately prepared, another important strategy to alleviate anxiety is relaxation techniques, which can be utilized before and during exams. Six strategies to help alleviate anxiety follow:

1. **Breathing exercises.** Breathing exercises are important for alleviating anxiety, since breathing and anxiety are interrelated. When a person is anxious, breathing becomes shallow and rapid. The resulting loss of oxygen can produce irritability and fatigue, which increase anxiety. Learning to breathe slowly and deeply by using abdominal muscles leads to a more relaxed, tranquil feeling and reduces tension in the skeletal frame.
2. **Meditation.** Meditation techniques, performed in conjunction with breathing exercises, can also lessen anxiety. Breathing deeply and repeating one word or sound again and again eases distractions and tension. Another method of meditation is to choose one object in a room to focus on. This intense focus, together with breathing slowly and deeply, shifts one's thoughts away from negative, painful ideas and sensations.
3. **Physical exercise.** Moderate exercise three or four hours before a test can ease anxiety and improve concentration. It helps the student to feel in control, which is self-affirming. Like deep breathing, exercise increases the oxygen intake and reduces tension. Vigorous exercise, however, leads to fatigue and probably reduces a student's ability to perform well.
4. **Self-dialogue.** Everybody has a negative voice and a positive voice. The negative voice says you are not going to succeed on the test and often goes on to elaborate on the dire consequences of failure. The negative messages naturally lead to anxiety. The first step to alleviate the harmful effects of negative messages is to identify them. The next step is to counter these messages with positive ones and bring balance into the situation. Will you ruin your life and all chance of future success if you fail a test? No. There will always be alternatives and there are always new opportunities for growth and success. Finally, make a list of positive statements to repeat slowly to yourself. Statements such as, "I am capable. I am safe. I can do it." will help calm anxiety. Develop three or four statements and say them to yourself slowly and calmly, until they have the desired effect.
5. **Focus on the present moment.** If you experience anxiety during the test, practice gently, calmly bringing yourself back to the task at hand, which is to write the answers you know on the piece of paper. By focusing on the present, the fears and

negative messages will be pushed aside, and you will be able to eliminate the negative "what if" thoughts that can lower your performance.

6. **Preparation of a success kit.** Another technique that might help you alleviate test-related stress is putting together a "success kit," which can include all kinds of test-related items. Your kit might include extra pens, pencils, a pencil sharpener, extra paper, paper clips, and a small stapler. You might want to include dried fruit, a quick energy snack, and gum to give you a feeling of security and comfort. You could even add a picture or lucky charm that has special meaning for you.

These techniques take practice. If you suffer from test anxiety, be patient with yourself and keep practicing. Don't be discouraged if your test anxiety doesn't vanish immediately; remember that some anxiety is normal and healthy. It can spur you on to do your best. In fact, like a runner before an important race, a certain level of anxiety can actually improve performance. Just keep studying and practicing these relaxation techniques, and slowly you will begin to feel more relaxed in test-taking situations.

PLANNING

Planning before and during the test can also alleviate test anxiety. This section describes techniques everyone can use to improve test performance, whether test anxiety is a problem for you or not. Planning a study schedule can help you feel in control and confident, and planning techniques on the day of the test can improve your concentration and your self-confidence.

Study Schedule

Making decisions about studying is paramount to achieving success. You need to organize your materials and make decisions about what to study because if you study the wrong information, your efforts will be unrewarded. You also need to answer the question of *where* to study. It is important to be in an area that is conducive to studying. Another area to consider is *when* to begin studying. Students often leave studying until the last minute, and when you cram, it is difficult to perform at your best. Preparation for taking a test should begin at least a week to three days before the test. In fact, continuous review and good study strategies are the best methods for preparing for taking tests. Finally, you need to consider *how* to study.

Following are guidelines to use when trying to determine the what, where, when, and how of studying for a test.

What

1. All major sources of information.
2. Textbook chapters.
3. Lecture notes.
4. Previous exams and quizzes.
5. Teacher handouts.
6. Course outline.
7. Any outside of class assignments.

Where

1. A place where there can be no interruptions.
2. The library
3. Your usual study place.

When

1. Several review sessions at least a week in advance of test.
2. Several hours for study each day of week.
3. The day before the exam—once through entire review.

How

1. Organize the review.
2. Begin by going through all your material.
3. Sort out those areas in which you need work and concentrate on them.
4. Select a procedure based on the type of exam. For objective tests, you only need to recognize information. For essay tests, you need to recall information.
5. Predict questions that will be asked on the test.
6. Develop a study system.

Study Systems

In addition to developing a study schedule to prepare for tests, you need to use some type of **study system.** Merely reading through the text or just reviewing class notes is not adequate to ensure optimal performance. You may feel that you have test-taking difficulties, when in reality you have not organized the material into any viable study system. We recommend the following four systems:

- Index card system
- Study sheet system
- Study group or study partner system
- Mapping and charting

Index Card System

The index card system is a particularly useful study system to use for taking objective exams on which there are multiple-choice, matching, and completion questions. Using index cards prevents learning information in a rigid order. This is an advantage when you need to recall and apply information for various situations in a test. For example, an instructor may indicate that you need to know the five elements of a good paragraph. However, you might not be required to list these elements in order on the test. Rather, you may have to apply knowledge and understanding of the various aspects of good paragraphing as well as recall the five elements. By putting the name of each element of good paragraphing on one side of a separate index card and the explanation on the other side, you can practice naming and explaining the five elements before the test. If you often feel that you know the material but complain that the questions asked are in a different order or form, using index cards can help you develop the flexibility to adapt to different formats.

Another advantage of the index card system is that the cards can easily be carried anywhere so that you can use any spare time you may have to study. Using index cards also allows you the flexibility of studying by yourself or with a partner. Although index cards may not be efficient for studying complex materials and ideas, they are quite effective for remembering definitions, lists, and facts.

Following is the procedure for using the index card system. An example of the index card system is shown in Figure 9-1.

1. Put a definition or fact on one side of the card; put an explanation on the other side.
2. Use cards to quiz yourself.
3. Sort out information you don't know.
4. Concentrate on reviewing information you don't know, but leave time for several complete reviews.

Study Sheet System

In contrast to the index card system, developing a study sheet requires you to do critical thinking in evaluating what the important

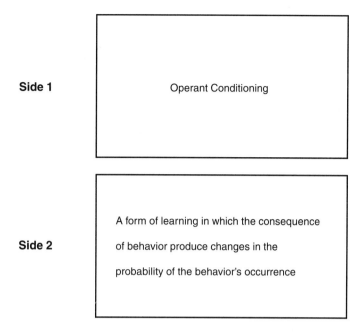

FIGURE 9-1 **Model of card system.**

issues are and what to focus on when studying. The study sheet system often works well in subjects such as history, religion, political science, and sociology.

Following is the procedure for using the study sheet system. An example of the study sheet system is shown in Figure 9-2.

1. Select important information to be learned.
2. Map or chart material.
3. Group together important facts and details.
4. Read through the entire review several times.
5. Study topic by topic.

Study Group or Study Partner System

The study group or study partner system works well in conjunction with prior preparation of index cards or study sheets. The advantage of working with a partner to study is that discussing ideas and repeating information are excellent ways of remembering material. This system also uses the auditory mode, which students often do not use when studying alone. Learning is easier when you write, read, and recite. This system also forces active involvement in the study process. Whether you discuss, teach, or listen, you will gain additional comprehension and knowledge.

Key Concepts of Jungian Psychology

Collective Unconscious: The impersonal, deepest layer of the unconscious mind shared by all human beings because of their common ancestral past

Archetypes: Primordial images of every individual's collective unconscious

1. Anima (woman)
2. Animous (masculine)
3. Self—represented in art, ex. mandala
4. The shadow—our darker self, ex. Satan, Darth Vader

Expressions of Archetype:

1. Primitive tribal lore
2. Myths
3. Fairy tales

Differences between expressions of archetypes and psychic experiences:

1. Experienced more directly in dreams and visions
2. Are more individual, less understandable, more naive in dreams than in myths
3. Archetype is essentially unconscious content

As scientific understanding has grown, so our world has become dehumanized. As a result:

1. People feel isolated
2. Nature has lost its symbolic significance. No river contains a spirit, no tree the life principle of humankind

FIGURE 9-2   Model of Study Sheet System

One potential problem with this system lies in not choosing the right partner or group. You need to study with someone with whom you are compatible, someone who attends to the task of learning and doesn't waste time socializing.

Following is the procedure for using the study group system:

1. Study first, and then socialize.
2. Quiz each other on material.
3. Teach each other material.
4. Clarify concepts, and learn other approaches.
5. Find answers to areas you don't understand.

Mapping and Charting

Mapping and charting is a study system that can be used for preparing for both objective and essay exams. One of the greatest advantages of mapping and charting is that both techniques organize the material, which in turn strengthens retention. You can map and/or chart individual text chapters, individual lectures, or whole sections of books and lectures to be covered on the test. This strategy is discussed in more detail in Chapter 7.

Following is the procedure for mapping and charting. An example of the mapping and charting system is shown in Figure 9-3.

1. Put material into logical order.
2. Select main ideas and important details.
3. Develop a configuration that reflects the organization of the information.

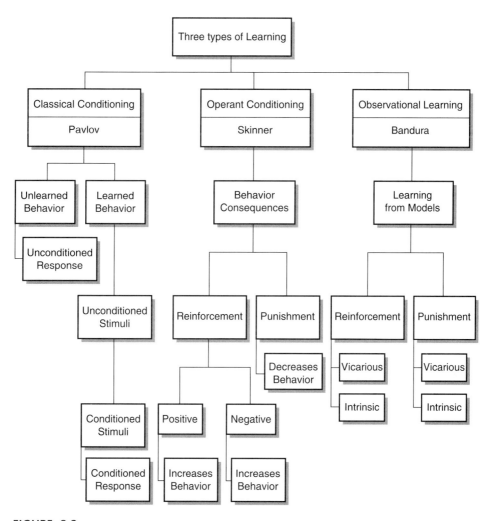

FIGURE 9-3

TEST-TAKING STRATEGIES

Budgeting Time While Taking a Test

It is important to apply time-management skills, as discussed in Chapter 4, on the day of the test. Be sure to allow enough time to arrive relaxed and at ease. Do not try to cram right before the test or to learn new material at the last minute. When you receive the test, look over the whole test briefly, and then plan by taking a minute or two to decide how much time to spend on each section. This will help you finish the test more efficiently. Budget your time in relationship to the points of each test section. In general, you should allow about thirty seconds to answer each objective question. When deciding how much time should be delegated for essay exams, note how many points each question is worth. The more points an essay is worth, the longer the time allotted should be. Remember that you don't have to begin answering questions with the first test item. You might wish to start your test where you best know the information, or you might want to begin with the simplest section. Be sure to leave a few minutes at the end of the test to review questions you were unsure of and to proofread your answers.

Before the Exam:

1. Take necessary materials to the exam.
2. Get there on time. Do not arrive too early.
3. Sit in the front of the room.
4. Use relaxation techniques to relieve tenseness.

During the Exam:

1. Look over entire test before you start to answer questions.
2. Set up a time schedule for each section.
3. Read the directions to each section carefully.
4. Don't leave anything blank.

    a. For true/false questions, you have a 50 percent chance of answering correctly.

    b. For multiple-choice questions, you have a 25 percent chance of answering correctly.

5. Mark an *X* on unanswered questions.
6. Look for clues included in the test itself.
7. If you get stuck, skip the question and keep going.
8. When you finish, go back to check for questions you didn't answer.

The following exercises will give you an idea of how you should divide your time.

◆ **EXERCISE B: BUDGETING TIME ON A CLASS TEST**

Indicate how you would divide your time for the following test, which is being given in a fifty-minute class period.

_____ 30 multiple-choice questions 30 pts.

_____ 20 true/false questions 10 pts.

_____ 1 application question 30 pts.

_____ 1 essay question 30 pts.

◆ **EXERCISE C: BUDGETING TIME ON A FINAL EXAM**

Indicate how you would divide your time for a final exam of two hours.

_____ 30 multiple-choice questions 15 pts.

_____ 30 true/false questions 15 pts.

_____ 10 sentence-completion questions 10 pts.

_____ 10 short answer 30 pts.
         (write 2–3 sentences)

_____ 2 essay questions   30 pts.

Objective Tests

Different kinds of tests pose different problems. Objective tests include true/false statements, matching, multiple-choice questions, and sentence completion. With the exception of sentence completion, successfully answering objective test questions relies on your ability to recognize the correct answer and to apply logical reasoning skills. In objective tests, you do not have to pull the answer from your storehouse of knowledge; instead, you need to be able to recognize the answer. Also, when answering the question, you need to apply deductive reasoning skills. For example, if *A* is true and *B* contradicts *A,* then you know it is not a valid answer.

True/False

When answering true/false questions, decisions should be based on what you have learned about the subject. Although you can look for certain clues to help you make correct decisions, do not analyze and "read into" the question, since these types of tests are not designed to measure your analytical skills.

When you answer a true/false question, assume that it is true unless you can determine that it is false. For a statement to be true, all parts of the statement must be true. The more facts included in a statement, the more likely it is to be false. Read each question carefully; often there is just one word that makes a statement true or false.

Usually indicates *false* response	Usually indicates *true* response
All	Some
Never	Usually
Always	Generally

If you are not penalized for incorrect answers , always guess even if you don't know the answer, because you have a 50/50 chance of getting a correct answer.

◆ **EXERCISE D: PRACTICING TRUE/FALSE QUESTIONS**

Answer the following questions by marking *F* if the statement is false and *T* if the statement is true. Mark your answers on the line that precedes each statement. Use the above strategies when answering the questions.

_____ 1. The American flag has fifty stripes.

_____ 2. The following vehicles are used in land transportation: automobile, bus, train, airplane, and taxicab.

_____ 3. Florida is a state in the southeast portion of the United States.

_____ 4. All doctors are more wealthy than all grocery clerks.

_____ 5. A concert pianist will never make an error during a concert.

_____ 6. Summers are usually warmer than winters.

_____ 7. A violin is a musical instrument.

_____ 8. A sick person must call a physician to get well.

_____ 9. A wealthy person is always happier than a poor person.

_____ 10. Health insurance always saves money for the person who has it.

_____ 11. All auto mechanics are experts in the repair of all kinds of automobiles.

_____ 12. Most people enjoy singing at one time or another.

_____ 13. Happiness, anger, jealousy, sleep, and love are examples of emotions.

_____ 14. The victim of a fatal heart attack will never recover sufficiently to return to his or her job.

_____ 15. It is never unwise to study for an exam.

Matching

When taking matching tests, students must discover the relationship between various items. A good way to approach this type of test is to look at both columns to see what type of relationship is being presented. Once you have determined the relationship between the items presented, answer the questions you know for sure. Use an elimination process to help you find the answer in a sequential way. Work systematically through the list, crossing off choices as you use them. The following quiz gives you a chance to practice these strategies.

◆ **EXERCISE E: PRACTICING MATCHING QUESTIONS**

The following names are those of past presidents of the United States. Match the name to the statement that best describes each president. Write the number in the space provided.

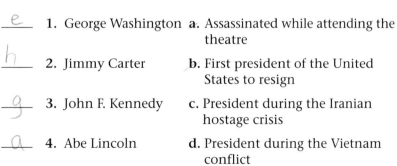

_e_ 1. George Washington **a.** Assassinated while attending the theatre

_h_ 2. Jimmy Carter **b.** First president of the United States to resign

_g_ 3. John F. Kennedy **c.** President during the Iranian hostage crisis

_a_ 4. Abe Lincoln **d.** President during the Vietnam conflict

_b_ 5. Richard Nixon

_____ 6. Gerald Ford

_____ 7. Lyndon Johnson

_____ 8. Franklin Roosevelt

_____ 9. Harry Truman

_____ 10. Woodrow Wilson

e. First president of the United States

f. Only president of the United States to serve more than three terms

g. Assassinated by Lee Harvey Oswald

h. President who made the decision to use the atomic bomb

i. President who was responsible for the League of Nations

j. President of United States not elected by the people

Multiple Choice

When answering multiple-choice questions, you need to use a logical reasoning approach as mentioned earlier in this chapter. Taking a multiple-choice exam requires that you get into the right rhythm, or mindset. Of course, knowing and understanding the information well is the first requisite for doing well on a multiple-choice test. However, if you add your critical-thinking skills to the task, you should do even better. For example, if you are taking a nursing exam and the questions pertain to a woman with heart trouble who comes to the hospital with leg problems, you need to see the relationship between the leg difficulties and the heart trouble. Specifically, you need to understand that the relationship has to do with the pumping of blood from the heart to the various parts of the body. Once you apply your reasoning skills, you can deduce that the real problem is poor blood circulation. Generally, it is relatively easy to narrow the choice of answers down to two. Once you accomplish this, you can use the following strategies to help you find the correct answer:

1. Read the directions carefully to find out if you are to:

   a. Select the single best answer.
   b. Select all possible answers.

2. Read the stem of the question, and then combine it with each of the options. Choose the option that best completes the statement. (The first part of a multiple-choice question is called a *stem*. The choices are called *options*.)

3. Exercise logic and common sense.

4. Use test clues to help you guess:

    a. *Length*—longer items tend to be correct.
    b. *Location*—correct answers are more often found in the middle.
    c. *Language*—overly technical language usually indicates an incorrect alternative.

5. The incorrect answers are called *distractors*. These types of options tend to be distractors:

    1. Absolute statements.
    2. Unfamiliar looking terms or phrases.
    3. Jokes and insults.
    4. High and low numbers.

These types of options tend to be correct answers:

    1. Complete, inclusive answers.
    2. "All of the above."
    3. One of two similar statements.

◆ **EXERCISE F: PRACTICING MULTIPLE-CHOICE QUESTIONS**

Take the following multiple-choice test, and apply the strategies described on the previous page.

1. Match the terms with the definition that makes the most sense.
    a. Passive behavior
    b. Passive-aggressive behavior
    c. Assertive behavior
    d. Aggressive behavior

    _____ **1.**   Behavior that is outwardly complacent but inwardly hostile

    _____ **2.**   Behavior that is hostile and offensive

    _____ **3.**   Complacent behavior—accepting the directions of others without objection or resistance

    _____ **4.**   Behavior in which expression is forceful and direct.

2. Which state has been the home of the greatest number of presidents starting with George Washington?

    a. Hawaii
    b. South Dakota
    c. Virginia
    d. Oregon

3. Cheese is considered a nutritious food because

   a. It is high in cholesterol
   b. It is high in protein
   c. It tastes good
   d. It is high in fat content

4. Rodents are considered noxious because they

   a. Eat contaminated food
   b. Carry rabies
   c. Are used for medical experiments
   d. All of the above
   e. A and B only

5. Which of the following characteristics is not hereditary?

   a. Color of eyes
   b. Height
   c. Skin color
   d. Egocentricity

Sentence Completion

Sentence-completion questions are more difficult than other objective tests, because you must rely on recall of previous information and the few clues provided by the sentence itself (minus the missing word). The grammatical structure of the sentence can often help you discover the missing word. Determine whether the missing word is a noun, a pronoun, or a verb. Be sure that the word you add is logically consistent with the rest of the sentence. Also consider the number and length of the blanks to be completed. Following is a practice test. Try to see what clues you can use to find the correct answer.

◆ **EXERCISE G: PRACTICING SENTENCE-COMPLETION QUESTIONS**

Fill in the blanks for the following questions using information learned from the previous chapters.

1. Visual and _____ learning styles are two major orientations to learning.

2. _____ brain dominance indicates keen verbal ability.

3. The most common place in a paragraph for a topic sentence is in the _____.

4. _____ are statements that prove or support the main idea.

5. The _____ method of note taking emphasizes review.

CRITICAL THINKING

Although test taking may seem like an alien idea imposed on us from the outside by teachers, administrators, or employers, it is a natural part of self-awareness, the foundation of thinking critically. One observes, draws a conclusion, and then observes further to test whether the conclusion or idea is true. Sometimes we need to test our ideas by trying them out; sometimes, we need to wait to see whether our ideas are true. One way to heighten our self-awareness is to question ourselves. Questioning and testing ourselves about our knowledge leads to learning, growth, and metacognition, one foundation for successful test taking.

With one other person, develop ten questions about the previous chapters of the book. These questions should include true/false, matching, multiple-choice, and sentence completion. Be sure to concentrate on what you feel are the most important ideas in the chapters and to develop questions that call for students to assess their learning strengths. Then share your test questions with the class.

_____

_____

_____

_____

_____

_____

_____

_____

_____

_____

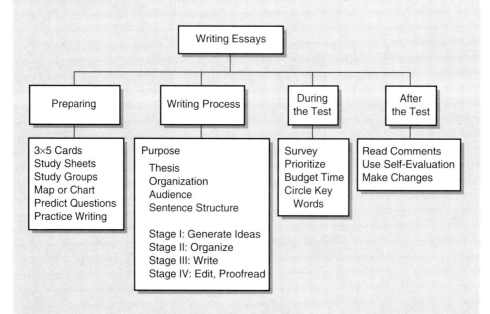

10

ESSAY WRITING FOR TESTS

Writing's not hard, no harder than ditch-digging.
—PATRICK DENNIS

Key Concepts

Audience The reader's point of view, which the writer needs to be aware of.

Mechanics The sentence structure, spelling, and punctuation that make writing clear to the reader.

Organization The overall plan of writing, showing a logical sequence of ideas with appropriate paragraphing.

Purpose The reason for writing, such as to inform, evaluate, analyze, or entertain.

Thesis The central idea of an essay or any other piece of writing.

Transitions Words, phrases, or sentences that show the relationship between ideas.

Essay tests are a common method of assessing students' knowledge in college courses. Teachers often assign essay questions instead of objective test questions because they want you to demonstrate your understanding of the concepts of the subject and to think creatively about the material. Writing essays demands that you make connections between ideas, evaluate those ideas, and come to your own conclusions. In fact, when responding to an essay question, you need to combine all levels of learning, which includes memorization of information, seeing relationships between facts and between ideas, applying the material to areas outside the course, and forming an opinion about the concepts. In other words, in answering essay questions, you need to use your critical-thinking skills. Not only do you have to recall the information, you then have to organize and synthesize it into a well-written, coherent form. Using some of the following strategies when writing essays can result in greater ease with writing as well as higher test scores.

PREPARING FOR ESSAY TESTS

As you learned in Chapter 9 on objective tests, your performance on all tests depends on thorough preparation. There simply is no substitute for careful studying, so you need to develop study strategies that will help you respond quickly, thoroughly, and insightfully to a question. Depending on the nature of the course and on what information you received from the instructor, you might begin preparing for the test by using one of the four study methods described in Chapter 9. For instance, if there are many new definitions and terms in the material, then using 3 × 5 cards might be helpful. If you know that the relationship between ideas will be emphasized on the test, developing a map or chart may be helpful. If you know there is a great deal of material to understand and remember, creating study sheets could give you a structure to work from as you review the information. Studying with a partner or a group might also be helpful in clarifying the ideas covered in the test.

Another study method for preparing for essay tests calls for you to *predict* the test questions and to *practice* writing an essay for that question. In order to anticipate possible test questions, you need to think back to what was discussed in class. For instance, the topics that the instructor emphasized will probably appear on the test. Thus, reviewing your notes will help you develop some possible essay questions. You will also need to look at relationships between ideas or at trends or ideas that appear throughout the material. You could also look at the summary questions at the end of the textbook chapters for questions that might be covered on the test, or you could work in a study group to develop possible essay questions.

Once you have anticipated some essay questions, practice writing answers for them. This step, of course, means you use the skills and strategies that produce effective writing in any situation.

THE WRITING PROCESS

Practice in writing essays gives you an advantage when you get to the test because how well you score on a test does not always depend on how well you know the material. As with any writing, essays on tests must demonstrate a clear purpose, a sense of audience, a thesis, organization, as well as correct punctuation and usage. These qualities are explained more completely in the information below:

Purpose: The writing reflects an understanding of the reason for the written response. Purposes include such tasks as listing, explaining, analyzing, comparing, contrasting, or evaluating. In a test situation, the purpose is usually indicated in the test question.

Thesis: The central idea is clear and insightful.

Organization: The overall plan is clear, with an apparent beginning, middle, and end. The paragraphing is logical and effective. The transitions are helpful to the reader.

Audience: The writing shows an awareness of the reader's point of view and gives enough information and transitions to enable the reader to follow the message.

Mechanics: The sentence structure, usage, spelling, and punctuation are close to flawless; errors do not distract from the message of the essay.

Transitions

Before evaluating the two samples of student writing that follow in Exercise A, it is worthwhile to consider the transitional elements of writing in more detail. **Transitions,** included under the Audience category above, are words, phrases, or sentences that act as signal words to the reader by making clear the connection between ideas. Words such as *first, next,* and *in addition* are commonly used transitional words, but you can also make connections clear by repeating key words or carefully using pronouns such as *this,* and *these* to refer to previous ideas. Sometimes, you may be able to connect two sentences with words such as *because, since, if,* and *so;* these words make the relationship between ideas clear. Using appropriate transitions will make your writing clearer and will probably improve your grade on essay exams.

Following is a list of commonly used transitional words:

Connection	*Word or Phrase*	
Addition	also	furthermore
	and	in addition
	as well as	next
	further	too
Cause or Effect	as a result	since
	because	so
	consequently	then
	for	therefore
	for that reason	thus
Conclusion	finally	therefore
	so	thus
Differences	although	on the contrary
	but	on the other hand
	despite	though
	however	yet
	nevertheless	
Direction	above	here
	among	in front of
	around	next to
	below	on top of
	beside	over
	between	there
	beyond	under
	down	where
Examples	for example	specifically
	for instance	such as
	in other words	
Likeness	all	both
	and	like
	as	similarly

Connection	*Word or Phrase*	
Sequence and Emphasis	after	first (second, etc.)
	always	last
	at last	least
	before	next
	consequently	primarily
	especially	then
	finally	when

◆ **EXERCISE A: QUALITIES OF A WELL-WRITTEN ESSAY**

Read the following essays. Break into groups of three or four, and complete the chart following each essay. Each group should choose a spokesperson to present the two charts' contents to the class.

Essay 1

Presidential Advertising on Television

The negative perspective of government, and the image's conceived of the candidates for office, as portrayed by their media blitz, was less than honorable. What we may have learned from this media manipulation and false focus, away from the important issues, is that: TV advertising has a pernicious effect on presidential campaigns.

Presidential candidates, rather than discuss issues, discuss each other's character. Thru using mis-information about other candidates, and their families, Presidential candidates attempt to rally votes. Bringing up questions about candidates personal ethics, leads to doubts about other candidates. An example was Pres. Bush discussing Clintons personal perspective on Vietnam. Perot said that after the election we will hear of hundreds more cases of S & L mischief.

Television advertising creates a pernicious effect by giving a negative perspective of government. When watching these ads, and each nominee ripping the others personal character and beliefs, one is immediately turned off and tends to just not believe any of it. These negative ad campaigns tend to make the voters choose not a "best" candidate, but just one that is less worse than the others. Voters do not look at voting as finding the candidate that will lead the country back up the hill, just the one who will slow the continuous roll down the hill.

Television advertising has a pernicious effect on presidential campaigns. Candidates use slander to discredit there opponents to try to create a negative perspective of government. They try to get the people to vote for the lesser of the 2 evils. There many purpose is try to confuse the public, so they don't vote. If people don't vote, the candidates have a greater chance of winning on false advertisements.

	Superior	Above Average	Average	Below Average	Poor or Absent
Purpose					
Thesis					
Organization					
Audience					
Sentence Structure, Usage Mechanics					

Essay 2

Rereading America *suggests that we need to reexamine accepted myths that are part of our society. This means that people have many misconceptions concerning others and that we need to change those misconceptions. Through my examination of stories from* Rereading America *I have learned that our ideas are in a constant evolution process.*

Throughout the semester I have been very focused on the gender myth. Before the women's movement in the 60's and 70's women were expected to stay home and take care of their children. Now, in the 90's, the majority of the women are busy developing successful careers. The stereotype of women staying home has drastically changed. Women have fought for a long time for the chance to get a decent job. People's attitudes have adapted to women in the work force. It is now acceptable and encouraged for a woman to be working. Girl, *the essay written by Jamaica Koncaid, portrays a young girl being taught what is expected of her as she grows up. The speaker in the story, possibly her mother, teaches the child how to clean and garden and how to act like a lady. I believe this essay is a good example of how life used to be for women. Women were supposed to cook, clean the house and care for their children. This stereotypical view is not found in very many American households today. In my family my father is the one who cooks our dinner meals. My mother has a full-time job teaching and does a lot of one-on-one instruction in the evenings. I have a part-time job and do the majority of my homework at night. This leaves my father to prepare supper and he is also the one who is left to clean up the dishes. This explana-*

tion represents how the myth of the woman, being at home cooking and cleaning, is violated by a man taking on her role. That is acceptable now, 20 years ago it would not have been, but society's views have changed and will continue to change.

People's attitudes have been altered concerning race as well as gender. Although, we did not study race specifically, it came through in many different discussions. White culture has always been the dominant group in this society. Minority groups have been fighting for equal rights for hundreds of years. African Americans have gone from being slaves to being severely injured just because of the color of their skin. The women's movement has moved faster than the black movement, but a least their has been a change. African Americans do not live without being discriminated against in the workforce or in schools. The song "Tennessee" by Arrested Development reflects how their ancestors were hung from trees (lynched), today that does not occur. It is very probable, though, that an African American will be shot and killed by a white man in the next 24 hours. Change is inevitable, in the coming years such violence will not be known on our city streets. Hopefully, people's views will continue to change and they will be open to equality.

	Superior	Above Average	Average	Below Average	Poor or Absent
Purpose					
Thesis					
Organization					
Audience					
Sentence Structure, Usage Mechanics					

Key Words

To understand the purpose of the essay question, you need to understand the key words in the question itself. Sometimes, the instructor wants to assess how much you know about a topic, so words such as *describe, trace, explain,* and *list* may appear in the question. Other times, the instructor may be interested in whether you are able to use the information to back up a well-reasoned evaluation of a topic. In that case, the key words in the question might be *argue, evaluate,* and *prove.* In order to do a good job of writing your essay, you need to have a clear understanding of the question. If you don't understand what is being asked, you will have difficulty writing a comprehensive essay. In order to perceive what is needed, you will need to understand the key words or verbs that are used in essay tests.

◆ **EXERCISE B: KEY TERMS**

The following list contains key words that are used in essay exams. Knowing these verbs will help you organize your essay. Write the definition of each. Then with a classmate develop an essay question for each. You can make up questions about any topic or use the reading selections in Exercises E and F.

1. **Analyze** _____

_____

Question: _____

_____

2. **Argue** _____

_____

Question: _____

_____

3. **Compare** _____

_____

Question: _____

_____

4. **Contrast** _____

_____

Question: _____

_____

5. **Criticize** _____

_____

Question: _____

_____

6. Define _____

_____

Question: _____

_____

7. Describe _____

_____

Question: _____

_____

8. Discuss _____

_____

Question: _____

_____

9. Elaborate _____

_____

Question: _____

_____

10. Enumerate _____

_____

Question: _____

_____

11. Evaluate _____

_____

Question: _____

_____

12. Illustrate _____

_____

Question: _____

_____

13. **Interpret** _____

_____

Question: _____

_____

14. **Prove** _____

_____

Question: _____

_____

15. **Summarize** _____

_____

Question: _____

_____

STAGES OF THE WRITING PROCESS

Now that you have read and discussed two essays and have considered the qualities of good writing, let's look at the writing process. When you practice writing a response to the essay questions you composed for Exercise B, keep in mind that this process moves through the same stages that apply to all writing tasks. Actually, you will move through these stages naturally as you plan, write, and revise your essay, but being aware of these stages can give you confidence and will probably strengthen your final written product.

Stage One: Generate Ideas

The first stage in the writing process is thinking and listing ideas. In some ways, this is the most crucial and the most uncomfortable stage because you know the demand for the final essay looms ahead of you. The tendency of most students is to rush over the thinking stage and to start writing. Taking time to think, however, can pay off in the final product. By giving yourself time to focus on the purpose of the essay question and to generate the ideas relevant to the response, you are streamlining the time you spend actually writing. Depending on how much time you have, you may want to use some thinking strategies during this first stage.

Some of these strategies include listing and mapping, or charting described in Chapter 7. During the exam, in the margin of your paper, you can simply list key words of the information and concepts you want to include in your answer. Writing these ideas down can lead you naturally to the second phase in writing: organizing and planning.

Stage Two: Arrange Ideas

After you have made a quick list or map of your ideas, decide how you want to organize them. Now is the time to think of your focus for the essay or to ask yourself what is the central idea you want to get across in the essay. (Refer to Chapter 5 if you feel unsure of the concept of the central idea.) This main idea will become your thesis, which naturally will depend to a great extent on the purpose or the directives in the essay question. You may want to rearrange your list of ideas, so the order of your topics will become more logical and convincing. You may also need to eliminate some topics you listed as you assess the amount of time you have to write the essay. For instance, if you're presented with the directions "Contrast the native American and European view of land use," your answer will naturally depend on the amount of time you have to write your response. Since this essay topic could easily become the subject of a book, framing your response in light of the amount of time you have becomes a crucial step in writing the essay. Therefore, when practicing writing essays at home, be sure to give yourself a time limit to answer the questions.

In some instances the question will contain the directions. For instance the question "Describe the symptoms, causes, and remedies for test anxiety" includes the overall plan in the directions. You may not need to jot down any notes if you feel sure you remember the material. However, a few notes or an informal outline such as the following may be helpful:

1. Symptoms

   —Physical
   —Emotional
   —Mental

2. Causes

   —Poor planning
   —Lack of confidence
   —Past experiences

3. Remedies

   —Relaxation techniques
   —Exercise
   —Effective studying
   —Positive self-talk

Of course, during actual test situations, you may want to have briefer outline notes, using phrases like "poor planning" written as "plan" or "symptoms" becoming simply "s." Since you're making notes for yourself and time is always important, only the briefest cues are needed.

Often the directions on essay tests do not indicate the organization or form of your response. Then you will need to spend longer thinking and organizing the topic. The following exercise gives you an opportunity to think through a more open-ended essay topic.

◆ **EXERCISE C: OUTLINING**

After listing some ideas for the following topic, develop a brief outline for a possible written response. Then share your outline with other class members. "Discuss the idea that test anxiety is a natural by-product of our educational system itself. In responding to this idea, you may want to consider factors such as competition, support systems, and classroom climate."

_____

_____

_____

_____

_____

_____

_____

_____

Stage Three: Write

If you know the material, if you've given yourself time to think, and if you have developed a brief outline, then the actual writing of the essay can be a fairly relaxed process, even though you may have to write quickly. You may find that as you write, you will think of additional ideas. Jot these new ideas in the margin. If you see a place where you can work these ideas in logically and without straying from the focus of the essay, add them to the essay.

As you write, keep in mind basic writing skills of paragraphs: center the paragraph around one idea with enough supporting details to demonstrate a clear understanding of the topic. As you write from your outline, you will be forming paragraphs around the topics of the outline and adding details to support statements about the topics. For example, a paragraph about the symptoms of test anxiety might begin with the sentence, "Test anxiety manifests itself in three ways: physically, mentally, and emotionally." This sentence becomes the topic sentence. The other sentences in the paragraph will support, or explain, that sentence by providing examples of exactly what the symptoms of each are. Other kinds of supporting details include facts, reasons, comparisons, contrasts, and the opinion of experts on a topic. The chart shown in Figure 10-1 illustrates some kinds of support that can be used.

◆ EXERCISE D: SUPPORTING INFORMATION

Below are five sentences that could be topic sentences in an essay. Describe the kinds of supporting information you could use to complete the paragraph for each.

1. Researchers differ in explaining the causes of depression in women.

2. The mental symptoms of test anxiety cause lower test scores, which, in turn, make the anxiety worse.

3. The media emphasizes violence and sex to a greater extent now than they did ten years ago.

4. The increase in violence in today's society has a negative effect on children.

5. If people watched only one hour of television a day, their lives would change considerably.

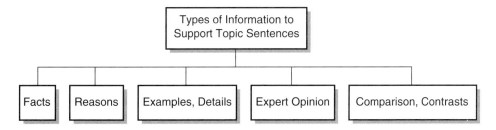

FIGURE 10-1   Support for topic sentences.

Now choose one of the five topics, and write your essay. Keep in mind that the following basic writing skills and practical strategies will improve the final grade you receive:

- Begin a new paragraph for each topic in your outline. Use topic sentences to highlight your ideas for the reader. (See Chapter 5 for a review of topic sentences.)
- Give details, examples, and definitions; even though your instructor knows the material quite well, remember that your task is to demonstrate *your* mastery of the material.
- Write legibly, or print your answer if your handwriting is hard to decipher. An essay that is hard to read will probably receive fewer points than one that is legible.
- Leave space to proofread and edit.
- Avoid writing in the first person unnecessarily. Use *I,* only when the directions clearly call for a personal response.
- Show some enthusiasm! Try to get yourself interested in the material, and write so even someone who is not in the course can understand and learn from your essay.
- Answer the essay question as completely as you can, but do not repeat ideas and pad your writing to stretch your essay.

Stage Four: Proofread

The last stage of writing will depend on your allowing yourself some time before turning your paper in to reread your essays. Although you probably won't have time for major revisions, you can correct careless grammar, spelling, and punctuation errors. Watch for unclear sentences, and try to restate these to clarify your ideas.

◆ **EXERCISE E: WRITING AN ESSAY**

Read the amendment and article shown here. Then write an essay responding to the essay test question that follows.

*Amendment I. Freedom of Opinion (1791)**

Religion, Speech, Press, Assembly, Petition. *Congress shall make no law respecting an establishment of religion, or prohibiting the free exercise thereof; or abridging the freedom of speech, or of the press; or the right of the people peaceably to assemble, and to petition the Government for a redress of grievances.*

*Frank A. Aukofer, *Milwaukee Journal Sentinel,* July 9, 1995, p. 16A. Reprinted with permission.

Debate over Internet Heating Up

Washington—With connected computers spreading across the country like an enveloping fog, a prolonged and bitter confrontation over obscenity and indecency is growing in Congress and the courts.

The debate is over whether the government should regulate postings on the Internet and the World Wide Web, those computer networks that now circle the planet and are becoming ever more accessible to children.

It pits advocates of free speech against family-oriented organizations and individuals, including members of Congress, who want to pass laws to punish people who disseminate indecent materials over computer networks.

The issue goes to the core of the Bill of Rights and the First Amendment's guarantee of free speech. The debate is over the constitutionality of laws that might restrict computer-disseminated materials—or punish people who distribute them.

Congress already has taken a step toward passing such a law. On an 86–14 vote last June 14, 1994, the Senate passed an amendment that would set fines of up to $100,000 and prison terms of up to two years for people convicted of knowingly making, creating, soliciting or initiating the transmission of indecent materials over electronic networks.

The legislation's fate in the House is uncertain because Speaker Newt Gingrich has criticized it as a violation of free speech and the rights of adults to communicate with each other. Among the small band of vocal opponents in the Senate was Wisconsin Democratic Sen. Russ Feingold.

Ultimately, the U.S. Supreme Court will have to decide the boundaries of First Amendment protection for Internet users. And that may not even settle the matter. Until then, the public debate will rage on center stage.

The issues have little to do with the recent case in which federal prosecutors charged a Las Vegas man with electronically soliciting sex from a 14-year-old Milwaukee girl. That sort of conduct is a crime unprotected by any free speech laws or principles—on or off the Internet.

Times Have Changed

In earlier times, in a simpler world, children rarely, if ever, encountered pornographic depictions of sex and violence—even if they were inclined to seek them out. Now computer-literate kids—many of them more familiar with the byways of the information superhighway than their parents—can easily gain access to materials that the vast majority of the people would regard as ranging from inappropriate to downright disgusting.

A recent study by researchers at Carnegie-Mellon University, described in an article in the Georgetown University Law Journal, found an array of pornographic materials on adult bulletin boards on the Internet. Included were depictions of bestiality, urination/defecation, incest, torture and mutilation. Among other things, the researchers found that 83.5% of the images stored by Usenet news groups were pornographic.

But several professors and lawyers with backgrounds in statistics and market research—all advocates for the free use of electronic highways—have fiercely attacked the study's methodologies and motives. They note that the study was not submitted for normal peer review before publication, and called it misleading research.

Even so, Cathy A. Cleaver, director of legal policy for the Family Research Council, a nonprofit organization that conducts education and research on pro-family issues, said the study was powerful evidence of a need for a federal law that defined right from wrong on the Internet.

Without it, she said, the only way to shield children would be through technological or software barriers, which she said computer hackers, including children, could quickly bypass.

Cleaver helped draft the Senate-passed legislation, which was introduced by Sen. James Exon (D-Neb.) and Sen. Daniel Coats (R-Ind.). She said she believed the bill, if it becomes law, would stand up under First Amendment scrutiny.

But Mike Godwin, the staff counsel for the Electronic Frontier Foundation, a public interest civil liberties group, said there was no way the Exon-Coats bill could withstand a constitutional review.

"This legislation, drafted by people who don't understand the Internet, amounts to a ban of so-called indecent material," Godwin said. "You're dumbing it down to what's appropriate for children, and no such ban has ever passed constitutional muster."

R. B. Quinn, legal director of The Freedom Forum First Amendment Center at Vanderbilt University in Nashville, said the time had come for the development of new legal and constitutional theories.

"The new technology will demand that we rethink existing precedents, not necessarily to change them but to recognize that the new communications vehicles—the new technology—are going to have an impact on how we define constitutional protections," he said.

Quinn said he doubted whether the Exon-Coats legislation would withstand congressional scrutiny.

Question: How does the Constitution's first Amendment affect possible laws concerning regulation of the Internet? What regulations would you recommend in light of the first Amendment?

DURING THE TEST

In addition to implementing the study strategies before the test and using effective writing skills while answering essay questions, you can employ other strategies for taking essay tests that will help you to maximize your knowledge of the material. When you receive the test, survey it to see how many questions are asked. Read the directions carefully to determine how many questions you are required to answer. Look at the point value for each question.

Next, make a rough time schedule for the entire test. Note the questions that are worth the most points; plan to give them more time. First, answer the easiest questions; next answer the questions with the highest point values. Be sure to identify the key words (listed in Exercise B) and to respond accordingly. For instance, if the essay question asks you to "argue" one side of an issue and you "describe" both sides, you'll lose points on the test. You may want to get in the habit of underlining or circling key words and then frame your response around those key words.

◆ **EXERCISE F: SAMPLE ESSAY TEST**

Below is a sample essay test that might be given in a class on contemporary issues that meets twice a week in one-hour-and-twenty-minute class periods. Assume you have a whole class period to complete the test. Read the questions, and then complete the activities following the test.

Contemporary Issues
Sociology 105
Professor Wiggins
Test #2

Answer *one* question in Part I. Then answer *three* from Part II.

Part I: Answer one of the following in a coherent, well-organized essay. (40 pts.)

1. What are some of the results of poverty in the inner city? Give three examples of the consequences, and discuss whether you think these consequences have benefited or harmed American society.

2. Trace the history of increased violence on TV programs and movies. Describe some of the criticisms of it, and explain whether you believe these criticisms are valid.

Part II: Choose *three* of the following, and answer each in one or two well-organized paragraphs.

3. Explain how the AIDS epidemic has changed our society. (20 pts.)

4. Explain the differences between the nuclear and blended family systems. What implications for society do you see in the increase of blended families? (20 pts.)

5. Argue either for or against limiting welfare payments to unwed mothers. (20 pts.)

6. Explain three reasons for the gender wage gap. (20 pts.)

7. List three different sources of authority and give an example of someone with that type of authority. (20 pts.)

8. In class we discussed commonly believed myths about poor people. Discuss two of these myths. (20 pts.)

1. Practice organizing your time for writing essays by deciding how many minutes you want to devote to each section of the test. Remember, the class period lasts one hour and twenty minutes.

Part I   _____ minutes

Part II   1. _____ minutes

          2. _____ minutes

          3. _____ minutes

2. In groups, choose one of the questions in Part II. Generate information by brainstorming possible ideas for answering the question. (Remember that when you brainstorm, you do *not* edit or eliminate *any* idea; you list *all* reactions and responses however improbable they may be.)

Question chosen: _____

Ideas for the paragraph(s): _____

_____

_____

_____

_____

_____

3. Individually or as a group, write the short essay response. Then share your essays with other class members.

AFTER THE TEST

When the test is returned, listen carefully to any comments the instructor makes to the class as a whole. Then review the graded test carefully, and use it as a learning tool. To analyze the test and to improve your performance on future essay tests, ask yourself some of the following questions:

1. What did I do well? Why?
2. What section of the test proved hardest for me? Why?
3. What comments were written on the paper?

   a. Do I understand the comments?
   b. How can I use these comments to increase my grade on future essay tests?
   c. Do I need to discuss the comments with the instructor?

4. Do I need to improve my performance while I am taking the test?

   a. Did I read the questions carefully?
   b. Did I answer the question that was asked?
   c. Did I budget my time effectively?

5. Did I perform poorly on the test because I didn't fully understand and remember the material?
6. Do I need to develop and/or use different study strategies for the next test?

CRITICAL THINKING

One characteristic of a critical thinker is knowing and respecting oneself enough to be able to respect and work well with others. The very basis of critical thinking calls for you to be open to new viewpoints and new perspectives. The following assignment calls for you to work with others to produce a polished essay.

Read the following article on militias and the Oklahoma bombing investigation.

1. Develop two possible essay questions about the article.
2. In groups, share your questions and choose one to answer.
3. List possible ideas for one of your questions, and make a scratch outline.

4. As a group, write an appropriate response to the question. Although writing as a group may seem strange at first, the following guidelines may ease the process:

    a. Choose a coordinator to direct the project.

    b. Choose a recorder to take notes and scribe the lists and the essay. (Two people may want to share this job.)

    c. Choose a spokesperson to communicate with the teacher and the rest of the class.

    d. Make sure each member contributes as well as listens.

New Message Fuels Militias*

Like the crisp, creased camouflage uniforms and spit-polished boots of its adherents, the radical right has gussied up and with cool calculation made its image and message increasingly more palatable to mainstream rural America.

From the Ku Klux Klan to the Posse Comitatus to neo-Nazi groups, the largely white supremacist hate movement has evolved into its current incarnation of state militias, whose well-spoken leaders direct their venom toward the federal government while softening the far right's historically harsh rhetoric toward Jews and racial minorities.

The strategy, experts say, has been wildly successful and placed the far-right movement in the enviable, and unaccustomed, position of being able to openly recruit members in Wisconsin and other states.

Michael Sandberg, Midwest civil rights director for the Anti-Defamation League of B'nai B'rith in Chicago, said, "The militia movement has been THE growth movement in the United States in recent years. The Ku Klux Klan is fractious and in decline."

Unlike the loosely organized Klan and Posse Comitatus, Sandberg said, "militias have regular membership, formal training and guiding principles. They have the language of discipline and purpose. That makes them more frightening.

"Some people who wouldn't want to be affiliated with the KKK, Posse or neo-Nazi groups can see themselves in militias. They see themselves as gun owners and that the federal government would come and take their guns from them.

"A lot of these people would shudder that their movement and the rhetoric produced from it would have been responsible for the tragedy in Oklahoma. But the language of militia leaders drips with references to violence relating to the federal government."

Sandberg said, "I'm sure a lot of the members are coming from the KKK and other white supremacist organizations. But I don't think that's

*Mike Mulvey, Milwaukee Journal Sentinel, April 30, 1995, p. 15. Reprinted with permission.

the majority. Some of the people coming from the white supremacist movement are looking for action, and they're bringing their guns.

"These militias are out front in the open recruiting members. I think a lot of people going to militia meetings aren't interested in breaking the law."

The watchdog group the Center for Democratic Renewal in Atlanta estimates that state militias have 80,000 to 100,000 members. The center said the largest militias are those in Michigan and Montana, with about 10,000 members each. The center said membership in the Wisconsin militia likely is much smaller, but that it is impossible to place a figure on the number of militia members here.

Sandberg and others who monitor the movements of the radical right say the militias' cloak of patriotism and avowed commitment to protect citizens' rights is nothing more than a calculated cosmetic makeover that thinly masks the ugly face of racism and hatred.

"After Oklahoma City, I think we're getting a true perspective of what they are all about," said Shawano County Sheriff's Sgt. Larry Roth, who has investigated members of the far right for 20 years.

"Over the years, I've confiscated their manuals in which they explain how to make bombs, carry out guerrilla warfare and other things that have no practical application unless one citizen intends to terrorize another.

"The various groups have had some of the same people over the years. It's the names of the groups that seem to change. But their philosophies are always the same: anti-tax, anti-government and white supremacist."

During a year in which much ado has been made about angry white males, the bombing of the Alfred P. Murrah Federal Building in Oklahoma City if investigators are correct chillingly demonstrates that some are angrier than others.

Klan Linkage

To get a clear picture of the evolution of the radical right, it is helpful to review the escalation of some of its members' violent run-ins with the law in recent years and the common threads that link the movement with the Ku Klux Klan of the 1960s.

After the Klan failed to halt integration efforts in the South, the Posse Comitatus formed in the early 1970s as white supremacists and tax protesters joined forces. The Posse and various neo-Nazi groups that followed never attained large membership, mostly because of the tarnished image of being simpatico with the Klan.

From the mid-1970s to the mid-1980s, however, the Posse made some footholds in rural areas of Wisconsin and other Midwestern and Western states, where farmers found their livelihoods threatened by bank failures and a sluggish agricultural economy.

Since 1980, Wisconsin in particular has been at the center of right-wing radicalism, in large part because of former national Posse Comitatus leader James P. Wickstrom. Wickstrom and his followers lived in Tigerton in Shawano County.

Wickstrom, who now resides in Munising, Mich., gained national attention during the manhunt for Posse member Gordon Kahl. After gunning down two deputy U.S. marshals in North Dakota in February 1982, Kahl fled and became a folk hero of the radical right. As national spokesman for the Posse, Wickstrom defended Kahl and his actions.

Kahl, 63, was finally tracked to Smithville, Ark., where he was killed in a shootout with police June 3, 1983. Thereafter, his fame grew, with Wickstrom and others claiming the authorities had "assassinated" him for his anti-government beliefs.

A Cairo, Neb., man who was influenced by Kahl and the Posse met a violent end Oct. 23., 1984. Arthur Kirk was facing a foreclosure action on his failing farm. He had threatened police with a gun and said a "Jewish conspiracy" had robbed him of his land. He was shot and killed on his farm by a State Patrol SWAT team.

Kirk, in turn, became a martyr during the so-called farm crisis when the changing agricultural economy made it increasingly difficult for small family farmers to hold on to their property.

Likewise, Robert Mathews in December 1984 became another flash point for elements of the radical right when the leader of the neo-Nazi group The Order died in a fire during a standoff with the FBI in his home state of Washington. Mathews' group was behind the June 1984 slaying of Alan Berg, an outspoken radio talk show host in Denver.

On Aug. 21, 1992, federal authorities killed the 14-year-old son and unarmed wife of white separatist Randy Weaver during a shootout at Weaver's Idaho compound. The killings enraged the radical right and some federal officials who criticized the FBI's handling of the case.

But no previous encounter with law enforcement matched the violence and firepower associated with the federal Bureau of Alcohol, Tobacco and Firearms raid of Feb. 28, 1993, of the Waco, Texas, compound occupied by David Koresh and his Branch Davidian cult. That incident left four federal agents and six cult members dead.

After a subsequent 51-day standoff, the FBI stormed the Waco compound. The wooden structures were set ablaze, perhaps by cult members, and Koresh and more than 80 of his followers died in the inferno.

The backlash from the Weaver and Waco cases, in particular, fueled the formation of the state militias in the past year.

Members of the Michigan militia have been tied to the April 19 bombing of the Oklahoma City federal building. The bombing, two years to the day after the Branch Davidians perished, is believed to be retaliation for the federal government's handling of the Waco case.

The death toll in Oklahoma City will be far higher than Waco.

Noah Chandler, a researcher with the watchdog group Center for Democratic Renewal in Atlanta, said the Oklahoma City tragedy won't necessarily stem the growth of militias.

"I think the environment is ripe in the U.S. for the formation of militias," he said. "There is a lot of intolerance. What used to be extreme is now mainstream. And militias are mainstreaming in a very successful fashion."

Chandler said a complex, rapidly changing society has made it easier for the militias to recruit members.

"These people see themselves as trying to go back to a time when white men ruled and women and people of color were second-class citizens," Chandler said. "We're living in a time when things are changing fast. National borders are coming down. Women and minorities are rising up in the world. This is a backlash."

Chandler fears the Oklahoma City bombing and the arrest and charging of Timothy McVeigh, who is known to have attended meetings of the Michigan Militia, may cause a further escalation of violence.

"This is part of their self-fulfilling prophecy," Chandler said. "Now, the ATF and other federal agencies are going to come after them. These groups are apocalyptic by nature. There is a lot of potential for future violence. They have been preparing themselves for this."

Sandberg, of the Anti-Defamation League, differed with Chandler and predicted the Oklahoma City bombing would force mass desertions from the militias.

REFERENCES

Aukofer, F. (July 9, 1995) Debate over Internet Heating Up. *Milwaukee Journal Sentinel.*

Mulvey, M. (April 30, 1995) New Message Fuels Militias. *Milwaukee Journal Sentinel.*

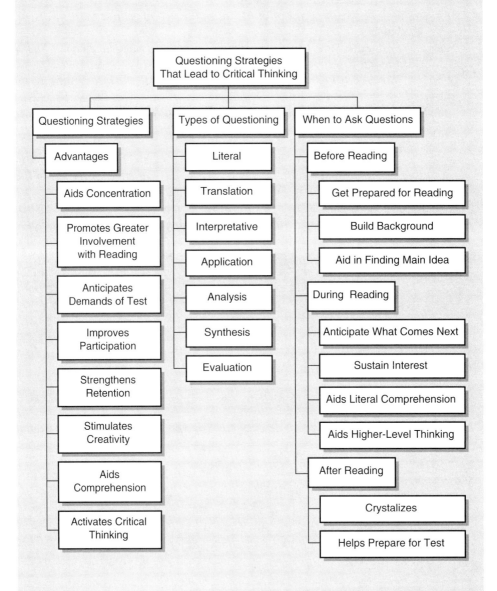

Questioning Strategies
That Lead to Critical Thinking

Questioning Strategies

Advantages

Aids Concentration

Promotes Greater
Involvement
with Reading

Anticipates
Demands of Test

Improves
Participation

Strengthens
Retention

Stimulates
Creativity

Aids
Comprehension

Activates Critical
Thinking

Types of Questioning

Literal

Translation

Interpretative

Application

Analysis

Synthesis

Evaluation

When to Ask Questions

Before Reading

Get Prepared for Reading

Build Background

Aid in Finding Main Idea

During Reading

Anticipate What Comes Next

Sustain Interest

Aids Literal Comprehension

Aids Higher-Level Thinking

After Reading

Crystalizes

Helps Prepare for Test

11

QUESTIONING STRATEGIES THAT LEAD TO CRITICAL THINKING

*Every sentence I utter must be understood not
as an affirmation, but as a question.*
—*NIELS BOHR*

Key Concepts

Analysis questions   Identify the logical steps used in the thinking
process to arrive at a conclusion.

Application questions   Transfer of ideas and concepts to other material.

Evaluation questions   Judgment of value.

Interpretive questions   Drawing relationships among facts, values,
and generalizations.

Literal questions   Recall of information.

Prior knowledge   What people know, feel, and believe before reading also is important in processing information.

Synthesis questions   Bring together information to create a new idea.

Taxonomy   The science, laws, and principles of classification.

Translation questions   Expression of information in a different form.

As we discussed earlier in Chapter 2 on Critical Thinking, students who are critical thinkers take an active part in their own learning. They often use questioning strategies while reading and studying to provide themselves with an effective method of taking control of their own comprehension and retention of information. Therefore, one way to increase your understanding of assigned reading is to become an active reader and to ask questions. This process leads to critical thinking, which further strengthens your understanding of the ideas and information you read.

Critical thinkers ask questions before, during, and after reading. Employing these questioning strategies provides the reader with a purpose that aids comprehension, prevents monotony and boredom, and also helps to develop critical thinking skills. Because the process of asking questions will help you to evaluate material critically, your focus will then be on defining issues and solving problems. In this chapter are explanations and examples of different kinds of questions to use during reading and studying. While studying, a student needs to keep his or her mind active, which helps in anticipating what information will be presented next, aids retention for test taking, and helps to make better test decisions. Answering the questions asked reinforces the learning process by confirming the validity of the questions.

QUESTIONING STRATEGIES

Asking questions is a natural thinking process for effective reading and studying. When you are studying, you need to keep your mind active so that you don't get bored, don't read the entire chapter without comprehending what you have read, and don't memorize information, but rather begin the process of thinking critically. It's possible to "read" a chapter by moving your eyes over every line of text but still have no clear idea of what the chapter is about. So, in order to concentrate, one strategy you can use is to ask yourself questions. For example, when you are reading a mystery story, what do you do? You always mentally ask yourself questions: "Who killed Mr. X?" "Who had a motive?" "Did the butler do it?" These types of questions keep you involved, thinking, and alert when you are reading an exciting story and can be applied to expository reading as well. At first, asking yourself questions will seem very contrived, and you might have to force yourself to form questions; however, after a while it becomes second nature. After you have practiced using questions for several chapters, the process will then become more automatic. Asking questions will also help you to think more critically. By asking and answering the questions *who, what, when,* and *where,* you will be gathering the facts needed to understand the material. Once you comprehend the material better, your test grades should improve because you will then be able to evaluate what is important and what is not. The following is a list of many of the advantages that questioning strategies provide:

Advantages

1. Aids concentration by stimulating your mind.
2. Allows greater involvement with reading by:

   • Eliminating passive reading.
   • Eliminating distractions.
   • Eliminating boredom.

3. Aids in anticipating test questions.
4. Improves classroom participation.
5. Strengthens retention.
6. Stimulates creativity and creates more questions.
7. Aids comprehension.
8. Activates critical thinking.

Levels of Questions That Lead to Critical Thinking

Questions can be asked at different levels. They can be as simple as factual information or as complex as synthesis type questions, which focus on higher-level thinking by combining information to create a new idea. Asking questions that relate both to what you are reading and what you have read, helps to build comprehension. Most reading and questioning begins at the literal level, which is the recall of information. It is probably a good idea to begin with the literal type of questions before using more complex questions. The following are the different levels of questions that you can ask yourself. These levels are based on Benjamin Bloom's *Taxonomy of Thinking and Reading* (1968).

Literal Questions	Recall of basic information
Translation Questions	Expression of information in a different form
Interpretive Questions	Drawing relationships among facts, values, and generalizations
Application Questions	Transfer of ideas and concepts to other material

Analysis Questions	Identification of logical steps used in the thinking process to arrive at a conclusion
Synthesis Questions	Bringing together information to create a new idea
Evaluation Questions	Judgment of value

Use **literal questions** to search for the basic information the author is presenting. For example, the type of questions that are asked at this level are as basic as asking yourself, " What are the facts I need to know?" or "What ideas or theories are presented?" You are really identifying and recalling main ideas and key details (see Chapter 5).

At the next level of comprehension, the **translation level**, you begin to use your critical-thinking skills. Instead of just recalling the information, you will begin to translate information into your own words. Paraphrasing and summarizing what the author has stated leads you to ask yourself questions such as "What is the author's message?" "What basic ideas is he or she trying to deliver?" "Is the message stated or unstated?"

At the next level, the **interpretation level**, or inferential level, you begin to draw relationships between the different facts and concepts. Inferential questions focus on the unstated messages, the information included between the lines. For instance, you could ask yourself questions that pertain to cause and effect: "If this is what has happened, what caused it to happen?" The author may not have stated the cause directly, but you can reason it out by asking interpretive questions.

Application, analysis, and synthesis questions each take you one step higher in the hierarchy of reading and thinking. As you progress through college, you will find that you will think more critically and begin to integrate these higher levels of comprehension into your framework of thinking. At the **application level**, you will transfer ideas and concepts to other materials. You will ask yourself questions such as, "If Shakespeare is important to understanding literature, then what importance does he have in history?" **Analysis questions** enable you to see the logical steps of your thinking and come to a conclusion. For example, you will be able to see the connection between history and religion because, as you begin asking questions at this level, you will see the big picture and not focus on just specific parts. **Synthesis questions** then bring together information that you have learned in order to create a new idea. You will be able to compose, design, assemble, and organize ideas and concepts and will be able to ask questions that will help you to integrate theory with practice. Lastly, **evaluation questions** can be equated with solving the problem. At this level of thinking, you be able to make decisions and support views based on an objective appraisal of all of the information you have gathered.

Although the levels of comprehension and critical thinking have been stated in a sequential way, you will not necessarily progress from level to level but will learn to integrate the various levels as needed. Critical thinkers have the ability to ask the questions that lead to a valid conclusion.

WHEN TO ASK QUESTIONS

There are three times to ask questions—**before, during, and after reading.** Questions asked before reading set the purpose for reading, direct your focus, and give you a better idea of what you need to learn. In a sense, they help you to preview the chapter before you begin the actual reading. Prereading, as mentioned in Chapter 4, can be done by reading the headings, summary, and questions at the end of the chapter. Questions asked during reading help you become an active participant in the reading process. You will not be able to think critically unless you are involved with the material. This can be done by turning the topic sentences into specific questions. You can anticipate what comes next by asking questions about the material you are reading. For instance, if you are reading about rape, you might ask yourself questions such as, "Does the rapist have a typical profile? Has he done this before? Can he be rehabilitated?" Questions raised during reading sustain interest, aid literal comprehension, and lead to higher-order thinking. Questions asked after reading help you test your comprehension. This can be done in conjunction with the Cornell note system or other study systems explained in Chapters 6 and 9. Postreading questions help you prepare for tests. If you try to answer the questions at the end of the chapter, and they seem like Greek to you, then you know you did not comprehend the material enough to perform well on a test.

Before Reading

Asking questions before reading helps you in a number of ways.

Questions Set a Purpose for Reading

It is important to know and understand why you are reading. Just reading a chapter in a text because it is assigned will not aid you in activating your thinking or help you to learn the material. For example, you need to ask yourself questions such as, "What are the main ideas?" "What information is most important to learn and understand?" "How does this information relate to what I am learning in lecture?" Setting the purpose for your reading will help you to focus on the material and learn the content more effectively.

Questions Build Background

The knowledge, experiences, beliefs, attitudes, and values that you bring to the material you are reading are invaluable because they provide insight into what is being read. For example, if you have a background in literature and have seen a variety of plays, reading Shakespeare will be easier for you than it will be for your fellow students who haven't had this experience. All students bring different backgrounds and different knowledge to text reading. The more varied a background you have, the better your comprehension will be.

It is important that you continue to build your background knowledge. The following ideas describe ways that students can actively work on bringing more knowledge structures to their background. The more knowledge you have, the easier it will be to ask questions and think critically. Sometimes adult students do better in classes because they have many more life experiences than the average freshman student. However, all students can build their background knowledge. As students progress through school, their knowledge base will broaden. Never underestimate introductory courses, since they contain the schema needed for understanding more complex concepts. Building a strong knowledge base should become an ongoing process, one that students are constantly involved in.

In order for you to activate your background knowledge, you need to find strategies that work. Use the following strategies to enhance your prior knowledge. They are are relatively easy to do and will help you build a broad base of background knowledge and information.

1. **Reading** is one of the most important factors for increasing your knowledge base. The more books you read, the better your background will be—through books you will have a chance to widen your horizons. Through reading you will be exposed to history, science, politics, and the arts. Gradually upgrade your reading so that your vocabulary will grow.
2. **Movies and TV** can be an enjoyable way to gain information. Try to watch programs that will expand your knowledge and relate to your academic courses. Public broadcasting stations offer a wealth of information that can be utilized for academic purposes. Even watching something as entertaining as *Gone with the Wind* can build schema for the Civil War era. When you lack sufficient background knowledge in a subject, movies and TV may be sources of information.
3. **Plays and the arts** offer a visual way of comprehending literature and can add to your knowledge of history. If you're studying Ibsen in school, why not see the play *A Doll's House*? If you're taking American history, why not visit a museum to view the various dis-

plays of American life such as Revolutionary War relics and Indian lore. Seeing Shakespeare's *Richard III* can help you to understand the social and political tenets of fifteenth-century England. These are some enjoyable ways to build your background.

4. **Reading something easier** is another way to build your background knowledge. Reading easier material to gain background information will help your comprehension of more complex materials. If you're reading a college text and it is hard to comprehend, go to the library to look for a high school text on the same subject. You will find the high school text will be easier to understand and will, in turn, make the college text easier to understand.

5. **Developing your vocabulary** is important because if you don't understand the language of the subject, your comprehension will be limited. A strong vocabulary enables you to recognize individual words and their meaning in context. In order to do well in a subject, you need to become familiar with its technical language. Each content area has its own language, and until you learn and understand the vocabulary, you will have difficulty learning the material. You can build a strong, precise vocabulary by doing a lot of reading and by learning words as concepts. Don't memorize the dictionary definition; try to understand the word. Then you can expand your working vocabulary by integrating a new vocabulary word into both your written and spoken language. This will help you identify the main ideas, another advantage of asking questions before reading.

Questions Find the Main Ideas

1. Ask, "What do I want or need to learn?" "What do I need to know?" Setting a purpose for reading will help you to focus on the most important information presented by the author. If you read without purpose, your comprehension will probably be minimal because you will not know what to look for. However, by asking questions you will help yourself understand the material more completely. You can gather literal information first by asking yourself the following questions.

2. Ask, "Who?", "What?", "When?", "Where?", "Why?", "How?", "What is the main idea?" These questions elicit the literal information you need to know. Once you have found the answers to these questions, you are ready to go to the higher-order questions.

3. Preread headings, summary, objectives, and questions at the end of the chapter.

Using these strategies before reading will keep you moving toward your main objective, which is to learn as much as possible.

◆ **EXERCISE A: USING PREREADING QUESTIONS**

Preread the following article by looking at the headings, terms in boldface print, and the first and last line of each paragraph. Use these strategies to develop three questions you might want answered by the article.

Schizophrenic Disorders*

Schizophrenia produces a bizarre set of symptoms and wreaks havoc on an individual's personality. **Schizophrenic disorders** *are severe psychological disorders characterized by distorted thoughts and perceptions, odd communication, inappropriate emotion, abnormal motor behavior, and social withdrawal. The term schizophrenia comes from the Latin word schizo, meaning "split," and phrenia, meaning "mind." The mind is split from reality and the personality loses its unity. Schizophrenia is not the same as multiple personality, which sometimes is called split personality. Schizophrenia involves the split of one personality from reality, not the coexistence of several personalities within one individual.*

Characteristics of Schizophrenic Disorders

Bob began to miss work, spending his time watching his house from a rental car parked inconspicuously down the street and following his fellow employees as they left work to see where they went and what they did. He kept a little black book in which he scribbled cryptic notes. When he went to the water cooler at work, he pretended to drink but instead looked carefully around the room to observe if anyone seemed guilty or frightened.

Bob's world appeared to be closing in on him. After an explosive scene at the office one day, he became very agitated. He left and never returned. By the time Bob arrived home, he was in a rage. He could not sleep that night, and, the next day, he kept his children home from school; all day he kept the shades pulled down on every window. The next night he maintained his vigil. At 4 A.M., he armed himself and burst out of the house, firing shots in the air while daring his enemies to come out (McNeil, 1967).

Bob is a paranoid schizophrenic, one of the schizophrenic disorders we will describe shortly. About 1 in every 100 Americans is classified as schizophrenic; the same percentage has been documented in other countries as well—Nigeria, Russia, and India, for example (Gottesman,

*John Santrock, *Psychology,* 3rd edition, 1991, p. 497, Wm. C. Brown Publishers. Reprinted with permission.

1989; Tsuang, 1976). Schizophrenic disorders are serious, debilitating mental disturbances; about one-half of all mental hospital patients in the United States are schizophrenic. More now than in the past, schizophrenics live in society and return periodically for treatment at mental hospitals. Drug therapy . . . is primarily responsible for fewer schizophrenics being hospitalized. About one-third of schizophrenics get better, about one-third get worse, and another one-third stay about the same once they develop this severe mental disorder. What are the symptoms these individuals develop?

Many schizophrenics have delusions, or false beliefs—one individual may think he is Jesus Christ, another Napoleon, for example. The delusions are utterly implausible. One individual may think her thoughts are being broadcast over the radio; another may think that a double agent is controlling her every move. Schizophrenics may also hear, see, feel, smell, and taste things that are not there. These hallucinations often take the form of voices. A schizophrenic might think that he hears two people talking about him, for example. On another occasion, he might say, "Hear the rumbling in the pipe? That is one of my men in there watching out for me."

Often schizophrenics do not make sense when they talk or write. Their language does not follow any rules. For example, one schizophrenic might say, "Well, Rocky, babe, help is out, happening, but where, when, up, top, side, over, you know, out of the way, that's it. Sign off." Such speech has no meaning. These incoherent, loose word associations are called word salad.

Schizophrenics' motor behavior may be bizarre, sometimes taking the form of an odd appearance, pacing, a statuelike posture, or strange mannerisms. Some schizophrenics withdraw from their social world, so insulated from others that they seem totally absorbed in interior images and thoughts.

Forms of Schizophrenia Disorders

Schizophrenic disorders appear in four main forms: disorganized, catatonic, paranoid, and undifferentiated schizophrenia.

__Disorganized schizophrenia__ is a schizophrenic disorder in which an individual has delusions and hallucinations that have little or no recognizable meaning—hence, the label "disorganized." A disorganized schizophrenic withdraws from human contact and may regress to silly, childlike gestures and behavior. Many of these individuals experienced an adolescence characterized by isolation or maladjustment.

__Catatonic schizophrenia__ is a schizophrenic disorder characterized by bizarre motor behavior, which sometimes takes the form of completely immobile stupor. Nonetheless, in this stupor, catatonic schizophrenics are completely conscious of what is happening around them. In a catatonic *state, the individual sometimes shows waxy flexibility; for example, if a person's arm is raised and then allowed to fall, the arm stays in the new position.*

Paranoid schizophrenia *is a schizophrenic disorder characterized by delusions of reference, grandeur, and persecution. The delusions usually form a complex, elaborate system based on a complete misinterpretation of actual events. It is not unusual for schizophrenics to develop all three delusions in the following order. First, they sense they are special and have been singled out for attention (delusions of reference). Individuals with delusions of reference misinterpret chance events as being directly relevant to their own lives—a thunderstorm, for example, might be perceived as a personal message from God. Second, they believe that this special attention is the result of their admirable and special characteristics (delusions of grandeur). Individuals with delusions of grandeur think of themselves as exalted beings—the Pope or the president, for example. Third, they think that others are so jealous and threatened by these characteristics that they spy and plot against them (delusions of persecution). Individuals with delusions of persecution often feel they are the target of conspiracy—for example, recall Bob's situation described earlier.*

Undifferentiated schizophrenia *is a schizophrenic disorder characterized by disorganized behavior, hallucinations, delusions, and incoherence. This category of schizophrenia is used when an individual's symptoms either don't meet the criteria for the other types or they meet the criteria for more than one of the other types.*

Questions Raised from Prereading Strategies

1. _____

   _____

2. _____

   _____

3. _____

   _____

During Reading

Asking questions during reading keeps you focused and helps you concentrate on the material being read. The more involved you are with the material being read, the more likely you will be to absorb and understand the information presented. Once you begin asking questions while you read, it will become an automatic process that will be as natural as the reading itself. Asking questions during reading helps you in a number of ways.

Questions Anticipate What Comes Next

Asking questions while you read leads you to think about what comes next. For example, if you are reading about a political crisis, you will be thinking about the outcome and through the process of critical thinking you will probably have an idea of the results. Your questions then will either be confirmed or refuted as you read, involving you intensely in the reading and studying.

Questions Sustain Interest

If you ask questions and are actively reading, your interest level will be higher than if you read passively and just try to get the assignment read. When your interest level is high, you tend to experience better comprehension and retention.

Questions Aid Literal Comprehension

Through the process of asking questions, you will be able to remember the information more readily and thereby retain the basic facts, which will help to improve your test results.

Questions Aid Higher-Order Thinking

As mentioned in Chapter 2, critical thinking becomes more and more important as you progress through college. Therefore, it is important to begin to put into practice critical-thinking skills as soon as possible because often, even in your Freshman year, teachers ask application questions on tests. If you have been asking questions as you read, you will be more able to think critically and at a higher level and to respond with understanding to application questions on tests. Often students say, "I understand the material, but the teacher stated it in a different way. That's why I got it wrong." If you think critically, you won't have any problems when questions are asked at different levels. You will be prepared.

Use the following strategies to form questions during reading:

1. Turn topic sentences into specific questions.
2. Ask yourself, "Could this be a test question?"

◆ **EXERCISE B: USING QUESTIONS DURING READING**

Read the selection about William James, and answer the questions that follow. Answering them will help you to comprehend the important information contained in this selection.

William James

*American psychologists at the end of the 19th century were more influenced by William James (1842–1910) than by Wilhelm Wundt. James preferred a more informal approach, emphasizing the kinds of questions we encounter in daily life. He wrote extensively about **consciousness**, which we now define as our awareness of the environment and ourselves. James also developed an influential theory that explained emotional reactions in terms of our perception of physiological responses.*

*James was deeply impressed with the theories of evolution proposed by biologist Charles Darwin. James believed that psychological processes had evolved in the same fashion as other human processes. He was particularly interested in the evolution and functions of consciousness, and he wondered how consciousness helps human beings. This emphasis on the functions of psychological processes inspired the name for James's approach to psychology: functionalism. **Functionalism** is the view that psychological processes are adaptive; they allow humans to survive and to adapt successfully to their surroundings.*

Whereas Wundt was known for his laboratory, James was known for his textbooks. For several decades, American psychology students read either the two-volume Principles of Psychology *(1890) or the shorter version,* Psychology, Briefer Course *(1892). Professors referred to the longer version as "James," and they nicknamed the shorter version "Jimmy." A century later, psychologists still admire these important books.*

Many of James's ideas seem remarkably modern. For example, he emphasized that the human mind is active and inquiring, a view still current today. James also suggested that humans have two different kinds of memory. This proposal was reemphasized nearly 80 years later. (Matlin, 1992, pp. 4 & 5)

Who? _____

_____

What? _____

_____

Where? _____

_____

Why? _____

_____

When? _____

_____

How? _____

_____

What is the Main Idea? _____

_____

◆   **EXERCISE C: USING QUESTIONS TO PREDICT THE OUTCOME**

While reading this story, jot down questions that come to mind. The last paragraph of this story is missing. Using your questions as a guide, write an ending for this story. After you have completed the assignment, turn to page 245 for the author's ending.

The Sniper   *QUESTIONS*

The long June twilight faded into night. Dublin lay enveloped in darkness but for the dim light of the moon that shone through fleecy clouds, casting a pale light as of approaching dawn over the streets and the dark waters of the Liffey. Around the beleaguered Four Courts the heavy guns roared. Here and there through the city, machine guns and rifles broke the silence of the night, spasmodically, like dogs barking on lone farms. Republicans and Free Staters were waging civil war.

On a roof top near O'Connell Bridge, a Republican sniper lay watching. Beside him lay his

*"The Sniper" from SPRING SOWING by Liam O'Flaherty, reprinted by permission of Harcourt Brace & Company.

rifle and over his shoulders were slung a pair of field glasses. His face was the face of a student, thin and ascetic, but his eyes had the cold gleam of the fanatic. They were deep and thoughtful, the eyes of a man who is used to looking at death.

He was eating a sandwich hungrily. He had eaten nothing since morning. He had been too excited to eat. He finished the sandwich, and taking a flask of whiskey from his pocket, he took a short draught. Then he returned the flask to his pocket. He paused for a moment, considering whether he should risk a smoke. It was dangerous. The flash might be seen in the darkness, and there were enemies watching. He decided to take the risk.

Placing a cigarette between his lips, he struck a match, inhaled the smoke hurriedly and put out the light. Almost immediately, a bullet flattened itself against the parapet of the roof. The sniper took another whiff and put out the cigarette. Then he swore softly and crawled away to the left.

Cautiously he raised himself and peered over the parapet. There was a flash and a bullet whizzed over this head. He dropped immediately. He had seen the flash. It came from the opposite side of the street.

He rolled over the roof to a chimney stack in the rear, and slowly drew himself up behind it, until his eyes were level with the top of the parapet. There was nothing to be seen—just the dim outline of the opposite housetop against the blue sky. His enemy was under cover.

Just then an armored car came across the bridge and advanced slowly up the street. It stopped on the opposite side of the street, fifty yards ahead. The sniper could hear the dull panting of the motor. His heart beat faster. It was an enemy car. He wanted to fire, but he knew it was useless. His bullets would never pierce the steel that covered the gray monster.

Then round the corner of a side street came an old woman, her head covered by a tattered shawl. She began to talk to the man in the turret of the car.

She was pointing to the roof where the sniper lay. An informer.

The turret opened. A man's head and shoulders appeared, looking toward the sniper. The sniper raised his rifle and fired. The head fell heavily on the turret wall. The woman darted toward the side street. The sniper fired again. The woman whirled round and fell with a shriek into the gutter.

Suddenly from the opposite roof a shot rang out and the sniper dropped his rifle with a curse. The rifle clattered to the roof. The sniper thought the noise would wake the dead. He stopped to pick the rifle up. He couldn't lift it. His forearm was dead. "I'm hit," he muttered.

Dropping flat onto the roof, he crawled back to the parapet. With his left hand he felt the injured right forearm. The blood was oozing through the sleeve of his coat. There was no pain— just a deadened sensation, as if the arm had been cut off.

Quickly he drew his knife from his pocket, opened it on the breast-work of the parapet, and ripped open the sleeve. There was a small hole where the bullet had entered. On the other side there was no hole. The bullet had lodged in the bone. It must have fractured it. He bent the arm below the wound. The arm bent back easily. He ground his teeth to overcome the pain.

Then taking out his field dressing, he ripped open the packet with his knife. He broke the neck of the iodine bottle and let the bitter fluid drip into the wound. A paroxysm of pain swept through him. He placed the cotton wadding over the wound and wrapped the dressing over it. He tied the ends with his teeth.

Then he lay still against the parapet, and, closing his eyes, he made an effort of will to overcome the pain.

In the street beneath all was still. The armored car had retired speedily over the bridge, with the machine gunner's head hanging lifeless over the turret. The woman's corpse lay still in the gutter.

The sniper lay still for a long time nursing his wounded arm and planning escape. Morning must not find him wounded on the roof. The enemy on the opposite roof covered his escape. He must kill that enemy and he could not use his rifle. He had only a revolver to do it. Then he thought of a plan.

Taking off his cap, he placed it over the muzzle of his rifle. Then he pushed the rifle slowly upward over the parapet, until the cap was visible from the opposite side of the street. Almost immediately there was a report, and a bullet pierced the center of the cap. The sniper slanted the rifle forward. The cap slipped down into the street. Then catching the rifle in the middle, the sniper dropped his left hand over the roof and let it hang, lifelessly. After a few moments he let the rifle drop to the street. Then he sank to the roof, dragging his hand with him.

Crawling quickly to the left, he peered up at the corner of the roof. His ruse had succeeded. The other sniper, seeing the cap and rifle fall, thought that he had killed his man. He was now standing before a row of chimney pots, looking across, with his head clearly silhouetted against the western sky.

The Republican sniper smiled and lifted his revolver above the edge of the parapet. The distance was about fifty yards—a hard shot in the dim light, and his right arm was paining him like a thousand devils. He took a steady aim. His hand trembled with eagerness. Pressing his lips together, he took a deep breath through his nostrils and fired. He was almost deafened with the report and his arm shook with the recoil.

Then when the smoke cleared he peered across and uttered a cry of joy. His enemy had been hit. He was reeling over the parapet in his death agony. He struggled to keep his feet, but he was slowly falling forward, as if in a dream. The rifle fell from his grasp, hit the parapet, fell over, bounded off the pole of a barber's shop beneath and then clattered on the pavement.

Then the dying man on the roof crumpled up and fell forward. The body turned over and over in space and hit the ground with a dull thud. Then it lay still.

The sniper looked at his enemy falling and he shuddered. The lust of battle died in him. He became bitten by remorse. The sweat stood out in beads on his forehead. Weakened by his wound and the long summer day of fasting and watching on the roof, he revolted from the sight of the shattered mass of his dead enemy. His teeth chattered, he began to gibber to himself, cursing the war, cursing himself, cursing everybody.

He looked at the smoking revolver in his hand, and with an oath he hurled it to the roof at his feet. The revolver went off with the concussion and the bullet whizzed past the sniper's head. He was frightened back to his senses by the shock. His nerves steadied. The cloud of fear scattered from his mind and he laughed.

Taking the whiskey flask from his pocket, he emptied it at a draught. He felt reckless under the influence of the spirit. He decided to leave the roof now and look for his company commander, to report. Everywhere around was quiet. There was not much danger in going through the streets. He picked up his revolver and put it in his pocket. Then he crawled down through the skylight to the house underneath.

When the sniper reached the laneway on the street level, he felt a sudden curiosity as to the identity of the enemy sniper whom he had killed. He decided that he was a good shot, whoever he was. He wondered did he know him. Perhaps he had been in his own company before the split in the army. He decided to risk going over to have a look at him. He peered around the corner into O'Connell Street. In the upper part of the street there was heavy firing, but around here all was quiet.

The sniper darted across the street. A machine gun tore up the ground around him with a hail of bullets, but he escaped. He threw himself face downward beside the corpse. The machine gun stopped.

Review your questions, and then write your ending for this story.

_____

_____

_____

_____

_____

After Reading

It is just as important to ask questions after you have read the assigned material as it is to do so before and during the reading. Many students feel that once they have done the assigned reading, they have accomplished the necessary work needed to succeed, but doing the reading is only part of what you need to do to be academically successful. Reading helps you to gain the basic information, but in order to learn, you need to work with the material. Studying the material means using study strategies that will aid your retention and comprehension. Developing after reading questions is one strategy that will help you to learn more effectively. After reading questions will help you in the following ways.

Questions Crystallize Information Read
If you ask yourself questions after you have read, this strategy will help you to integrate all the information you have read. You will see the whole picture and not just individual pieces of information, which will broaden and deepen your understanding.

Questions Prepare for Tests
Asking questions after reading will prepare you for the questions that might be asked on tests. You will probably get an idea of what type of questions the teacher will ask. You will also be summarizing and paraphrasing as you answer the questions you have posed. This is one good way of preparing yourself for tests.

Use the following strategies to form questions after reading.

1. Test for comprehension by asking yourself questions about the material read.

2. Answer questions at the end of chapters.
3. Start with literal types of questions, and eventually work toward more complex ones.

◆ EXERCISE B: USING QUESTIONS AFTER READING

Read the following selection. After you have read the article, develop three questions that could possibly be used as test questions. Make sure that each question is at one of the different levels presented earlier in this chapter. Be sure you have read the article carefully enough so that you can include the answer.

American Diversity*

Voting Ethnic

Although in many ways America has been a melting pot of different races and religions, we have not melted so far as to be indistinguishable. One visible sign of ethnic and cultural differences is in voting behavior. In general, socioeconomic class is a very important predictor of the vote: the lower the income, the more likely to vote Democrat. But this general rule is cross-cut with distinctive ethnic patterns (we use ethnic here to refer to differences of religion, national origin, and race).

For example, Jews are much more likely to vote Democratic than other whites of similar income. On the whole, they have a higher-than-average income, yet in 1992 about three-fourths of Jewish voters voted Democratic. As a group, they were exceeded in their Democratic allegiance only by blacks.

Catholics used to be predominantly Democratic. They still are, but not consistently. Although 60% supported Democratic congressional candidates, and they favored Clinton over Bush by 44% to 36%, only half voted for Dukakis and a majority voted for Reagan in 1980 and 1984.

Blacks are probably the most distinctive group politically. About 90% consistently vote Democratic, and this loyalty has increased over the past 25 years.

Hispanics, who also have lower-than-average incomes, are not as universally Democratic as blacks and have voted Republican in significant numbers in recent elections. Although almost three-quarters voted Democratic in congressional elections, just about 60% voted for Dukakis in 1988 and Clinton in 1992.

Hispanics vote Republican more than they previously did for several reasons. One is that many Hispanics are moving into the middle class. Another is that Republicans have made a great effort to lure Hispanic voters. Moreover, a growing number are Cuban Americans, largely located in Florida, whose most intense political opinion is anticommunism. Cuban Americans are much more likely to be Republican than either Mexican Americans or Puerto Ricans.

White Protestants generally give a majority of their vote to the Republicans and have done so for decades. However, as for other groups, income differences are important in determining the vote of Protestants.

Why is ethnicity important in determining the vote? There is nothing genetic about it. Rather, ethnicity is a shorthand term for many other factors influencing political behavior—class, historical treatment within the society, and basic culture and values. Jews are predominantly Democratic, for example, because as a persecuted minority throughout much of their history, they have learned to identify with the underdog, even when their own economic circumstances move them into the middle or upper class. Catholics were sometimes discriminated against too; this discrimination plus their working-class status propelled them to the party of Roosevelt. As Catholics have moved into the middle class and as tolerance toward Catholics has grown, Catholics, like Protestants, have tended to vote their income.

◆ **EXERCISE C: QUESTIONS BEFORE, DURING, AND AFTER**

Now that you have had the opportunity to practice using questions before, during and after your reading, read the following paragraphs to combine using all three with one reading selection. Read the article "Feeding Frenzy," and answer the following questions. Note at what point during reading these questions should be answered.

Topic of reading (Before):

_____

_____

Questions to think about while reading (Before):

1. _____

2. _____

3. _____

Answers arrived at (During):

1. _____

2. _____

3. _____

Names and dates to remember (During):

1. _____

2. _____

3. _____

New terms and meanings (During):

1. _____

2. _____

3. _____

How does this relate to something you already know (After)?

_____

_____

Why is this information useful or important for you to know (After)?

_____

_____

Feeding Frenzy*

Overwhelmed by conflicting advice, most Americans have thrown in the napkin on healthy eating. Here's how to cut through the controversy.

There's a new American way of living today . . . Americans care about physical fitness and good nutrition now as never before . . . We eat less red meat and more poultry and fish, more fresh vegetables and fruits, more whole grain cereals . . . *"Betty Crocker's Light and Easy Cooking."*

*It's breakfast time at Atlanta's Dunk & Dine Restaurant, where the special of the day is barbecued pork and a sign on the cigarette machine reads, **Thank You For Smoking.** Police Capt. Arthur Williams, 45, whose cholesterol level is so high that his doctor has warned him to change his eating habits or expect a heart attack, is enjoying a bacon, lettuce and tomato sandwich on white, with mayonnaise. His effort to start the day with fruit lasted only two weeks. "I couldn't stay with it," he says, not very repentantly. "It's hard to find food that's good for you, and tastes good."*

Williams' approach to the bewildering world of food choices is a simple one: give up and hope for the best. It seems to be shared by millions. Assaulted by a blitz of nutrition advice in recent years—lower your cholesterol, eat more fiber, throw out the salt shaker, forget red meat, get more calcium, reduce your fat intake, use more olive oil, grill everything, avoid barbecuing, eat more fish, watch out for shellfish, choose margarine, beware of transfatty acids in margarine—many Americans have thrown up their hands. "Basically, I eat junk," says Sharon, a 53-year-old telephone-company employee, downing a hot dog at a Santa Monica, CA, mall. "I don't listen to any of those claims that eggs are bad for you and everything else that causes cancer. The next thing they'll be telling us is you can't drink water."

Nonsense! Of course you can drink water (as long as it's been tested for lead). But recently Americans woke up to some particularly discouraging headlines: the latest dietary bugaboo is food itself. Or so it seemed. The basic four food groups, long touted as the healthiest organizing principle for American meals—two servings of meat a day, two of dairy products, six of grains and five of fruits and vegetables—are under attack. The U.S. Department of Agriculture, along with many nutrition experts, wants to reconfigure the groups to emphasize the importance of grains, fruits and vegetables, with a corresponding de-emphasis on meat and dairy products. Meanwhile, the Physicians Committee for Responsible Medicine, a Washington-based nonprofit group, wants to throw out the traditional groups entirely. PCRM favors what it calls the new four: fruits, vegetables, grains and legumes (which include peas and beans). Meat, poultry, fish, eggs and dairy would retire to the far fringes of the American diet.

Both these plans reflect a growing body of scientific evidence that American eating habits are killing us. Our rates of heart disease and some cancers, particularly of the breast and colon, are among the highest in the world. Many factors contribute to cancer and heart disease, including an individual's genetic inheritance, but when epidemiologists trace the course of diseases across the globe, the role of diet stands out sharply. Japan offers the starkest example. The traditional Japanese diet is the direct opposite of ours: typically they eat rice, vegetables and a little fish, while Americans put a big portion of meat in the center of the plate and add a few french fries. Consuming only about a quarter as much fat as we do, and far more carbohydrates, the Japanese live longer than anybody else in the world. That is, until they move here. "The Japanese in Japan have one fifth or one sixth the rate of breast cancer that we do," says Dr. Peter Greenwald, director of the Division of Cancer Prevention and Control at the National Cancer Institute. "When they move to Hawaii, the rate goes up." In the last few decades, moreover, as hamburgers, ice cream and other high-fat foods have become popular in Japan, higher rates of cancer and heart disease have followed. Similar patterns are emerging all over the globe. "I've been in Mauritius, Cuba and Hungary, three completely different countries, advising their governments on nutrition education," says Marion Nestle, professor of nutrition at New York University. "People in all three countries are starting to imitate our diet, they're eating more animal fat and dairy products, and their rates of disease are skyrocketing."

Precisely how our diet fails us is a matter of continuing debate, but nutritionists agree that its proportions are all wrong. That half-pound sirloin in the center of the plate carries nearly one and a half times the amount of protein you need in a whole day (the excess can make you fat), and it's packed with saturated fat. True, many Americans know the bad news about meat by now and have cut down, but substituting chicken or fish doesn't go to the heart of the problem. What's missing from the plate is just as important as what's on it. According to recent dietary studies, nearly half of all Americans eat no fruit on a given day and nearly a quarter eat no vegetables. Eleven percent eat neither, and only 9 percent of us get the recommended five servings a day. "For a great many people, a day without meat is somehow inadequate," says Gladys Block, a nutritional epidemiologist at the National Cancer Institute. "That just isn't so for a day without fruits or vegetables." Block and other scientists are now convinced that fruits and vegetables actively protect against cancer, and new evidence suggests that they may also protect against heart disease.

The theory is that an excess of free radicals—oxygen compounds generated in the course of normal metabolism—can travel through the body doing damage to its cells, thus initiating both cancer and atherosclerosis (hardening of the arteries). The body's best defense against these marauding molecules are nutrients known as antioxidants—the mineral selenium, vitamins C and E, and betacarotene, which turns to vitamin A in the body. They're found in fruits, vegetables and grains. Antioxidants neutralize the free radicals, at once protecting the body against disease and vindicating generations of mothers, nutritionists and home-ec teachers.

"For years, the National Academy of Sciences and the National Cancer Institute have been telling Americans to eat more vegetables," says Bonnie Liebman, nutritionist at the Center for Science in the Public Interest, a Washington, D.C. based consumer group. "But we aren't eating fruits and vegetables. No one has succeeded in getting that message across."

That message is very much at the center of the current flap over the four food groups; unfortunately, the controversy seems more likely to end in public frustration than public enlightenment. Ever since 1956, when the USDA began promoting the food groups, they have reflected political reality as well as nutrition policy. "The standard four food groups are based on American agricultural lobbies," says NYU's Nestle. "Why do we have a milk group? Because we have a National Dairy Council. Why do we have a meat group? Because we have an extremely powerful meat lobby." As the science of nutrition grew more sophisticated, and the relative roles of fats and carbohydrates became better understood, the food groups came up for revision—not in content but in graphic design. Rather than simply list the groups or show them on a pie chart, suggesting they are equals, the USDA created "The Eating Right Pyramid" with grains taking up the large space on the bottom, fruits and vegetables the next largest, meat and dairy products in a narrower slice above them and fats and sweets in a tiny space on top. Nutritionists applauded, but after the graphic had gone to the printer Agriculture Secretary Edward R. Madigan suspended its publication indefinitely. Meat and dairy representatives had objected to the new design for its purported slighting of their products. Madigan says the pyramid "was and is under review."

PCRM's far more radical proposal to dump the four food groups has received a great deal of publicity, but surprisingly little attention has been paid to its practical implications—or to the politics embodied by PCRM. The group has two stated purposes: to address nutrition issues and to work against the use of animals in medical experiments. Its president, Neal Barnard, is a psychiatrist; he has also served as a scientific advisor to People for the Ethical Treatment of Animals, an animal-rights group, although he says he has "no official role" with the organization. According to PCRM, some 3,000 of its members are medical doctors; more than 50,000 "associate members" are not. While PCRM's new four food groups purport simply to place fruits, vegetables, grains and legumes at the diet's center, leaving other foods as options, Barnard himself is a strict vegetarian who eschews all animal foods including dairy products. The menus and food lists that PCRM has circulated with its proposal are similarly extreme, eliminating even low-fat animal and dairy products.

CRITICAL THINKING

The critical-thinking process of solving problems involves generating and answering questions. Some of the questions might be as follows:

1. What is the problem?
2. What are some possible solutions?
3. What are the advantages of each solution?
4. What are the disadvantages of each solution?
5. What's the best solution?

Read the following selection. Then, on a separate piece of paper, answer the first four questions above. Next, write a paragraph describing your recommended solution to the problem.

Heading for Apocalypse?*

A new U.N. report says global warming is already under way—and the effects could be catastrophic. *By Michael D. Lemonick*

Like street-corner prophets proclaiming that the end is near, scientists who study the earth's atmosphere have been issuing predictions of impending doom for the past few years without offering any concrete proof. The atmospheric scientists' version of the apocalypse is global warming, a gradual rise in worldwide temperatures caused by man-made gases trapping too much heat from the sun. If the theory is correct, the world could be in for dramatic changes in climate, accompanied by major disruptions to modern society. So far, though, even the experts have had to admit that while the earth has warmed an average of up to 1.1 degrees F over the past 100 years, no solid evidence has emerged that this is anything but a natural phenomenon. And the uncertainty has given skeptics—especially Gingrichian politicians—plenty of ammunition to argue against taking the difficult, expensive steps required to stave off a largely hypothetical calamity.

Until now. A draft report currently circulating on the Internet asserts that the global-temperature rise can now be blamed, at least in part, on human activity. Statements like this have been made before by individual researchers—who have been criticized for going too far beyond the scientific consensus. But this report comes from the International Panel on Climate Change (IPCC), a respected U.N.-sponsored body made up of more than 1,500 leading climate experts from 60 nations.

Unless the world takes immediate and drastic steps to reduce the emissions of heat-trapping gases, says the panel, the so-called greenhouse effect could drive global temperatures up as much as 6 degrees F by the year 2100—an increase in heat comparable to the warming that ended the last Ice Age and with perhaps equally profound effects on climate. Huge swaths of densely populated land could be inundated by rising seas. Entire ecosystems could vanish as rainfall and temperature patterns shift. Droughts, floods and storms could become more severe. Says Michael Oppenheimer, a senior scientist with the Environmental Defense Fund: "I think this is a watershed moment in the public debate on global warming."

This shift in scientific consensus is based not so much on new data as on improvements in the complex computer models that climatologists use to test their theories. Unlike chemists or molecular biologists, climate experts have no way to do lab experiments on their specialty. So they simulate them on supercomputers and look at what happens when human-

generated gases—carbon dioxide from industry and auto exhaust, methane from agriculture, chlorofluorocarbons from leaky refrigerators and spray cans—are pumped into the models' virtual atmospheres.

Until recently, the computer models weren't working very well. When the scientists tried to simulate what they believe has been happening over the past century or so, the results didn't mesh with reality; the models said the world should now be warmer than it actually is. The reason is that the computer models had been overlooking an important factor affecting global temperatures: aerosols, the tiny droplets of chemicals like sulfur dioxide that are produced along with CO_2 when fossil fuels are burned in cars and power plants. Aerosols actually cool the planet by blocking sunlight and mask the effects of global warming. Says Tom Wigley, a climatologist at the National Center for Atmospheric Research and a member of the international panel: "We were looking for the needle in the wrong haystack."

Once the scientists factored in aerosols, their models began looking more like the real world. The improved performance of the simulations was demonstrated in 1991, when they successfully predicted temperature changes in the aftermath of the massive Mount Pinatubo eruption in the Philippines. A number of studies since have added to the scientists' confidence that they finally know what they're talking about—and can predict what may happen if greenhouse gases continue to be released into the atmosphere unchecked. Just last week, a report appeared in Nature *that firmly ties an increase in the severity of U.S. rainstorms to global warming.*

In general, the news is not good. Over the next century, says the IPCC report.

- *Sea levels could rise up to 3 ft., mostly because of melting glaciers and the expansion of water as it warms up. That could submerge vast areas of low-lying coastal land, including major river deltas, most of the beaches on the U.S. Atlantic Coast, parts of China and the island nations of the Maldives, the Seychelles and the Cook and Marshall islands. More than 100 million people would be displaced.*
- *Winters could get warmer—which wouldn't bother most people—and warm-weather hot spells like the one that killed 500 in Chicago this past summer could become more frequent and more severe.*
- *Rainfall could increase overall—but the increase wouldn't be uniform across the globe. Thus areas that are already prone to flooding might flood more often and more severely, and since water evaporates more easily in a warmer world, drought-prone regions and deserts could become even dryer. Hurricanes, which draw their energy from warm oceans, could become even stronger as those oceans heat up.*

- *Temperature and rainfall patterns would shift in unpredictable ways. That might not pose a problem for agriculture, since farmers could change their crops and irrigate. Natural ecosystems that have to adapt on their own, however, could be devastated. Observes Oppenheimer dryly: "They cannot sprout legs and move to another climate." Perhaps a third of the world's forests, he says, might find themselves living in the wrong places.*

These are all worst-case scenarios, and the report's authors acknowledge that plenty of uncertainties remain in their analysis. For example, as the world warms up, it should get cloudier; depending on what sort of clouds predominate, their shadows could offset the warming effect. And nobody knows how the deep ocean currents—which play a major but still murky role in world climate, channeling heat from one part of the globe to another—would respond to global warming.

Some researchers argue that even with these caveats the report overstates the case. Says Richard Lindzen, an atmospheric scientist at M.I.T.: "The margin of error in these models is a factor of 10 or more larger than the effect you're looking for."

Even if Lindzen is wrong and the IPCC report is right, there might not be much anyone could do. Slashing emissions of greenhouse gases to stave off global warming would be straightforward enough, but that doesn't mean it would be easy. Among the strategies recommended in the new report: switching from coal and oil to natural gas, turning to nuclear and solar energy, slowing deforestation, altering land-use and traffic patterns, curbing automobile use, changing life-styles and employment patterns.

In other words, people in the developed world would have to completely transform their society, and rich countries like the U.S. would have to subsidize poor but fast-developing nations like China. And that's just to roll CO_2 emissions back to 1990 levels, the goal most environmentalists endorse. To stave off global warming completely, Lindzen maintains, "you would have to reduce emissions to where they were in 1920." Despite noble proclamations issuing from meetings like the 1992 Earth Summit in Rio, that is virtually inconceivable. As economist Henry Jacoby of M.I.T.'s Sloan School of Management puts it, "If you said, 'Let's design a problem that human institutions can't deal with,' you couldn't find one better than global warming."

Even a Democrat-controlled, Al Gore–inspired Congress would shrink from passing draconian emissions-control measures. And the current Republican House and Senate are unlikely to consider such regulations no matter how many scientists are convinced that global warming is real. Other industrial nations probably won't do much better, and poor countries can't afford to try. A more realistic strategy, some scientists argue, is to spend what research money there is figuring out how best to deal with global warming when it comes. It's already too late, they say, to do much else.

Author's Ending for Selection in Exercise C:

Then the sniper turned over the dead body and looked into his brother's face.

REFERENCES

Lemonick, M. (Oct. 2, 1995). Heading for Apocalypse. *Time,* 54–55.

Matlin, M. (1992). *Psychology.* Orlando, Fla: Holt, Rinehart and Winston, Inc.

O'Flaherty, L. (1977). Sniper. *Spring Sowing.* Orlando, Fla: Harcourt Brace Jovanovich, Inc.

Santrock, J. (1991). *Psychology.* Dubuque, IA: W. C. Brown Publishers.

Shapiro w Koehl/Springen/Manly/Pyrillis/Hager/Starr. (May 27, 1991). Feeding Frenzy. *Newsweek,* 46–49.

Welch, S., Gruhl, J., Steinman, M., Comer, J., Rigdon, S. (1994). *American Government.* St. Paul, MN: West Publishing Company.

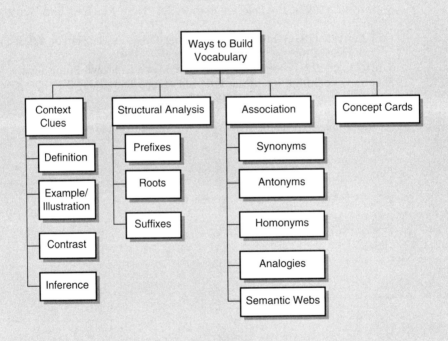

12

WAYS TO BUILD VOCABULARY

A word is dead
When it is said,
Some Say.
I say it just
Begins to live
That day.
—*EMILY DICKINSON, "A WORD"*

Key Concepts

Analogies   Comparisons that show similar relationships between dissimilar objects or ideas.

Context clues   Words around unknown words that contain clues to their meaning.

Homonyms   Words that sound alike but have different meanings.

Prefix   The part of a word that appears at the beginning of many words and helps to change its meanings.

Root   The part of a word that carries the meaning.

Structural analysis   Breaking down words into parts to find meaning.

Suffix   The ending of a word that changes its part of speech.

Synonyms   Words that have similar meanings .

Vocabulary   The sum of words used by, understood by, or at the command of a particular person or group.

Building a strong working **vocabulary**, the words you understand and use, is important because the words you know affect your ability to comprehend messages through print and speech. Since the scope of your vocabulary influences both reading and writing, adequate vocabulary will enhance your effectiveness as a student when you read textbooks and listen to lectures.

Studies have shown that one common characteristic of highly successful people is an extensive vocabulary. That is not to say that increasing your vocabulary will automatically ensure your success, but the characteristics that are common to both building a solid vocabulary and building a successful lifestyle include curiosity, a desire for knowledge and learning, and perseverance. A strong vocabulary has a positive effect both in college and in the business world because it indicates your interest in learning and the richness of your ideas and experiences.

Developing a stronger vocabulary involves much more than memorizing words and definitions. It requires applying critical-thinking skills, and it is through the process of asking questions, analyzing, and evaluating concepts that you will become aware of the important role vocabulary plays in helping you to comprehend ideas better. As you become proficient in using a wide range of words effectively, you will extend your word knowledge to concept knowledge, because as you progress in your college career, you will see that finding a definition of a word is not adequate. It is understanding the words as concepts that will enhance your learning. For example, think of the word *democracy*. The dictionary definition of democracy is a "government by the people, exercised either directly or through elected representatives" (*The American Heritage Dictionary,* 1992). However, the whole concept of democracy encompasses much more than the definition. It includes knowledge of democracy's beginnings, its influences on history, and its significance in world culture and geopolitics. All of these ideas help you to understand the information and situations related to the word and its content more clearly and help you to think in a more objective and critical way.

There are many methods of increasing your reading, speaking, and listening vocabulary. As you study the strategies for vocabulary development in the following pages, remember that building an excellent vocabulary takes effort and that you will need several encounters with a new word before it becomes part of your working vocabulary. Before we begin to discuss ways to increase your vocabulary, it is important for you to get an idea of your vocabulary skills. The following self-assessment will give you a sense of your vocabulary proficiency.

◆ **SELF-ASSESSMENT**

Look at the following words. Then put checks in the appropriate columns to indicate your familiarity with the words.

Vocabulary	*Recognize?*	*Define?*	*Use in Writing?*	*Use in Speaking?*
acquiesce				
affluent				
alienate				
ambivalent				
apropos				
bourgeois				
catharsis				
concurrent				
contentious				
credibility				
dogmatic				
eclectic				
esoteric				
infamous				
intercede				
loquacious				
myriad				
paradigm				
prolific				
provincial				
relent				
stoicism				
subservient				
superfluous				
surreptitious				
tenacious				

Vocabulary	*Recognize?*	*Define?*	*Use in Writing?*	*Use in Speaking?*
terrestrial	_____	_____	_____	_____
valid	_____	_____	_____	_____
veracity	_____	_____	_____	_____
variable	_____	_____	_____	_____

If you can't use at least half of the words from the self-assessment test in a sentence, then you need to develop strategies or a program to improve your vocabulary for reading comprehension, as well as for effective speaking and writing.

◆   **EXERCISE A: VOCABULARY FAMILIARITY**

Form groups of three of four, and, by combining your word knowledge, try to write a definition or/and use each of the above words in a sentence. As college students, you need to have a familiarity with a variety of words, and this exercise will give you the opportunity to work at increasing your vocabulary.

There are many strategies for improving your vocabulary; however, we will focus on the following strategies.

1. Context Clues.
   Getting meaning from surrounding words

2. Structural analysis
   Learn parts of word
   Prefixes
   Suffixes
   Roots

3. Association
   Synonyms
   Antonyms
   Homonyms
   Analogies
   Semantic Webs

4. Concept cards
   One way to improve your vocabulary is to keep a file of new words that you wish to add to your working vocabulary. Put each new word on a 3x5 card with its definition, and then go to your file each day to repeat the word and its definition. At the same time, begin to integrate the new word into your speaking and writing vocabulary. After a week of this type of practice, the word belongs to you.

CONTEXT CLUES

Context clues are words around unknown words that contain clues to their meaning. There are four types of context clues:

1. Definition
2. Example/illustration
3. Contrast
4. Inference

Definition clues are obvious direct statements of meaning. The author includes definitions in text to assist the reader's comprehension. Being aware of this clue is one way of enhancing your comprehension.

◆ **EXERCISE B: DEFINITION CLUES**

Write a definition for each <u>underlined</u> word in the sentences that follow.

1. Nora was <u>ambidextrous</u> and could write equally as well with both hands.

_____

2. Alan hated women, and these <u>misogynistic</u> tendencies caused him to remain a bachelor.

_____

3. David <u>exacerbated</u> the argument by increasing the disagreement with his negative view.

_____

4. <u>Behaviorism,</u> the branch of psychology stressing the role of environment in determining animal and human behavior, was advocated by Skinner.

_____

5. She belonged to a <u>subculture,</u> a specific group, that believed in taking psychedelic drugs.

_____

6. Because of its democratic tendencies, the United States is considered a <u>republic,</u> a political order in which the head of state is
not a monarch but usually a president.

_____

7. Ashes are an example of <u>residue,</u> matter remaining after a chemical or physical process is completed.

_____

8. The Bermuda Triangle has a dangerous <u>current,</u> a continuous
flow of water, that has mystified scientists for ages.

_____

Example/Illustration clues are ideas that are explained by giving
specific, concrete examples or illustrations. You can figure out the
meaning of an unknown word from the example.

◆ **EXERCISE C: EXAMPLE CLUES**

Write a definition for each of the <u>underlined</u> words in the sentences
that follow.

1. Martha was a <u>meticulous</u> person; she was neat and kept everything in perfect order.

_____

2. Arthur was <u>pernicious</u> to his coworkers because he was abusive
both psychologically and emotionally.

_____

3. Mark was <u>vindictive</u> when he took the car keys away from his
son who had unavoidably destroyed the car.

_____

4. She was a <u>flamboyant</u> character; she dressed in colorful clothes,
spoke loudly, and used dramatic gestures.

_____

5. Dressed severely in a gray cloth robe and having a stern expression, the monk had a very <u>austere</u> appearance.

_____

6. The <u>prognosis</u> for her cancer was that she would be dead within the year.

_____

7. He gave a <u>lucid</u> explanation about AIDS, and, as a result, everyone in the class understood it.

_____

8. He was a <u>venerable</u> leader; the people stood up and applauded as he entered the room.

_____

Contrast clues are clues that help the reader figure out the meaning of unknown words from other words or a phrase in the context that has an opposite meaning.

◆ **EXERCISE D: CONTRAST CLUES**

Write a definition for each of the <u>underlined</u> words in the sentences that follow.

1. His friends wanted him to join a club, but he wished to remain <u>solitary.</u>

_____

2. Instead of a <u>cogent</u> report on the problem, the man gave a rambling, disorganized presentation.

_____

3. The teacher found that her class was <u>apathetic</u> instead of eager and enthusiastic.

_____

4. Teenagers are often <u>belligerent</u> instead of contented and peaceful.

_____

5. The feelings of the people at the rally were <u>congenial</u> to the speaker and did not display the expected hostility.

_____

6. He was <u>proficient</u> in speaking but lacked the necessary analytical skills to join the debate team.

_____

7. His appearance was <u>robust</u> despite his recent loss of weight.

_____

8. They <u>inadvertently</u> disclosed the scheme before they had planned to.

_____

Inference clues are the use of general reasoning skills to figure out words by reading an entire paragraph to figure out an unknown word.

◆ **EXERCISE E: INFERENCE CLUES**

Write a definition for each of the <u>underlined</u> words in the sentences that follow.

1. The senator from Massachusetts delivered a <u>diatribe</u> against the proposed legislation on abortion.

_____

2. The gypsy's style was <u>eclectic</u> as she wore many different types and colors of clothing.

_____

3. The boy <u>fabricated</u> a story in order to deceive his mother so that she wouldn't find out about his accident.

_____

4. The old man was <u>frugal</u> and saved his money because he was afraid of being poor.

_____

5. The man committed a <u>heinous</u> crime when he hacked the limbs off his victim.

_____

6. The woman secretly knew she was <u>fallible</u> even though she acted as if she could never make a mistake.

_____

7. The <u>covert</u> operation was successful; no one ever found out about it.

_____

8. His <u>altruistic</u> nature helped him in the end when those he had helped repaid him.

_____

STRUCTURAL ANALYSIS

Structural analysis is a method of learning new words by analyzing parts of words. Words can have more than one prefix, root, or suffix. Words do not always have a prefix and a suffix. A root may change in spelling, since it may be combined with a suffix.

- *Prefixes* appear at the beginning of many English words. They alter the meaning of the root word. Prefixes can give direction, location, or placement.
- *Roots* carry the basic or core meaning of a word. They help to unlock the meaning of a word.
- *Suffixes* are word endings that often change the part of speech of a word. Several different words can be formed from a single root word with the addition of different suffixes.

The following are lists of prefixes, suffixes, and roots. These lists can be used to do the following exercises and for reference.

Prefixes of Number Words

Prefix of Number	Meaning	Example
uni	one	uniform
mono	one	monologue
du(O)	two	duet
bi	two	biped
tri	three	triangle
tetra	four	tetrameter
quad	four	quadruplets
penta	five	pentagon

Continued

Prefixes of Number Words   *Continued*

Prefix of Number	Meaning	Example
quint	five	quintet
sex	six	sexagenarian
hex	six	hexagon
sept	seven	septet
oct	eight	octopus
nov	nine	novena
dec	ten	decade
cent	hundred	percent
hect	hundred	hectogram
mil	thousand	millimeter
kil	thousand	kilometer
semi	half	semicircle
hemi	half	hemisphere
demi	half	demitasse

Suffixes

Suffix	Meaning	Example
able, ible	able to	readable
al	pertaining to	musical
ar, er, or	one who	liar, teacher, moderator
ful	full of	hopeful
ic	pertaining to	allergic
ish	like, close to	foolish, twentyish
ist	one who	psychologist
less	without	hatless
logy	study of	cosmetology
ous	full of	cancerous

Prefixes and Roots

Root or Prefix	Meaning	Example
ab	away (from)	absent
acer, acr	sour, bitter	acerbity, acrid
ad	to, toward	adhere
ambi	both	ambivalent
ante	before	anteroom
anthropo	man, mankind	anthropoid
anti	against, opposed	antipathy
aqua	water	aquatic
aster, astro	star	asteroid, astronaut
aud	hear	auditory

Prefixes and Roots   *Continued*

Root or Prefix	Meaning	Example
auto	self	automatic
bene	well, good	beneficial
bio	life	biology
cap	take, seize	captive
cede, ceed	go, move	recede, proceed
chron	time	chronological
circum	around	circumference
co, con, com	together, with	cooperate, conspiracy, comfortable
cogni	know	recognize
corp	body	corpse
counter, contra	against, opposite	counteract, contrary
cred	believe	credential
de	from, away	depart
dent	tooth	dentist
derm	skin	dermatitis
dic, dict	say	dictate
dis	apart, from, away from	distract
duc, duct	lead	aquaduct
ex, exo	out (of)	excise, exodus
fact, fac	make, do	factory, facile
fid	faith, faithful	fidelity, confident
gamy	marriage	monogamy
geo	earth	geophysics
graph	write	graphology
gress	go, move	progress
inter	between	interrupt
log, logo, logy	study of, thought	psychology
man	hand	manicure
mega	big	megaphone
mis	wrong, wrongly	mistake
miso, misa	hatred	misology, misanthrope
mit, miss	send	remit, dismiss
morph	form, shape	amorphous
mort	death	mortality
multi	many	multitude
neb	hazy, cloudy	nebulous
neo	new	neotropical
non	not	nonadjustable
path	feeling, suffering	apathy
ped, pod	foot	pedal, podiatrist
pel	push	repel
phone	sound, voice	telephone

Continued

Prefixes and Roots *Continued*

Root or Prefix	Meaning	Example
photo	light	photosensitive
poly	many	polygamy
port	carry	porter
post	after	postpone
pre	before	preamble
pro	forward	propel
re	back, again	return, redo
retro	backward	retrospect
rupt	break	rupture
scop	seeing	microscope
scrib	write	transcribe
sect	cut	dissect
sen, sent	feel	insensitive, sentiment
spect	see, look	spectator, inspect
sub	under	submarine
super	over, above	superior, supersonic
syn, sym	with, together	synchronize, symmetry
ten	hold	tenacious, tentacle
tend	stretch	extend
terr, terre	land, earth	territory, terrestrial
theo	god	theology
tort	twist	distort
trans	across	transport
ven, vent	come	venue, convention
vert, vers	turn	invert, versatile
vis, vid	see	invisible, video
viv	life	convivial
voc	call	vocation

◆ **EXERCISE F: PREFIXES, ROOTS, AND SUFFIXES**

From the choices given, decide the meaning of each of the following made-up words created from a variety of prefixes, roots, and suffixes. Refer to the meanings of these word parts if you need to. Circle the letter of your choice.

1. Ambident
   a. yellow teeth
   b. any tooth
   c. both teeth
   d. loose teeth

2. Aquaderm
   a. wet skin
   b. poolside
   c. to live in water
   d. green skin

3. Subman
   a. kind person
   b. healthy man
   c. sick man
   d. inferior person

4. Demisex
   a. playboy
   b. three
   c. six
   d. devilish

5. Audrupt
   a. broken stereo
   b. type of crime
   c. hearing device
   d. ruptured membrane

6. Megapod
   a. large apartment
   b. large pea
   c. big foot
   d. good crop

7. Mortscrib
   a. epitaph
   b. death rite
   c. afterthought
   d. death song

8. Monomorph
   a. many shapes
   b. one shape
   c. fat form
   d. twin

9. Ruptgamy
   a. ill spouse
   b. separated married couple
   c. single parent
   d. unfaithful spouse

10. Audmort
    a. place where speeches are made
    b. cemetery
    c. soft spoken
    d. deaf

♦ **EXERCISE G: USING ROOTS**

Use the list of common roots on pages 256–258 to determine the meanings of the following words. Write the meaning next to the word.

1. dictate _____

2. biophysics _____

3. photosensitive _____

4. apportion _____

5. visibility _____

6. credible _____

7. spectacles _____

8. auditory _____

9. terrestrial _____

10. astrology _____

11. denture _____

12. dermatologist _____

13. monacle _____

14. morphology _____

15. circumspect _____

◆ EXERCISE H: USING ROOTS, PREFIXES, AND SUFFIXES

Use your knowledge of roots, prefixes, and suffixes to match these words with the definitions that follow.

a. autocrat
b. monosyllabic
c. antipathy
d. adverse
e. subspecies
f. transcribe
g. cognition
h. exodus

i. patricide
j. megaphone
k. propel
l. transverse
m. tenacious
n. hemisphere
o. intergalactic

_____ 1. A ruler with absolute power.

_____ 2. A feeling of aversion, repugnance, or opposition.

_____ 3. A departure, usually of a large number of people.

_____ 4. The mental process or faculty by which knowledge is acquired.

_____ 5. A word or utterance of one syllable.

_____ 6. Between galaxies.

_____ 7. A subdivision of a toxonomic species.

_____ 8. The act of killing one's father.

_____ 9. Tending to hold on to an idea or object.

_____ 10. Antagonistic in design or effect.

_____ 11. Situated or lying across; crosswise.

_____ 12. To cause to move or sustain in motion.

_____ **13.** Half of a sphere bounded by a great circle.

_____ **14.** A device used to amplify the voice.

_____ **15.** To write or type a copy of something.

ASSOCIATION

Another way to increase vocabulary is to create associations or see the relationships between words. Below are four different types of word relationships that can help you to increase your vocabulary.

- *Synonyms* are words that have similar meanings: pretty/cute.
- *Antonyms* are words that have the opposite meaning: pretty/ugly.
- *Homonyms* are words that sound like another word but have a different meaning: there/their.
- *Analogies* are similar relationships between dissimilar objects. An example is: Up is to down as fast is to slow. An analogy deals with relationships between two pairs of words. The two pairs are usually dissimilar (not the same), but the relationship between the words are the same.

◆ EXERCISE I: SYNONYMS

In each of the groups below, three words are synonyms. Circle the letter of the *unrelated* word, and then write a definition for the related synonyms

1. a. attraction   **c.** aversion
   b. appeal   **d.** affinity

Definition: _____

_____

2. a. pertinent   **c.** inappropriate
   b. relevant   **d.** germane

Definition: _____

_____

3. a. aptitude   **c.** flair
   b. knack   **d.** unskillful

Definition: _____

_____

4. **a.** finale   **c.** prologue
    b. conclusion   **d.** epilogue

    Definition: _____

5. **a.** instability   **c.** vacillation
    b. constancy   **d.** insecurity

    Definition: _____

6. **a.** conciliatory   **c.** appeasing
    b. pacifying   **d.** antagonistic

    Definition: _____

7. **a.** mercenary   **c.** selfish
    b. altruistic   **d.** avaricious

    Definition: _____

8. **a.** drivel   **c.** ramble
    b. babble   **d.** speak

    Definition: _____

9. **a.** ostentatious   **c.** pompous
    b. conservative   **d.** grandiose

    Definition: _____

10. **a.** loquacious   **c.** laconic
    b. garrulous   **d.** verbose

    Definition: _____

◆ EXERCISE J: SYNONYMS

Circle the letter next to the word that is closest in meaning to the underlined word.

1. Canine
   a. cans
   b. foxes
   c. dogs
   d. cats
   e. horses

2. Hoax
   a. public deception
   b. loud cry
   c. scandal
   d. blasphemy

3. Lachrymose
   a. tearful
   b. milky
   c. cheerful
   d. caustic
   e. catastrophic

4. Neophyte
   a. disciple
   b. beginner
   c. proselyte
   d. mixed breed
   e. convert

5. Progeny
   a. genius
   b. ancestor
   c. offspring
   d. follower
   e. prophecy

6. Renegade
   a. recruit
   b. salutation
   c. withdrawal
   d. denial
   e. turncoat

7. Hedonist
   a. skeptic
   b. idealist
   c. mystic
   d. assailant
   e. lover of pleasure

8. Idiosyncrasy
   a. form of government
   b. original opinion
   c. strong desire
   d. peculiar habit
   e. ambition

◆ EXERCISE K: ANTONYMS

From the list below, choose two antonyms for each of the words in the exercise and write them in the space provided.

credulous	animation	lavish	embrace	accept
warm hearted	maladroit	rigid	detached	gullible
incompetent	incurious	generous	vigorous	lively
magnanimous	thoughtless	imprudent	obstinate	energy

1. ostracize _____ _____

2. lethargic   _____   _____

3. pliable   _____   _____

4. judicious   _____   _____

5. proficient   _____   _____

6. parsimonious   _____   _____

7. rapt   _____   _____

8. malevolent   _____   _____

9. skeptical   _____   _____

10. torpor   _____   _____

◆ **EXERCISE L: ANTONYMS**

Circle the letter next to the word that is opposite the meaning of the underlined word.

1. <u>Zenith</u>
   a. apogie
   b. peak
   c. valley
   d. desert
   e. nadir

2. <u>Ambiguous</u>
   a. evasive
   b. solitary
   c. miniature
   d. nebulous
   e. explicit

3. <u>Haggard</u>
   a. gaunt
   b. energetic
   c. obese
   d. attentuated
   e. pale

4. <u>Raucous</u>
   a. well cooked
   b. tranquil
   c. demure
   d. mellifluous
   e. decursive

5. <u>Mandatory</u>
   a. interrogative
   b. unassigned
   c. objectionable
   d. imperative
   e. voluntary

6. <u>Understatement</u>
   a. simile
   b. superscription
   c. hyperbole
   d. truth
   e. equivocation

7. <u>Deviate</u>
   a. circumscribe
   b. conform
   c. unite
   d. divide
   e. bond

8. <u>Moderate</u>
   a. temperate
   b. inebriate
   c. misjudge
   d. drastic
   e. diffident

◆ **EXERCISE M: HOMONYMS**

Choose the homonym that best completes the sentence.

1. The _____ dome in Madison is gold.
       (capitol, capital)

2. He _____ me against joining the army.
       (counciled, counseled)

3. The chair remained in a _____ position.
                            (stationary, stationery)

4. _____ is a place that lies between Avalon and Camelot
   where it never rains.
   (There, Their)

5. The king _____ for ten years.
          (reigned, reined)

6. She was _____ by the change in weather.
          (affected, effected)

7. The clown gave the _____ of being happy.
                      (illusion, allusion)

8. The teacher _____ a negative response from her students.
       (elicited, illicited)

9. She decided to go to the party rather _____ go to school.
                                         (than, then)

10. The doctor was an _____ physician.
               (imminent, eminent)

◆ **EXERCISE N: ANALOGIES**

Circle the correct letter of the words that complete the following analogies.

1. Decade is to century as
   a. dime is to dollar.
   b. penny is to dime.
   c. little is to much.
   d. time is to number.

2. Alchemy is to chemistry as
   a. geography is to geology.
   b. magic is to superstition.
   c. superstition is to astronomy.
   d. astrology is to astronomy.

3. Uncle is to nephew as
   a. aunt is to niece.
   b. patriarch is to tribe.
   c. son is to father.
   d. parent is to child.

4. Bull is to cow as
   a. deer is to doe.
   b. ram is to ewe.
   c. horse is to colt.
   d. fawn is to deer.

5. Brain is to heart as
   a. critic is to philosopher.
   b. rational is to emotional.
   c. rhyme is to rhythm.
   d. skeptic is to idea.

6. Creek is to river as
   a. mountain is to valley.
   b. Pomeranian is to greyhound.
   c. bay is to ocean.
   d. man is to pygmy.

7. Tradition is to reverence as
   a. custom is to respect.
   b. prestige is to respect.
   c. authority is to defer.
   d. society is to law.

8. Tree is to fruit as
   a. patriarch to progeny.
   b. source is to origin.
   c. pod is to seed.
   d. acorn is to oak.

◆ **EXERCISE O: ANALOGIES**

Fill in the word that best completes the analogy. The first one is done for you.

1. Barometer is to air pressure as thermometer is to **temperature** .

2. Hops are to beer as grapes are to _____.

3. Leash is to dog as handcuffs are to _____.

4. Island is to ocean as oasis is to _____.

5. Tadpole is to frog as caterpillar is to _____.

6. Plane is to cockpit as locomotive is to _____.

7. Century is to decade as dollar is to _____.

8. Woodsman is to axe as draftsman is to _____.

Semantic Webs

If you can think of something you already know and can connect this meaning to a new word, your retention and comprehension will improve. For instance, for a class in government you may need to remember the definition of *consensus,* which is a collective opinion or general agreement. Associating *consensus* with the word *census,* which you are already familiar with and has a related meaning, will make *consensus* easier to remember. If you have a list of unfamiliar vocabulary to remember, you can create a semantic web for each word to help you remember the word, as shown in Figure 12-1.

By creating a semantic web for each word as shown in Figure 12-2, you are creating associations.

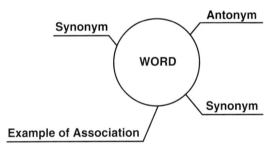

FIGURE 12-1   Semantic web structure.

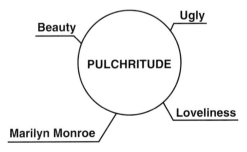

FIGURE 12-2   Semantic web model.

◆ **EXERCISE P: FOR THE FOLLOWING LIST OF WORDS, DEVELOP YOUR OWN SEMANTIC WEBS**

1. paltry
2. doldrums
3. cacophony
4. behemoth
5. charlatan

◆ **EXERCISE Q**

Completing crossword puzzles is an excellent way to increase vocabulary. The one here includes a word list. Choose a partner, and work together to decide where the words or word parts below go in the puzzle.

Down

teem	Elle	diet
sacred	for	I do
tens	scrap	elevator
Lane	adds	tor
husk	ala	wig
elephant	ashe	seals
and a	a ha	boy
shoo	Pisans	Sada
chin	robes	left
loo	eye	rag
knit	ecce	deep

Across

Teds	fit	Sela
Elia	ode	clad
electron	rend	Metro
shaves	eras	up a
awed	seas	tab
Lil	shank	O ho
age	held	pray
pro	sari	school
asked	Ahab	elegance
dine	Foy	nice
ants	toe	step

ACROSS

1 Kennedy and Koppel
5 Healthy
8 "Sisters" actress Ward
12 Director Kazan
13 Tribute in verse
14 Dressed
15 Particle of matter
17 Rip
18 French underground?

DOWN

1 Rain cats and dogs
2 Model Macpherson
3 Japanese parliament
4 Holy
5 Backing
6 Altar affirmative
7 Change for a fifty
8 Remnant
9 It's good for a pick-me-up

ACROSS

19 Splits heirs?

21 Epochs

24 ___ ___ tree (cornered)

25 Dumbstruck

28 The Red and the Black

30 Paper-doll dress flap

33 Abner's adjective

34 Leg

35 Discoverer's cry

36 Census datum

37 Contained

38 Supplicate

39 Paid player

41 Rani's wrap

43 Where there's room
    for improvement?

46 Mailed invitations

50 Obsessed seaman

51 Panache

54 Eat

55 Eddie of vaudeville

56 Agreeable

57 Hill dwellers

58 Place-kicker's pride

59 Dance lesson

DOWN

10 Daily Planet staffer

11 Puts together

16 Craggy peak

20 Peel ears

22 "Days of Grace"

23 Christmas-card decorations

25 Miss neighbor

26 Falsehood?

27 He may turn up his nose
    at you

29 "_____ partridge . . ."

31 Discoverer's cry

32 Role in a Tarzan movie

34 "Ske-daddle!"

38 Tower city's locals

40 Judicial closetful

42 Scott Joplin's specialty

43 Actress Thompson

44 Chew the fat

45 Remaining

47 Create a cardigan

48 "— homo!"

49 Profound

52 Old card game

53 Peacock tail coloration

CRITICAL THINKING

The class should divide into groups of four. Each group should then choose a director, recorder, typist, and narrator. The task of the group is to write a short story using at least half of the following vocabulary words. The final story must be typed and handed in, and the narrator from each group will read the story aloud to the class. You will be graded on presentation and finished story. Underline the vocabulary words used from this list.

The final copy is due _____ .

accurate	egoistic	meddle
alter	geriatrics	misdemeanor
boarder	hypersensitive	moderate
collaborate	hypertension	packed
conformed	hypotension	physicist
congenital	impress	power
consequences	inappropriate	seclusion
conversation	introspective	shanty
courage	irresponsibility	sympathy
dehydrate	magnanimous	unimportant
dermatology	magnify	
disseminate	matricide	

REFERENCES

Sheffer, E. (June 9, 1995). The Daily Puzzler. New York: King Feature Syndicate.

INDEX